CRAZY SUNDAYS

CRAZY SUNDAYS

F. SCOTT FITZGERALD

IN HOLLYWOOD

Aaron Latham

NEW YORK / THE VIKING PRESS

ACKNOWLEDGMENTS

Esquire Magazine: From "Old Scott" by Budd Schulberg. © 1960 by Esquire, Inc. Reprinted by permission of *Esquire* Magazine.

Samuel Goldwyn Productions: From the film script *Raffles*. Reprinted by permission.

Holt, Rinehart and Winston, Inc., and Cassell & Co. Ltd.: From *Beloved Infidel* by Sheilah Graham and Gerold Frank. Copyright © 1958 by Sheilah Graham and Gerold Frank. Reprinted by permission of Holt, Rinehart and Winston, Inc., and Laurence Pollinger Limited.

Metro-Goldwyn-Mayer Inc.: Material from *Red Headed Woman* on pages 66–68 © 1932 by Metro-Goldwyn-Mayer; copyright renewed 1959 by Loew's Incorporated. Material from *A Yank At Oxford* on pages 113–14 © 1938 by Loew's Incorporated; copyright renewed 1965 by Metro-Goldwyn-Mayer Inc. Material from *Three Comrades* on pages 137–43 © 1938 by Loew's Incorporated; copyright renewed 1965 by Metro-Goldwyn-Mayer Inc. Material from *Infidelity* on pages 166–67 © 1971 by Metro-Goldwyn-Mayer Inc. This material is from an unpublished manuscript, the copyright in which is owned by Metro-Goldwyn-Mayer Inc. Material from *The Women* on pages 186–90 © 1939 by Loew's Incorporated; copyright renewed 1966 by Metro-Goldwyn-Mayer Inc. Material from *Madame Curie* on pages 204–206 © 1943 by Loew's Incorporated; copyright renewed 1970 by Metro-Goldwyn-Mayer, Inc. Material from *The Last Time I Saw Paris* on pages 247–54 © 1944 by Loew's Incorporated.

New Directions Publishing Corp. and The Bodley Head: F. Scott Fitzgerald, *The Crack-Up*. Copyright 1934, 1936 by Esquire, Inc., 1945 by New Directions Publishing Corporation. Reprinted by permission of New Directions Publishing Corporation and The Bodley Head.

Paramount Pictures Corporation: From the film script *This Side of Paradise*.

Charles Scribner's Sons and The Bodley Head: The following material is reprinted by permission of Charles Scribner's Sons and The Bodley Head from the works of F. Scott Fitzgerald: *The Last Tycoon* (Copyright 1941 Charles Scribner's Sons; renewal copyright © 1969 Frances Scott Fitzgerald Smith), *The Letters of F. Scott Fitzgerald*, edited by Andrew Turnbull (Copyright © 1963 Frances Scott Fitzgerald Lanahan), and *The Stories of F. Scott Fitzgerald*, edited by Malcolm Cowley (Copyright 1951 Charles Scribner's Sons).

Twentieth Century-Fox Film Corporation: For permission to reproduce excerpts from the screen play by F. Scott Fitzgerald, based upon the play by Emlyn Williams entitled *The Light of Heart*.

Warner Bros. Inc.: Material quoted from *Lipstick* on pages 56–58. Copyrighted © 1971 by Warner Bros. Inc. All Rights Reserved. This material is from an unpublished manuscript, the copyright in which is owned by Warner Bros. Inc.

For my sister, Sharon
1945–1967

☆ ☆ ☆

Preface

As long past as 1930, I had a hunch that the talkies would make even the best-selling novelist as archaic as silent pictures.[1] *

More than anything in the world he wanted to make pictures. He knew exactly what it was like to carry a picture in his head as a director did and it seemed to him infinitely romantic.[2]

Hollywood had Scott Fitzgerald down as a drunk. He himself had helped to shape that image by writing a story called "Crazy Sunday" which immortalized a party where he had too much to drink and "made a fool of himself in view of an important section of the picture world, upon whose favor depended his career."[3] And there *were* recurrent bouts during Fitzgerald's Hollywood years, from 1937 to his death in 1940, when all his days seemed to be turning into crazy Sundays, when he seemed to be caught up in a drunken party which would not end, when he went on making a fool of himself day after day. Toward the end he couldn't find work.

Most of the time, however, he was not drinking: he was bitterly sober. Most of the time he shunned parties: he had given them up when his success and his wife crumbled at the same time. Most of the time he worked almost desperately hard: the movies seemed to him to offer his last hope of recapturing the fame he had won young and lost young. Unlike William Faulkner

* Numbers refer to Notes, beginning on page 279.

and other novelists who went to Hollywood only for the money, Fitzgerald wanted much more: he had come to believe that he could no longer write novels and short stories, but he thought that he could write pictures. "There are no second acts in American lives,"[4] he had once written, but in Hollywood he hoped to prove himself wrong. He had gone there for nothing less than to save himself as a writer.

I went to California in the fall of 1968 to look for the scripts which were supposed to put Fitzgerald back on top again. Most of them I found in the basement of the Metro-Goldwyn-Mayer studio. The scripts had been down there in the "morgue" for over three decades, undisturbed, waiting in long cardboard boxes the size of coffins. I was given an office in the Thalberg Building, and the keeper of the morgue brought Fitzgerald's screenplays, notes, letters, and endless memos up to me in a shopping cart. For six weeks I stayed on at the studio reading.

One day while I was quietly working in my borrowed office, I was interrupted by a tall man wearing a bow tie, who burst in and, without so much as acknowledging my existence, picked up my telephone, dialed a number, and with all the charm of a used-car salesman offered someone sixty-seven thousand dollars for something. When he had finished making his expensive deal, I introduced myself. Unable to ignore my presence any longer, the tall figure said that he was H. N. Swanson, the agent, and went on to ask if I was writing a script. I explained that I was writing my dissertation for Princeton on Fitzgerald's motion-picture career.

"Really?" said Swanson. "I used to be his agent. I got him the job here."

We talked for ten or fifteen minutes about Fitzgerald; then another deal still to be made pulled the agent out the door.

After I left MGM, I found the rest of Fitzgerald's screenplays —the ones he wrote for Selznick International, Goldwyn Pictures, 20th Century–Fox, First National, and United Artists—in the rare-book room of the Princeton University Library. And I continued what I had begun accidentally at Metro, interviews with people who had known and worked with Fitzgerald in Hollywood. I would like to thank the following for sharing their memories with me: Helen Hayes, Maureen O'Sullivan, Anita Loos, Joseph Mankiewicz, Charles Marquis Warren, Arnold Gingrich, Edwin Knopf, George Oppenheimer, Ogden Nash, Nunnally Johnson, Shirley Temple, Frances Kroll, Frances Goodrich, Albert Hackett, Lillian Hellman, George Cukor, and Sheilah Graham. I am indebted to Fitzgerald's daughter, Scottie (Mrs. Grove) Smith, not only for our conversations about her father, but for generously allowing me to quote from previously unpublished material. (Where it is clear from the context who told me what, I have not footnoted information obtained through interviews.)

I would also like to thank the motion-picture companies— some more than others—for their cooperation in allowing me to quote from Fitzgerald scripts which they own. MGM, for whom Fitzgerald did the most, was least generous in permitting quotation.

My special gratitude also goes to: Mary Reid Chambers, my editor; Professor Richard N. Ludwig, my Princeton advisor; the late Professor Alan S. Downer, who read the dissertation and made important suggestions; Sigourney and Sylvester Weaver, who helped locate the scripts; Wanda Randall, in the Princeton University Library rare-book room, who helped guide me through the sprawling Fitzgerald collection; and Thomas Plate, who originally suggested that I write on Fitzgerald.

Fitzgerald was notorious for his bad spelling. In *This Side of Paradise* he went so far as to misspell the name of the man to whom he dedicated the book: Father Sigourney Fay (he left out the *u*). In general, I have regularized his spelling in all quotations.

Princeton, New Jersey   AARON LATHAM

☆ ☆ ☆

Contents

	Preface	*vii*
1.	A Day at the Studio, 1938	*3*
2.	Flashback	*26*
3.	Beginning in Hollywood	*45*
4.	The Wrong Kind of Picture	*62*
5.	*Tender Is the Night* and the Movies	*76*
6.	*A Yank at Oxford:* Pictures of Words	*97*
7.	*Three Comrades:* Words, Words, Words	*120*
8.	*Infidelity:* A Picture Worth a Book of Words	*150*
9.	*The Women:* Epitaph for the Spoiled Heroine	*174*
10.	*Madame Curie:* Brave New Heroine	*196*
11.	Free-Lancing	*213*
12.	*Cosmopolitan:* Splicing It Together	*238*
13.	"Action Is Character"	*259*
	Epilogue	*275*
	Notes	*279*
	Index	*301*

CRAZY SUNDAYS

A Day at the Studio
1938

At the sound of a light knock on the door of her office in the Thalberg Building on the Metro-Goldwyn-Mayor lot, Anita Loos looked up from a script. She was an old friend, but at the same time she was precisely what her visitor was not—a successful screenwriter.

"Come in," Miss Loos said to the man standing in her doorway but making no move to enter.

"No," he said diffidently, "you don't really want me to come in."

"Of course I do," she assured him. "Come in."

"No," he said, "you're just being nice."

"Scott!"

In the old days his own confidence and enthusiasm had been the only invitation F. Scott Fitzgerald had ever needed to go anywhere. An editor would be working at his desk when suddenly a hat would plop down in the middle of his papers. That meant that the hat's brash young owner was on his way in. And then there he would be in the doorway looking—said a floundering young contemporary—"so successful he made me feel dirty."[1]

But in Hollywood Fitzgerald's habit of barging in had reversed itself.

Scott dropped by to see Miss Loos often—to reminisce about the old days in New York, to speculate about the future in Hollywood—but all the visits began the same way, with a knock followed by a self-imposed catechism of self-doubt which made them both uncomfortable, but which became a ritual between them. On one occasion Fitzgerald wrote a poem for his successful friend. It was a nonsense poem, one of which the Mad Hatter could have been proud, since it had to do with the Hatter's chief interest—a birthday:

> This book tells that Anita Loos
> Is a friend of Caesar, a friend of Zeus
> Of Samuel Goldwyn, and Mother Goose
> Of Balanchine of the Ballet Russe
> Of Tillie the Viennese papoose
> Of Charlie MacArthur on the loose
> Of shanks, chiropodist—what's the use?
> Of actors who have escaped the noose
> Lots of Hollywood beach refuse
> Comics covered with Charlotte Russe
> Wretched victims of self-abuse
> Big producers all obtuse
> This is my birthday, but what the deuce
> Is that sad fact to Anita Loos.

After Miss Loos read the poem, she laughed at first. She had written enough comedies to appreciate wit; then she came to those last lines about the birthday and felt their unexpected tug. A decade before, Fitzgerald had written in his ledger, "32 and sore as hell about it"; now he was turning forty-two and was more sore than ever. And what the deuce, Miss Loos did care—yet she could not help hearing a kind of echo: *Come in, no you're only being polite.*

At the beginning of his assault on Hollywood, when he had hoped to be really at home there, even make a home for his daughter, Scottie, there, he had written Scottie about the friends she would have. "I know Freddie Bartholomew will love taking you around to birthday parties in the afternoons," he said, "and you'll find Shirley Temple as good a pal as Peaches and more loyal."[2] But it had not worked out that way. Scottie was still in the East, and it was her father who often needed a "good and loyal pal."

Anita Loos had known Fitzgerald in his great days in the twenties. One day, she remembers, she had been walking along Fifth Avenue when he drove up beside her:

"He asked me where I was going, and I said that I was not going anywhere. I didn't know that he was tight. We had a wild ride to Great Neck; I thought that he was going to kill us both. When we finally arrived, Zelda was at home and we sat down to dinner. Scott was very moody, not saying much. Zelda and I ignored him, and that seemed to make him angry. Finally he jumped up from the table and said, 'I'm going to kill you two.' And he tried. He jerked off the tablecloth with everything on it and then started throwing the candelabra and other big, heavy things at us. Scott had locked all the doors, but the butler—he will always be a hero to me—broke through a glass pane in one of the doors and came in and held Scott. Then Zelda and I ran across to Ring Lardner's house. Ring decided to go out looking for Scott. He looked for quite a while before he found him. When he did, Scott was kneeling in the road eating dirt. 'I'm a monster,' he was saying. 'I tried to kill those two darling girls and now I've got to eat dirt.'"

The old candelabra-hurler was preferable to this timid knocker at the office door. "Scott had that unhealthy humility of the reformed alcoholic," says Miss Loos. "It was an embarrassing humility. It convinced me that you should never sober up a chronic drunk." Still she would put aside her work and try to entertain him, to reassure him, whenever he came calling.

These visits never lasted long. After some minutes Fitzgerald would feel that he had rested as much as he could afford, at which point he would take his leave and head back down the corridor to his own office. On his way he would pass by the doors of other offices, and even these would put him in his place; some actually glittered with success. The Army sews chevrons on sleeves or pins medals to chests, but at MGM the door was the thing. The studio caste system had long ago separated writers and department heads from producers by giving the latter gold name plates. (Some department heads were actually known to take cuts in salary in exchange for the gold-plated status that went with the title "producer.") Fitzgerald would pass these success stories all written out in fourteen carats and finally come to the door where his own name was typed out on a little square of white paper. He would go in once again to *Madame Curie* or *Marie Antoinette* or *Three Comrades* or *A Yank at Oxford*—as the 1930s were drawing to a close he worked on them all. At one point he even spent several weeks on the big one, *Gone with the Wind.*

On his desk were the inevitable pencils and legal-size pads on which he wrote; impatient scripts in their blue cardboard covers waited beside the typewriter. On the floor, lined up against the walls, there were the Coca-Cola bottles he collected; an army of them would gather in a row as if on parade. They were his own private palace guard, a thin line which protected not a monarch but a mind: Coke was what Fitzgerald drank to keep from drinking something stronger. The novelist-turned-screen-writer threatened that when the column of bottles reached all of the way around the room so that the vanguard overtook the rear guard, he would celebrate the completion of the circle by going off the wagon.[3]

Sometime between twelve and one, Fitzgerald would knock off for lunch. He would take his leave of the pencils and pads, scripts and Coke bottles, and set off down the third-floor hall for the elevator of the writers' and producers' building. The long, barren hallway belonged as much in a hospital corridor as it did in a place where movies were made up and written down. In fact, the building looked so much like a *Krankenhaus* that everybody called it the Iron Lung—which would have seemed funnier if Fitzgerald had not been such a sick man. Out the window he could see a small green building which looked like a drugstore but was in fact a mortuary—and that too would have been funny, death house and fantasy land sharing the same block, if Fitzgerald had not been so sick.

Since the Metro-Goldwyn-Mayer empire believes, with considerable justice, that it is under constant siege from hoards of aspiring movie stars, it has built its plant like a fortress. Spiked fences surround everything and there are police stationed at every entrance. From the outside looking in, it has the air of the world's most exclusive country club, but from the inside it can have the air of a prison camp. To reach the MGM commissary, known as the Lion's Den, Fitzgerald had to leave the Thalberg Building and walk along a fenced-in corridor which led to the main lot, a sprawling, crowded place that looked like a blind city: almost none of its buildings had windows. There were rows of huge structures which from the outside were as shapeless and uninteresting as four-story cardboard boxes but were actually the sound stages where movies were being made. There were also a few office buildings, which in his unfinished Hollywood novel, *The Last Tycoon*, Fitzgerald described as "old building[s] with . . . long balconies and iron rails with their suggestion of [a] perpetual tightrope."[4]

The commissary was wedged between one of those office buildings and a theatre-size projection room. In *Tycoon* Fitzgerald remembered this huge dining hall as being "gay with gypsies and with citizens and soldiers, with the sideburns and braided coats of the First Empire. From a little distance they were men who lived and walked a hundred years ago . . ."[5] In this commissary he would sit down quietly by himself.

Isolated in that crowd—this is how Frances Goodrich Hackett remembers Fitzgerald. Like Anita Loos, Mrs. Hackett was another successful screenwriter: with her husband Albert, she had scripted all kinds of movies for Metro, ranging from the classic *Ah, Wilderness!* to such popular hits as *The Thin Man* series. "The first time I saw Scott," she says, "he was in the commissary sitting alone at a table. He just sat there but he didn't order.

What I noticed were his eyes. Never in my life will I forget his eyes. He looked as if he were seeing hell opening before him. He was hugging his brief case and he had a Coke. Then suddenly he got up to go out. I said to Albert, 'I just saw the strangest man.' He said. 'That's Scott Fitzgerald.' "

Like Manny Schwartz in *Tycoon,* Fitzgerald

was obviously a man to whom something had happened. Meeting him was like encountering a friend who has been in a fist fight or collision, and got flattened. You stare at your friend and say: "What happened to you?" And he answers something unintelligible through broken teeth and swollen lips. He can't even tell you about it.[6]

Later the Hacketts persuaded Fitzgerald to eat at the writers' table, where he sat down with Ogden Nash, Dorothy Parker, George Oppenheimer, S. J. Perelman, and a battalion of other name writers. "We did get him to do that," Mrs. Hackett remembers, "because I never forgot that tormented face." Nash remembers Fitzgerald "at lunch with his Coca-Cola," where he was "very quiet indeed but extremely attractive with a sweet nature that came through." Some days Groucho Marx would join the writers for lunch and would prove Fitzgerald's exact opposite. Nash says that Marx "turned things upside down so that you couldn't have a coherent conversation—everything had to be a joke." While Groucho kidded and talked all the time, Scott would sit as voiceless as Harpo, not even laughing. He and Groucho had been neighbors in Great Neck in the twenties. "Scott was drunk a good deal of the time back then," the comedian remembers, "but that didn't distinguish him from anyone else in Great Neck." In Hollywood, sober now, Fitzgerald struck Marx as "a sick old man—not very funny stuff."

The MGM writers' table, which was long and stood against the wall of the commissary, existed in contradistinction—sometimes even open opposition—to what Fitzgerald called "the Big Table."[7] The Big Table meant the producers' table and it sat like a road hog in the middle of the room. Mrs. Hackett considered the writers who crossed the line and ate with the producers "an awful lot of finks."

George Oppenheimer remembers that some people called the writers' table the Left Table both because it stood against the left wall and because its politics were much more liberal—some thought "pinko." Fitzgerald later wove the politics of the Left and Right, of the screenwriters versus the producers and bosses, into the novel on which he was still working at his death.

So the writers would eat and joke and with it all keep an eye on the executive camp. They would watch, for example, as the producers rolled dice to see who would pick up the check for the whole table. "When they saw they wouldn't have to pay that day," Mrs. Hackett recalls, "they would order all kinds of things." And through it all the legendary Fitzgerald sat quietly listening, saying almost nothing, his presence as bland as the potato soup.

Other days Fitzgerald would absent himself from the table against the wall to eat with another crowd, a group of writers and actors who thought of themselves as "the clique." Those days he would walk down the spiked-fence corridor to the vast Monopoly board of a lot and sit down in the commissary at a table with Anita Loos and veteran gag writer Robert "Hoppie" Hopkins, Johnny Meehan and Howard Emmett Rogers, Spencer Tracy and Clark Gable. Sometimes Carole Lombard would be there. And while Aldous Huxley was at Metro working on *Pride and Prejudice* and *Madame Curie*, he was a part of the clique, too. "Huxley thought that we were a bunch of queer fish," Miss Loos remembers. The group was snobbish, she says, accepting only people with brains, which meant that almost all the fabled actresses on the lot were excluded.

"Scott didn't stand out in a group like that," Miss Loos says, "but we accepted him because we respected him. He wasn't a phony and there were a lot of phonies at Metro in those days." Again, what Miss Loos remembers best about lunching with Fitzgerald is not what he said but his long silences. He was sick sober, she remembers, and "people treated him like an invalid."

On rare days Fitzgerald would quit the studio entirely to lunch on the outside with his agent, or an actor or director. Occasionally he went to what he called "the Bev Brown Derby, a languid restaurant, patronized for its food by clients who always look as if they'd like to lie down."[8]

George Cukor, who directed *The Women* and part of *Gone with the Wind,* both of which Fitzgerald worked on, remembers that he once had the author out to his house for lunch. Back in 1926, Cukor had also directed Owen Davis's Broadway version of *The Great Gatsby*—a play Fitzgerald had never seen, having been in France all the while Jay Gatsby was on stage. The author who created Jay and the man who directed him had waited over a decade to lunch together, and now as they met in Hollywood it seemed that they had waited too long, that they had almost nothing left to say to one another. Cukor describes a "very grim, very dim, slightly plump" man who "ate very quickly." In fact, all the director remembers of their conversation is their talking about how fast they both ate. "I've only known two people to eat faster than you and I," Cukor told Fitzgerald, "and they are both dead now." They finished the meal "in five minutes flat."

Scott had more to say when he lunched with his agent, H. N. Swanson. "He was always complaining about the stories they assigned him," the agent remembers all too well. Swanson had been the editor-founder of *College Humor* in the twenties and had published many Fitzgerald stories, but in Hollywood the ex-editor and the ex-fiction writer had tense, strained meetings. Swanson thought of his client as "burned out," "a magnificent failure in the picture business." Fitzgerald felt the "poor Scott" condescension. In his notes to *The Last Tycoon* he wrote, "no mercy for Swanie."

After lunch, it would be time again for characters like Marie and Pierre Curie—or Louis XVI and Marie Antoinette, or Rhett Butler and Scarlett O'Hara, or whoever it happened to be that day—to begin once again shouting inside his head. He would sit down and, scratching at one of his pads, try to be a screenwriter. Or, pacing up and down his office, he would dictate dialogue to his secretary.

Up above Fitzgerald as he wrote, like an Old Testament God, was Louis B. Mayer. Mayer and most of his fourth-floor crowd were Jewish, but people called them the College of Cardinals, and sometimes Fitzgerald, on the floor below, felt them weighing down heavily, as if part of his job were to hold them up. He knew they treated themselves well up there with masseurs and steam baths. "We used to say," the Hacketts remember, " 'You're keeping all the wrong people healthy. While the producers are getting rubbed down up above, the writers are going crazy down below.' "

After fighting the good fight with his imaginary people for hours, getting their lines down, it would be time for another break, and that often meant a visit to the writers in Hunt Stromberg's unit. Stromberg, respected as one of Hollywood's most creative producers, had gathered under him people like Dorothy Parker, her husband, Alan Campbell, and the Hacketts. Down the hall Fitzgerald would come, hoping to get away from dialogue for a moment, and what would he walk into but Parker and Campbell composing dialogue out loud.

Campbell would ask Parker, "What does Jane say?"

And Dorothy Parker would say a word softly so that only her coauthor heard.

"Don't use that word," Campbell would say, and then he would go on to the next question. "What does John say?"

Soft response.

"Don't use that word. What does Jane say?"

Soft response.

"Don't use that word."

Sometimes Fitzgerald would swoop down for only a hit-and-run visit, like the time he wanted some professional advice. "One day," the Hacketts remember, "Scott popped in and said some line. 'Is that funny?' he asked. 'Oh, never mind.' Then he popped out again. We didn't understand what he was up to." What he was probably up to was that same old insecurity treadmill—

—Is that funny?
—Come in, no you're . . .
—Oh, never mind.

Other days Fitzgerald would stay longer. "He would write letters to his daughter," Mrs. Hackett recalls. "She was at Vassar and I had been at Vassar and so he would come and read the letters to me. They were beautiful letters."

The first epistles to Vassar had spoken of succeeding in Hollywood, of working his way up to the top as if he were starting out in business. "I must be very tactful but keep my hand on the wheel from the start," he had written, "—find out the key man among the bosses and the most malleable among the collaborators—then fight the rest tooth and nail until, in fact or in effect, I'm alone on the picture. That's the only way I can do my best work. Given a break I can make them double this contract in less [than] two years."

But now these hopes were bankrupted too and the letters had come to speak with a different, tired voice. "I'm convinced," he wrote after he had been in Hollywood for a year and a half, "that maybe they're not going to make me Czar of the Industry right away, as I thought ten months ago. It's all right, baby—life has humbled me—Czar or not, we'll survive. I am even willing to compromise for Assistant Czar!"[9]

About four o'clock Fitzgerald could get away to a saloon built right on the Metro lot. The place was called The Trap, so named because management seemed to think that it was poaching on their workers' time. There Fitzgerald could be seen with one of his omnipresent Coke bottles in his hand; and there he would rejoin the clique—Loos, Gable, Tracy, Huxley, and the others. The way to make a hit was to say something funny, but true to what had become his style in those days, Fitzgerald rarely said anything at all.

The studio day ended, officially, at six o'clock. Having earned two hundred fifty dollars for his day's work, Fitzgerald could go home.

2

Evening. During the years of his young success, evenings meant to Fitzgerald, as they had to Jay Gatsby, that a party would be starting soon. "The lights grow brighter as the earth lurches away from the sun."[10] But now something had happened to Fitzgerald. Edwin H. Knopf, who was story editor at MGM and therefore one of Fitzgerald's bosses, remembers that the author who had once personified The Prom, The Bonne Fête, The Wild Party, now shied away from large gatherings. "If it was to be a big party," Knopf says, "he didn't want to come."

Knopf worried about Fitzgerald. After all, it was he who had offered the novelist the job at Metro in the first place and gotten him to come to Hollywood. "If he was lonely, he would call me," Knopf says. "I finally trained him to do that." On the lonely days when Fitzgerald did call, he would be invited out to the Knopfs' sprawling home on La Mesa Drive in Santa Monica. The author would drive over, sit and talk and drink a Coke. "He always seemed frightened," Knopf says of those visits. "He didn't want to say anything wrong. But he trusted us to the extent that he didn't think we would hurt him."

It must have seemed to the author that Knopf had everything that he himself did not. To begin with, there was the Knopf home itself with its big entrance, huge dining room, two living rooms, seven bedrooms, and six baths. In one of his screenplays Fitzgerald had a woman wonder aloud, "I never understood what you'd do with a big house unless you had a thousand children." To which the man replied, "Nothing but vanity. Or else sometimes you think you're so much in love that your love could fill the biggest palace conceivable."[11] The Knopfs' love *had* filled their mansion—filled it with children. Meanwhile Fitzgerald, like Last Tycoon Monroe Stahr, had only "the house he rented," and there "the empty floor stretched around him— the doors with no one sleeping behind."[12] And a man without a house meant, in Fitzgerald's symbol-studded mind, a man without a family—daughter away at school, wife away at the asylum.

There was another big, picture-filled house which Fitzgerald visited regularly. Set in Beverly Hills, it belonged to the author's lunch-time companions, the Hacketts. Once a week the couple gave a dinner party for their studio friends. It was essentially the writers' table picked up and moved to the Hacketts' house—plus a few stars like Joan Blondell, who made a pretty centerpiece.

And what did the writers do when they got together for a dinner party? They took a writer's holiday and played writing games. "Scott would pass a paper around," the Hacketts remember, "and we would all try writing jingles in imitation of Ogden." As Fitzgerald reached the end of his life, he still took an almost childlike delight in organizing such contests. In fact, that is how he autographed the Hacketts' copy of *The Great Gatsby*—with a jingle:

> When anyone dances
> It's liable to be Frances
> While a quiet and malicious racket
> Is liable to proceed from Albert Hackett
> (Writing this way is rash
> In the presence of Ogden Nash)
>> For Albert and Frances Hackett
>>> 1939

There were other contests too. "One night," the Hacketts recall, "Scott was playing some childish game sitting on the stairs with Joan Blondell." No one could quite make out what the rules of the game were, but there on the stairs, moving up and down and around, they looked like two kids playing on a slide. Fitzgerald was very fond of the actress, and yet the reformed alcoholic wrote in his notebook, "Joan Blondell always a little drunk."[13]

Sundays Fitzgerald and everyone else went to lunch at Charles and Elizabeth Brackett's. "I think it likely that the Bracketts posed for the words 'lady' and 'gentleman,'" George Oppenheimer says of the man who wrote the film *The Lost Weekend* and his wife. "Certainly they were two of the most civilized people in Hollywood. . . . They surrounded themselves not only with many of the more intelligent members of the movie colony, but they even invited 'civilians' (nonmovie people) to their house for Sunday lunch, an occasion to look forward to . . . and savor, a meeting place of natives and outlanders, a crucible of Western [Hollywood] and Eastern [New York] culture with excellent Bloody Marys."[14]

One of the outlanders, of course, was Fitzgerald; another was Aldous Huxley. One Sunday the author of *The Great Gatsby* looked on as a crowd taught the author of *Brave New World* how to play a popular word game. His first time at bat, Huxley spelled out C-O-V-E-N.

"*Coven?*" someone asked. "Whazzat?"

Fitzgerald smiled as Huxley answered, "A congregation of thirteen witches."

The game proceeded smoothly for a time. After "coven," everyone saw that Huxley could take care of himself when it came to using words. Then someone used three letters to spell out the enigmatic A-G-O.

"Ah-goo?" asked Huxley politely. "What may I ask is that?"

"*Ago,*" someone said. "Two hundred years *ago* England owned America."

"Oh," said Huxley.

Yes, some of the small Hollywood gatherings which Fitzgerald attended were fun. But then there were some of the other kind, too. He described one unidentified fête as follows: "The dinner party in fact looked just like a Metro movie—except for the lines. Since the writers could not balance the actors on their knees like ventriloquists and give them dialogue, everything was a bit flat—[William] Powell was facetious without wit—Norma [Shearer] heavy without emotion. Selznick snoring." Perhaps the party *was* a bomb, or perhaps Scott simply did not feel well that night. At another point he observed in his notebook, "The people of Hollywood are not very nice outwardly—there is too much unwelcome familiarity, too much casual snootiness."[15]

Then the parties, good and bad, changed for Fitzgerald: he no longer went out of loneliness. In fact, he no longer went alone; he started bringing Sheilah Graham. She was twenty-eight when Fitzgerald met her, and had spent most of those years getting as far away as she could—socially, economically, and geographically—from her beginnings in the London slums. Edwin Knopf didn't like her and many other people felt the same way, but Fitzgerald had escaped from the emptiness of the empty house. "Suddenly he had no attitude left except the sense that the day, at least, was complete," he wrote of his alter ego, Stahr. "He had an evening—a beginning, a middle, and an end."[16]

Miss Graham wrote in her book *Beloved Infidel* that when they went to parties, Fitzgerald

> mingled briefly with his friends and then found his place beside me in a corner of the room, and there we remained, quite content, while the wit and repartee flowed about us. Once Alan Campbell came up to us to say, almost enviously, "You two always look as though you had a secret you were going to talk about later." He was right. Our secret was us. . . .
>
> At night, when we did not go out, we put on records and danced as we had done at the Clover Club: wheeling and pirouetting, or tap dancing together or separately, brushing past each other and bowing with an elaborate, "Pardon me," if we touched. Or as I watched choking with laughter, Scott performed his own little stiff-legged dance while reciting Swinburne's "When the Hounds of Spring." Or we'd box together, Scott bouncing about me on his toes, making ferocious faces as he sparred with me: "Sheilo, keep your chin in or I'll slug you!" Or, while I prepared coffee, he whipped together a batch of fudge in my kitchen and we gorged ourselves, as happy, as uncomplicated, as two children together.[17]

Even in the evenings, however, Fitzgerald could not relax from work completely. The Pittsburgh steel mills keep trains running day and night to feed raw materials into their ovens, and the Hollywood movie machine keeps its writers running in much the same way. The studio was always following Fitzgerald home: once it even followed him to a party at the Hacketts.

Fitzgerald, like the Hacketts, was working for producer Hunt Stromberg at the time. "We asked Scott and Sheilah Graham to come to dinner," the Hacketts recount. It was to be Miss Graham's debut at the Hacketts' weekly gathering. "The actors were scared to death of her," the hosts remember. After all, the columnist had once written of King Gable: "Clark Gable threw back his handsome head and exposed a chin line upon which a thin ridge of fat is beginning to collect"; and of the girl who had come up all of the way from San Antonio, to be every shopgirl's heroine: "If they hadn't said to me, 'Miss Graham, we want you to meet Joan Crawford,' I would never have recognized her in this tired, sallow-faced woman."[18] When Joan Blondell heard that Miss Graham was going to be there, she said, "I'm not going to open my mouth."

When the couple arrived, Fitzgerald took the Hacketts aside and explained to them that he had just gotten a call from Stromberg. "As often happened with Stromberg," according to the Hacketts, "he wanted an evening conference. Scott would have to leave Sheilah and go." Only he hadn't told her yet. "He didn't dare say he had to go to a conference, he told us. She had gotten her hair all fixed for the party and he didn't want to disappoint her." When the author finally did work up the courage to tell his "Sheilo" that he would have to leave her alone and go talk things out with Stromberg, he broke the news in typical fashion. He wrote an Ogden Nash–styled poem which explained all about the call and what he would have to do—and then he read it to her. It was that same old shyness acting up again. *Come in, no you're just being polite.* "The conference went on until all hours," the Hacketts remember.

Other times the studio invaded the privacy of Fitzgerald's evening recluse hours in a more subtle and damaging way, seeping through the cracks in his self-confidence. There was, for instance, a night when George Oppenheimer drove Fitzgerald home from some Hollywood function—home at that time being one of a group of bungalows known as the Garden of Allah. Since Oppenheimer was a cousin of Edwin Knopf's wife, the conversation soon turned to MGM's head of stories, the man whose great house and great family had always been open to the novelist. Fitzgerald would later write: "Eddie Knopf and I have always been friends . . . I think I'd rather work for him than any man I've met here."[19] But that night on the way home he talked very differently of his studio superior. The toil and trouble of paranoia had begun in earnest and now even friends seem to select their weapons and join the attack.

"Eddie Knopf doesn't like me," moaned the man on the car seat beside Oppenheimer.

Oppenheimer assured Fitzgerald that Knopf did like him and liked his work.

No, Fitzgerald would not believe it. The boss had turned on him. What he could not understand was why.

Oppenheimer tried again.

Fitzgerald refused once again to be comforted.

And that was while the author still had a job. When MGM fired Fitzgerald, the paranoia got worse. Or was it all paranoia?

"Looking at it from a long view," Fitzgerald wrote his agent during the last year of his life, "the essential mystery still remains, and you would be giving me the greatest help of all if you can find out why I am in the doghouse. . . . Once Budd Schulberg told me that, while the story of an official black list is a legend, there is a kind of cabal that goes on between producers around a backgammon table, and I have an idea that some such sinister finger is upon me."

Fitzgerald wondered in his letter if the producer blackballing him might be David Selznick or Edgar ("Eddie") Mannix or Bernard ("Bernie") Hyman? "Wouldn't it be well when another offer comes up," he suggested, "for you to tell the producer *directly* that certain people don't like me? That I didn't get along with some of the big boys at Metro? And refer them to people who *do* like me like Knopf, Sidney Franklin and I think, Jeff

Lazarus. . . . In any case, it seems to me to be a necessity to find out what the underground says of me. I don't think we'll get anywhere till we *do* find out, and until you can steer any interested producers away from whoever doesn't believe in me and toward the few friends that I've made. This vague sense of competence unused and abilities unwanted is rather destructive to the morale. It would be much better for me to give up pictures forever and leave Hollywood. When you've read this letter will you give me a ring and tell me what you think?"[20]

One summer night in 1937 Fitzgerald was forced to measure his diminished stature against an old friend who loomed as a giant in both physical size and writing output, and he came away shaken. Ernest Hemingway had come to Hollywood to raise money for the Spanish Republic which was fighting for its life in yet another war which Ernest would see but Scott would miss. He had brought with him the final cut of a motion picture called *Spanish Earth* which he, Lillian Hellman, Joris Ivens, and Archibald MacLeish had made. They ran off their movie for the very rich of Hollywood and raised thirteen thousand dollars to buy ambulances for Spain. Fitzgerald attended the screening and afterward agreed to give Miss Hellman a ride over to Dorothy Parker's, where Hemingway and many others were to toast their success.

"I had met Scott Fitzgerald years before in Paris," Miss Hellman later wrote,

> but I had not seen him again until that night, and I was shocked by the change in his face and manner. He hadn't seemed to recognize me, and so I was surprised and pleased when he asked if I would ride with him to Dottie's. My admiration for Fitzgerald's work was very great, and I looked forward to talking to him alone. But we didn't talk: he was occupied with driving at ten or twelve miles an hour down Sunset Boulevard, a dangerous speed in most places, certainly in Beverly Hills. Fitzgerald crouched over the wheel when cars honked at us, we jerked to the right and then to the left, and passing drivers leaned out to shout at us. I could not bring

myself to speak, or even to look at Fitzgerald, but when I saw that his hands were trembling on the wheel . . . I put my hand over his hand. He brought the car to the side of the road.[21]

By way of explanation, Fitzgerald said, "You see, I'm on the wagon. I'll take you to Dottie's, but I don't want to go in." When they finally reached Mrs. Parker's, Fitzgerald opened Miss Hellman's door and almost whispered, "It's a long story. Ernest and me."

Ten years before, the small, yellow-haired author had helped convince Scribner's to publish his hulking, black-haired friend, but Hemingway could never forgive a favor and for the past few years the canary and the bull had circled one another warily. The reversal of roles had always been a big theme in Fitzgerald's fiction—the healer falling ill while the patient grew stronger—and now with Ernest he was living his theme. Hemingway was a success and Scott considered himself a failure.

Miss Hellman tried to change Fitzgerald's mind about not going in, but he replied, "No, I'm riding low now." Miss Hellman protested once again and Scott said, "I'm scared of Ernest, I guess, scared of being sober when—"

Miss Hellman took Fitzgerald's hand and he saw that he could not refuse. The playwright and the former novelist entered Mrs. Parker's living room just as Hemingway threw a glass against the fireplace. Fitzgerald's unsteady hold on himself seemed to shatter with the crystal. He stayed only a few minutes, evidently never spoke to Ernest, then disappeared into the night where he faced still another fear: the slow drive home at ten miles an hour.

The next day Fitzgerald decided to send a wire to the man who had made a cult of bravery and whom he had been afraid to face. The telegram said: THE PICTURE WAS BEYOND PRAISE AND SO WAS YOUR ATTITUDE.[22] Scott wrote Maxwell Perkins, who had long been both his and Ernest's editor at Scribner's, "Ernest came like a whirlwind, put Ernst Lubitsch the great director in his place by refusing to have his picture prettied up and remade for him à la Hollywood at various cocktail parties. I feel he was in a state of nervous tensity, that there was something almost religious about it."

At the studio a few days later, Ogden Nash drew Fitzgerald into a rare conversation. "It's no use writing," Scott said, "so long as Ernest is around."[23]

3

Night. To help the man get through that night there was the woman, Sheilah Graham; but to stretch those hours and make them unbearable came Fitzgerald's chronic insomnia. The author had once written an article called "Sleeping and Waking" about what the dark was like when the voices inside his head hammered:

I need not have hurt her like that.
Nor said this to him.
Nor broken myself trying to break what was unbreakable.[24]

Sometimes it would be hours before the voices died down to a whisper followed by "real sleep, the dear, the cherished one, the lullaby." Now his dreams would carry him back to that same old dream, the one which played over and over again in his sleep like a song in an old juke box:

In the fall of '16 in the cool of the afternoon
I met Caroline under a white moon
There was an orchestra—Bingo-Bango
Playing for us to dance the tango
And the people all clapped as we arose
For her sweet face and my new clothes[25]

With the morning, the author would awaken in the Capital of Escapism to find that he could no longer escape. He would pull on a gray suit that he had bought back east some years ago; then as he was going out the door, he would stuff his head into an old Homburg. He was obviously in no hurry to adjust to California's open, sunshine dress or manners. He was expected at the studio between nine and ten. When he arrived he would wearily sense what he once jokingly called "the smell of old dialogue in the writers' building."[26]

Secretaries, even technicians, had to punch in at the beginning of the day, out and in again at lunch, and out at the end of the day. The writers were spared this, but there was still that time-clock atmosphere. And yet beneath the workaday rhythm there was for Fitzgerald the excitement of an author's last gamble willingly taken up. He was betting everything on The Big Talent which he had once felt: "You know, I used to have a beautiful talent once, baby. It used to be wonderful feeling it was there."[27] Everything was riding on that number and that number only, with no energy left over to spread among friends up and down the hall.

Fitzgerald would go to the studio and he would know, as he had written in *The Crack-Up:* "I have now at last become a writer only. The man I had persistently tried to be became such a burden that I have 'cut him loose' with as little compunction as a Negro lady cuts loose a rival on Saturday night. . . . The old dream of being an entire man in the Goethe-Byron-Shaw tradition, with an opulent American touch, a sort of combination of J. P. Morgan, Topham Beauclerk and St. Francis of Assisi, has been relegated to the junk heap of the shoulder pads worn one day on the Princeton freshman football field and the overseas cap never worn overseas."[28]

In place of the Goethe-Byron-Shaw hero with his shoulder pads on and his combat fatigues too—ah, the nonsense of which dreams are made—he now strove to create a rougher beast: a screenwriter. He was quiet in the halls, but at his yellow writing tablet he could still be loud.

From that tablet came a polish job on A Yank at Oxford (1938), a funny, predictable story about a Yank who began his Oxford career by getting his pants taken off. The picture would make screen history not for what it was but for where it was made—England. It was one of the first "runaway" productions, but the script was prepared back home in Hollywood, which meant that it was built on an assembly line. Fitzgerald was asked to rewrite someone else's half-finished script, and then, when he was finished, a whole string of writers rewrote what he had written.

After *Yank* came *Three Comrades* (1938), and this time Fitzgerald wasn't rewriting anyone; he got first crack at the script. But after the screenplay was finished, the producer wanted to make some changes. "He wanted Margaret Sullavan to live," Fitzgerald wrote later, remembering one of the many battles fought over the script. "He said the picture would make more money if Margaret Sullavan lived. He was reminded that Camille had also coughed her life away and had made many fortunes doing it. He pondered this for a minute; then he said, '*Camille* would have made twice as much if Garbo had lived.' 'What about the greatest love story of all?' he was asked. 'How about *Romeo and Juliet*—you wouldn't have wanted Juliet to live, would you?' 'That's just it,' said the producer, '*Romeo and Juliet* [a 1936 Metro film] didn't make a cent.' "[29] The writer and the producer quarreled bitterly, but they nonetheless managed to put together a sound script, and their movie was selected by the *New York Times* as one of the best of the year.

The novelist-turned-screenwriter was off to a good start; his salary was raised from one thousand to twelve hundred fifty dollars a week. Then suddenly, just as the apprenticeship was ending and Fitzgerald was beginning to write his best scripts, his work stopped reaching the cameras. Inexplicably, his chance to conquer Hollywood was already behind him, lost somewhere back in the vast obscurity of the Hollywood machine. After *Comrades*, Fitzgerald wrote *Infidelity* (1939), his best script yet; it was an original screenplay which looked back to the luxurious New York apartments and fashionable Long Island estates where Gatsby had loved a woman and lost his life. But the industry censor stopped the film because infidelity simply was not allowed in the movie houses in the thirties. The studio changed the title to *Fidelity*, hoping that no one would come out against *that*, but the trick did not work and the picture was never made.

Fitzgerald's next assignment was to write a screen adaptation

of Clare Booth's fingernail-sharp comedy *The Women* (1939). As
he worked on the project, he began to toy with the idea of a new
kind of heroine, something more exciting than a warmed-over
flapper. But again he began to quarrel with his producer, a man
whose original genius had been blunted by drugs. After completing two drafts of the script, he was moved to another picture,
Madame Curie.

In *Madame Curie* (1939) Fitzgerald found his modern heroine.
In a letter to his daughter, Scott said, "The more I read about
the woman the more I think about her as one of the most admirable people of our time. I hope we can get a little of that
into the story." Fitzgerald's bosses, however, thought that there
were too many test tubes and not enough romance in his screenplay; the author was fired from the studio.

For several months he moved about like a traveling salesman
from one studio to another, working on *Winter Carnival, Air
Raid, Raffles,* and the great one, *Gone with the Wind.* Then he
got a job with an independent producer, adapting his own short
story "Babylon Revisited" for the screen. Fitzgerald called his
screenplay *Cosmopolitan* and it was quite simply the best script
he ever wrote. But the star whom the producer wanted to hire
asked too high a price, so Fitzgerald's best screenplay took its
place alongside his other trophies: the pads never worn in a
game, the overseas cap never worn overseas, the movie never
shown on the screen.

Fitzgerald died in Hollywood shortly after two o'clock on a
winter afternoon in December 1940. He had arrived in the sum-
mertime just three and a half years before. He had come into Los
Angeles by plane, and as they dropped down for the landing the
air had gotten rougher, causing more bumps, but Scott had not
been thinking of bumps then. He had been looking out the plane's
window at the flashing neon signs of the city. He said that they
looked like "fireworks" and that they gave him a "feeling of new
worlds to conquer."[30] At the very beginning as he looked down
on all those lights, he must have known the same wonder which
struck Gatsby "when he first picked out the green light at the

end of Daisy's dock."[31] He had come a long way to this sprawling Western city, and his goal "must have seemed so close that he could hardly fail to grasp it." He could hardly wait to get down to work. He already had some ideas for that college film they wanted him to do.

Flashback

1

When the Horn Brothers finished their act, the house lights went down. Koster and Bial's vaudeville theatre, located on New York's Herald Square, went as black as a mustachioed villain's thoughts. The Gay Nineties were about to receive a spark which would make them even gayer, but for one moment that spark lay incubating in total darkness. The first-nighters giggled, squirmed in their seats, whispered like children, "What is it?" A machine which the *New York Times* said looked like "the double turret of a big monitor" began to make "a loud buzzing and roaring." The eighth act on the vaudeville bill was beginning, but it was like no other act ever seen by an audience before. A shaft of light hung itself like a clothesline from the projector to the screen, and on that screen a picture not only moved but actually danced.

Two pretty girls were wearing pink and blue dresses, their picture as real as if Peter Paul Rubens had painted it, and they were twirling their parasols, doing a dance-step routine. The *Dramatic Mirror* said, "The effect was the same as if the girls were on stage."

Then the screen went black and white and suddenly there was the ocean, its waves washing the screen and tickling the inner ear: whoever heard of getting seasick in a vaudeville theatre? The sea rolled for several seconds and the audience seemed to think they rolled, too. The scene changed again as two slapstick comics came on and began swatting at one another. After the comics a tall blonde danced a skirt dance, and the show was over. The act, billed as "Thomas A. Edison's Latest Marvel, the Vitascope," was a hit.[1] The *Times* said that the theatregoers cheered "vociferously."

The historic year was 1896: the movies, as a popular entertainment, had been born. That same year marked the birth of F. Scott Fitzgerald. The novelist and the film industry grew up together. In 1906, as Marcus Loew—later the founder of Loew's Theatres and MGM—was beginning to move primitive projectors into his New York penny arcade, Fitzgerald was beginning in show business, too. It was then that the actor Dustin Farnum entered his life, trailing clouds of stage romance. Fitzgerald was living in Buffalo at the time, and Farnum was acting in a Buffalo summer-stock company; he often gave Scott complimentary tickets to his shows. "He used to go to the Wild West movies and the Tech Stock Company," Fitzgerald's ledger reports (in the third person); Scott even memorized many of the speeches. Inspired by the theatre world which Farnum had opened to him, Fitzgerald "made up shows in Ingham's attic," according to the ledger; these plays were "all based on the American Revolution and a red sash and three-cornered hat." He even rigged a sheet as a curtain, invited the neighborhood children, and then charged them admission to see his dramas; money and the theatre were already fused in the young impresario's imagination. There was competition for the boy Fitzgerald, however, just as there was for the young Loew. "Gus Shy's play put him temporarily in the shade," Fitzgerald wrote of himself. "Finally the moving-picture machine Lucky's uncle gave him eclipsed Gus Shy."[2]

In 1908, the year the Fitzgeralds moved to St. Paul's Summit Avenue, the movies themselves attempted their own move uptown. A company known as Film d'Art, formed in France for the express purpose of introducing the lowly movie audiences to the world's greatest stage artists, released its first film, *The Assassination of the Duc de Guise*. American producers soon took up the idea and, among other things, turned out a completely silent *Hamlet* which ran just ten minutes. The movies were beginning to mold themselves into a form which might have bored the boy who loved his "Wild West movies," but which would later interest the grown-up artist in Fitzgerald.

For his third year of preparatory study, Fitzgerald left St. Paul for the Newman School on the outskirts of Hackensack, New Jersey. In his ledger he wrote: "Poor marks and on bounds. Trips to New York." That year movie audiences around the world were introduced to the fabulous Sarah Bernhardt in a film version of her play *Queen Elizabeth* (1912), but Fitzgerald paid more attention to Ina Claire, star of *The Quaker Girl*, and Gertrude Bryan, star of *Little Boy Blue*. "Confused by hopeless melancholy love for them both," the author wrote, "I was unable to choose between them—so they blurred into one lovely entity, the girl."[3] In one of his autobiographical stories Fitzgerald remembered The Girl this way: "Yes, she was, indeed, like that song—a Beautiful Rose of the Night. The waltz buoyed her up, brought her with it to a point of aching beauty and then let her slide back to life across its last bars as a leaf slants to earth across the air. The high life of New York!"[4] Or put more simply: "She didn't have wings, but audiences agreed generally that she didn't need them."[5] So it was that Fitzgerald could hardly think of New York without thinking of the theatres there, and the girls who made them luminous.

Before long he wanted to do more than just "sit in the audience without helping to make the play."[6] "In school I went off on a new tack," he wrote. ". . . my desk bulged with Gilbert and Sullivan librettos and dozens of notebooks containing the germs of dozens of musical comedies."[7]

That summer, as Mack Sennett was setting up his Keystone studio where "kops" would run riot, Fitzgerald was busy, too. On the train home for summer vacation, the fifteen-year-old author wrote his first full-length play. It was about a cat burglar and it was called *The Captured Shadow*. Enjoying an autonomy which he would never have once he turned pro, Fitzgerald cast himself not only as the author but also as director-producer and bit player. The other roles were played by his St. Paul friends. The show was performed at Mrs. Backus' School on August 23, 1912, and the next day the young showman pasted his first notices into his scrapbook. One review said that "much favorable comment was elicited by the young author's cleverness"—the young author cleverly underlined the words in red. Then, beside all of the reviews, he wrote in big block letters: ENTER SUCCESS.[8]

Later, Fitzgerald wrote a short story, also called "The Captured Shadow," about writing and staging the play; in it he described what he had learned from his first real attempt at playwriting. For example, there had been one laugh he had not expected. Chinaman Rudd had been entrusted with one of the young playwright's favorite jokes. When asked what an alderman was, the Chinaman said candidly, "An alderman is halfway between a politician and a pirate." The audience sat unmoved. A moment later "Bill Kampf absent-mindedly wiped his forehead with his handkerchief and then stared at it, startled by the red stains of make-up on it—and the audience roared. The theatre was like that."[9]

Years later in Hollywood, as Fitzgerald watched child stars like Judy Garland, Mickey Rooney, and Freddie Bartholomew moving about the sets, they reminded him of the boys and girls of St. Paul getting up their show. They even gave him an idea. He began to imagine Judy and Mickey and Freddie in a movie based on his story about his first play. It sounded so good that he sent off a memo to Edwin Knopf proposing that Metro do a film called *The Captured Shadow*. "There is my theme," he wrote, "the Impresario in the Days of his Youth." Fitzgerald went on to say that the plot should turn on the hero's discovery that the only way to get his play staged was "by reducing his ideas (just as we have to do in pictures)."[10] The project ended, however, with Fitzgerald reducing his own ideas and working on a picture assigned him by his bosses.

Since *The Captured Shadow* did so well in St. Paul it was followed the next summer by *The Coward,* which played to a sellout crowd at the YWCA auditorium and made a hundred and fifty dollars for the Baby Welfare Association—twice what *Shadow* had made. Fitzgerald wrote, directed, produced, and this time starred in the play, which concerns a Southerner who at first refuses to fight in the Civil War, then finds the courage to enlist, and becomes a hero. In his scrapbook the author wrote large THE GREAT EVENT. He underlined in red a review sentence which said, "Scott Fitzgerald, the author, played the part of Lieut. Charles Douglas with great success."[11]

Show business even helped Fitzgerald pick out a university. "Near the end of my last year at school I came across a new musical-comedy score lying on top of the piano," he remembered. "It was a show called *His Honor the Sultan,* and the title furnished the information that it had been presented by the Triangle Club of Princeton University. That was enough for me. From then on the university question was settled. I was bound for Princeton."[12]

In September of 1913—the year Charlie Chaplin entered the Keystone studio at a salary of one hundred fifty dollars a week— Fitzgerald entered Princeton. The moment he passed his entrance examination, he wired his mother: ADMITTED SEND FOOTBALL PADS AND SHOES IMMEDIATELY.[13] But instead of playing football—or studying either, for that matter—Fitzgerald spent most of his freshman year at the university doing what he had come there to do: working for the Triangle Club. His ledger entries for that year are spotted with the club symbol. "Oct [1913]—The △ meeting"; "Nov—Working on △ lyrics"; "Dec—Working on lights in Casino"; "Feb [1914]—Began △ play"; "Mar—Working hard on △ play." The results of all this work for Triangle were summed up by Fitzgerald as follows: "I failed in algebra, trigonometry, coordinate geometry, and hygiene."[14]

By tutoring over the summer, however, the shaky student managed to come back to Princeton the next fall as a sophomore. But
more important to Fitzgerald, he came back not only as a second-
year man but also as a successful college playwright. His ledger
tells the story: "Sept—Play accepted"; "Nov—△ rehearsing";
"Feb [1915]—Secretary of △ Club on 26th"; "April—New York
△ show." The Fitzgerald musical which the Triangle accepted,
rehearsed, and then took on a road trip all the way from New
York to St. Paul, was called *Fie! Fie! Fi-Fi!* It was the story of a
Chicago gangster who took over Monaco as easily as if it had
been a floating crap game. But the gangster is undone by his
estranged wife Fi-Fi who, reduced to the position of manicurist
in a Monacan hotel, sides with the Monacans and helps them win
their country back. The play went well. The *Brooklyn Citizen*
declared: "This delicious little vehicle was announced as a
musical comedy and the name can only be disputed to the extent
that it is also given to innumerable Broadway productions that
possess less vivacity, less sparkling humor, and less genuine
music."[15]

The year *Fie! Fie! Fi-Fi!* hit New York, so did D. W. Griffith's
The Birth of a Nation. With this one film the movie industry's
labor pains ended and the modern motion picture was born. The
camera panned; it rode with the Klansmen when the Klan rode;
it rushed in for dramatic close-ups—all Griffith innovations. No
less a critic than Woodrow Wilson said that the picture was "like
writing history in lightning."[16] Fitzgerald saw the film and felt
the lightning, too; in 1920 he visited Griffith's New York studio
and "trembled in the presence of the familiar faces of *The Birth
of a Nation.*"[17]

The academic year which followed the success of *Fie! Fie!
Fi-Fi!* might well have been entitled *Fie! Fie! Fitzgerald!* What
happened was this: Edmund Wilson, later a sometimes forbid-
dingly serious critic, turned out a zany musical drama called *The
Evil Eye.* Fitzgerald, however, was not left out: he wrote the
lyrics for Wilson's book. A quarter-century later the two men

would collaborate again—except that it would not really be collaboration, for Wilson's work on the unfinished manuscript of *The Last Tycoon* would not begin until Fitzgerald was already dead.

Besides his efforts as lyricist, the author also served the Triangle as photographers' *femme fatale*. That is, he posed for publicity pictures dressed, in traditional Triangle kick-line fashion, as a chorus girl. His picture appeared in newspapers all across the country accompanied by the caption: "Considered the Most Beautiful 'Show Girl' in the Princeton Triangle Club's New Musical Play."[18] Charles Bornhapt, a producer, saw the photograph in the *New York Times* and offered to find the lovely Fitzgerald a role on Broadway.

But again the busy author-actor was in academic trouble. He was on the point of failing at Princeton when what doctors diagnosed as malaria allowed him to retire from school gracefully. "I wore myself out on a musical comedy," he wrote later, "which I . . . organized and mostly directed while the president played football. Result: I slipped way back in my work, got [sick], lost a year in college—and, irony of ironies, because of [a] scholastic slip I wasn't allowed to take the presidency of the Triangle."[19] Elsewhere he said: "Almost my final memory before I left was of writing a last lyric on that year's Triangle production while in bed in the infirmary with a high fever."[20] Fitzgerald sat in the audience when *The Evil Eye* played in St. Paul that spring.

At home convalescing, the young dramatist had plenty of time to write another Triangle play—one which, like many of his Hollywood scripts, was never produced. His ledger says "April [1916]—Writing △ play," and then adds, "May—Play refused." So once again he wrote the lyrics for another author's play, a production called *Safety First*.

In September of 1917, his senior year, Fitzgerald achieved the rank of professional author, making his first sale—a poem for which *Poet Lore* paid two dollars. The same year Charlie Chaplin, twenty-seven, made a sale also: he signed a contract with First National for one million dollars a year. Appropriately, one of Chaplin's first pictures, filmed in 1914, had been called *Making a Living*.

In November Fitzgerald moved out of his Princeton dormitory room and into a barracks at Fort Leavenworth, Kansas. So far as the author was concerned, the university had lost its savor. When he had failed to reach the top of the Triangle, Fitzgerald felt that he had lost more than a few hundred watts of limelight: from the beginning, the stage had been to him a political and social instrument. The Triangle presidency would have given him real stature at Princeton, perhaps even gotten him onto the Senior Council. By way of the Triangle, later by way of Broadway and Hollywood, Fitzgerald was to have arrived. But as he later wrote, "There were to be no badges of pride, no medals, after all."[21]

There were no medals awaiting the author in the Army either: he joined too late to "get over" to the war in Europe. There was something to take the place of decorations, however. In 1918, while Chaplin was filming *Shoulder Arms*, Fitzgerald, stationed at Camp Sheridan, Alabama, met Zelda Sayre. After the war he went north to New York where he got paid for writing advertising copy and got nothing for writing in a number of other genres. "I had one hundred and twenty-two rejection slips pinned in a frieze about my room," he remembered. "I wrote movies. I wrote song lyrics. I wrote complicated advertising schemes. I wrote poems. I wrote sketches. I wrote jokes."[22] It looked as though Fitzgerald's writing career would go the way of his football career. Then in 1919 the author scored.

That year the original Metro Company paid out twenty thousand dollars for Blasco Ibáñez' popular novel *The Four Horsemen of the Apocalypse*, and Charles Scribner's Sons bought *This Side of Paradise*. In 1920, the year the novel was published, Marcus Loew bought Metro itself for over three million dollars. Already Fitzgerald as a novelist faced a kind of competition of which Dickens and George Eliot had never dreamed, but he was not worried. He liked show business, all kinds of show business, and that meant movies too.

2

To read *This Side of Paradise* is to see again that love, dreams, money, and drama were in some ways wound up on the same reel in Fitzgerald's imagination. Love was not only the thing all those plays and movies were about. Love itself *was* a kind of play. It had been that way since those first dramas he made up in the attic. In describing Amory Blaine's feelings, the author recalled his own love for the theatre, a love which is entwined with his love for The Girl. "The play was *The Little Millionaire*," he wrote of one of Amory's trips to New York, "with George M. Cohan, and there was one stunning young brunette who made him sit with brimming eyes in the ecstasy of watching her dance." Amory's friend Paskert puts his own admiration into strong words: "Yes, sir, I'd marry that girl tonight!" But Amory is a more complex lover; he feels a certain ambivalence toward the star and the stage, an ambivalence which would stay with his creator right through his life to his Hollywood days. "I wonder about actresses," he says. "Are they all pretty bad?"[23]

There were shows in Princeton, too: for Amory, like Fitzgerald, soon discovers that about the only way romance ever entered that isolated college town was by way of the mailman's pouch or the movie house. The girls on the screen were, in fact, the only members of the opposite sex whom he saw regularly. He enjoyed going to the movies and sitting in the dark while other boys shouted:

"Clinch!"

"Oh, *clinch!*"

"Kiss her, kiss 'at lady, *quick!*"

"Oh-h-h——!"[24]

When Amory meets Rosalind, love and drama become so entangled in the book and in the author's mind that the romantic scenes are actually written in dramatic form, as if they were to be enacted in the theatres of New York or on the moving-picture stages of California. For example:

AMORY: Suppose—we fell in love.
ROSALIND: I've suggested pretending.
AMORY: If we did it would be very big.[25]

And if love to the young Fitzgerald was drama, then lovers
were likely to be actors. As a boy he had once tried to instruct
his shy sister on how to *act* with men: "Expression, that is facial
expression, is one of your weakest points," he wrote. "A girl of
your good looks and at your age ought to have almost perfect
control of her face. It ought to be almost like a mask. . . . Get
before a mirror and practice a smile and get a good one."[26] Much
later at the age of forty he would write in his *Crack-Up* essays:
"And a smile—ah, I would get me a smile. I'm still working on
that smile. It is to combine the best qualities of a hotel manager,
an experienced old social weasel, a headmaster on visitors' day,
a colored elevator man, a pansy pulling a profile, a producer
getting stuff at half its market value. . . ."[27] Yes, Fitzgerald took
acting seriously. Rosalind is always playing the little actress and
Amory the actor. "He sees himself constantly not as a human
being," wrote Heywood Broun, "but as a man in a novel or in a
play. Every move is a picture and there is a cameraman behind
each tree."[28]

For love, life, and drama to become confused past all un-
tangling, the only thing that remained was for Fitzgerald and
Zelda to act out their real-life love in play form, and that is
exactly the job one movie producer offered them. He wanted
Scott and Zelda to play their fictional alter egos, Amory Blaine
and Rosalind Connage, in the movie version of *This Side of
Paradise*. Fitzgerald's editor Maxwell Perkins, with ancestors
buried in Puritan New England, was horrified by the idea. The
author tried to win him over by promising that this would be his
"first and last appearance positively."[29] After all, why shouldn't
the Most Beautiful Show Girl of Princeton's Triangle Club (and
his wife) be seen by all who were willing to buy tickets? Fitzgerald could still remember those days when the movies—as well

as magazine editors and publishers—had regarded him as if he
were invisible. Now he was beginning to enjoy visibility. But
before Fitzgerald could give the producer a definite yes or no,
the project was shelved, only to be revived three years later in
1923.

3

In September of 1920, as the undergraduates were going back to
classes and homework at Princeton, Scribner's brought out a
collection of Fitzgerald's short stories called *Flappers and Philosophers.* These stories won for the author his first success with
motion-picture sales. To Zelda, who had refused to marry him on
the grounds that he was poor, he wired the following love note:
I HAVE SOLD THE MOVIE RIGHTS OF HEAD AND SHOULDERS TO THE
METRO COMPANY FOR TWENTY FIVE HUNDRED DOLLARS I LOVE YOU
DEAREST GIRL.[30] Metro quickly produced a movie based on the
story, calling it *The Chorus Girl's Romance.* Not long after, Fitzgerald sold "The Offshore Pirate" to the same company for another twenty-five hundred, and again the story was quickly
filmed. It was the kind of success that the author would not fully
appreciate until twenty years later, when as a Metro screenwriter
he would see how hard getting stories onto the screen could be.

It was appropriate that, of all the stories which Fitzgerald had
published, the movie studio should pick the two it did, for both
have to do with the world of entertainment. In "Head and Shoulders" the heroine is an actress named Marcia Meadow, and the
hero, by contrast, a precocious, monklike student named Horace
Tarbox, who is "leading the sophomore class by several lengths."[31]
When Horace and Marcia meet, Horace falls in love and therefore puts aside his life of passive contemplation to enter the
world of action: he joins a circus. So the circus, that passing show,
becomes one of Fitzgerald's metaphors for the active world and
life itself.

"The Offshore Pirate" is linked to show business more obliquely.
The story is about a girl named Ardita who is bored because she
is pursued by too many run-of-the-mill heirs to industrial for-

tunes. Kidnaped by a band of offshore pirates, Ardita asks the leader to tell her the story of his life. "Why?" he wants to know. "Going to write a movie about me?"[32] When Ardita is finally rescued and it is revealed that her pirate is no pirate at all but a young millionaire, she is neither relieved nor disappointed. She simply says in a low voice, "What an imagination! I want you to lie to me just as sweetly as you know how for the rest of my life."[33] It would seem that in courtship the play is indeed the thing to catch the admiration of a heroine worth having.

In October 1921 the Fitzgerald's only child, Scottie, was born. The author wired Zelda's parents: LILLIAN GISH IS IN MOURNING CONSTANCE TALMADGE IS A BACK NUMBER A SECOND MARY PICKFORD HAS ARRIVED.[34] Half a year later in 1922 there was another new arrival, a novel called *The Beautiful and Damned*. It told the prophetic story of a heroine who loses her beauty and a hero who sinks into alcoholism. One of the characters in the book is a novelist who begins his career with a brilliant novel and ends it "making a great fortune writing trash for the movies."[35]

The novel, however, does not dismiss all movies as trash. In fact, the world of the movie studio is once more seen as a metaphor for the world of action. Again and again Gloria Gilbert Patch is offered the opportunity to enter this world, but Anthony is opposed. "It's so silly!" he argues. "You don't want to go into the movies—moon around a studio all day with a lot of cheap chorus people." "Lot of mooning around Mary Pickford does!" says Gloria. ". . . Perhaps if I *did* go into this for a while it'd stir you up so you'd do something."[36] She finally relents, however, and—like Anthony—does nothing. Her failure to go into the movies pairs with Anthony's failure to go to war, even as a war correspondent. Neither *acts*.

While Scott worked on his book about Gloria Gilbert, the star who never was, Zelda herself was trying to make up her mind about a movie career. One of the Fitzgeralds' friends posed the problem in his diary. "What shall Zelda do?" he asked. "I think she might do a little housework—[apartment] looks like a pig sty. . . . I told her she would have to make up her mind whether she wanted to go in movies or get in with young married set. To do that would require a little effort & Zelda will never make an effort."[37]

Happily, the fictional Gloria did finally make her way to the screen, her chance coming in the movie version of *The Beautiful and Damned*. Fitzgerald sold the novel to Warner Brothers in 1922 "for $2,500 which seems a small price. . . . Please don't tell anyone what I got for it."[38] The movie starred Marie Prevost as Gloria and Kenneth Harlan as Anthony, and was described by one reviewer as "one of the most horrific motion pictures of memory."[39]

4

Fitzgerald followed *The Beautiful and Damned* with a collection of stories called *Tales of the Jazz Age*. In that volume he gave the world a larger-than-life symbol of absolute wealth: it was a "diamond bigger than the Ritz-Carlton Hotel." In his story "The Diamond as Big as the Ritz," this emblem of extravagance is paired with another larger-than-life symbol: Hollywood. For who besides Hollywood would be more suited for the job of fashioning a setting for such a gem? When hero John Unger asks about the architect who planned the mansion built atop the great diamond, Percy Washington answers, "I blush to tell you, but it was a moving-picture fella. He was the only man we found who was used to playing with an unlimited amount of money. . . ." The moving-picture man did, however, have his drawbacks—"he did tuck his napkin in his collar and couldn't read or write."[40] It would therefore seem that even in his twenties, before any real exposure to the medium, Fitzgerald felt the same love-hate for Hollywood that he felt for the very rich. Just as he saw that the rich could be both romantic and cruel, so he saw the two faces of the movies. If one mask smiled and dispersed "an unlimited amount of money," another mask wore its napkin at its chin and was illiterate.

In his quest for the kind of wealth represented by the imaginary diamond, Fitzgerald turned to the stage with a play

called *The Vegetable, or from President to Postman.* He wrote
Perkins that he was writing "an awfully funny play that's going
to make me rich forever. It really is. I'm so damned tired of the
feeling that I'm living up to my income."[41] Of course the near-
miss aspirant for president of the Triangle Club had his designs
on more than wealth. In another letter to Perkins, and in an
equally self-assured tone, he wrote, "It is, I think, the best American comedy to date and undoubtedly the best thing I have ever
written."[42]

The year 1923 was an important one in the history of enter-
tainment. That year René Clair released his first film, *Paris Qui
Dort;* Cecil B. De Mille premièred his landmark extravaganza
The Ten Commandments; and Irving Thalberg, about whom
Fitzgerald would later write *The Last Tycoon,* went to work for
Louis B. Mayer. Fitzgerald himself opened *The Vegetable,* "the
best American comedy to date," and it bombed. The unlucky day
was November 20, the place the Apollo Theatre in Atlantic City.

The play was the story of Jerry Frost, a downtrodden railroad
clerk who dreams the American Dream of becoming President. In
the second act the clerk's fantasy was acted out so that the
audience actually saw Jerry functioning as President. Of course
the satire worked the other way, too. Fitzgerald was also showing
the clerkishness of the then President Harding. In the last act
Jerry wakes up and becomes the postman he had wanted to be
in the first place—happy ending. "His main point," writes Arthur
Mizener, "is that the American dream of rising from newsboy to
President is ridiculous and that the Jerry Frosts of this world are
far happier being the postmen nature made them than being
presidents."[43] Even Edmund Wilson, sometimes a harsh critic
of Fitzgerald's thought processes, seemed pleased with the intellectual content of the drama: "I think you have a much better
grasp on your subject than you usually have," he wrote his old
Princeton friend, "—you know what end and point you are
working for as isn't always the case with you."[44] But if the play
made points, it did not make people laugh—or so the audience
seemed to think. Playing on his hero's cold name, Fitzgerald

described opening night as follows: "It was a colossal frost. People left their seats and walked out, people rustled their programs and talked audibly in bored impatient whispers. After the second act I wanted to stop the show and say it was all a mistake but the actors struggled heroically on."[45] One of those who walked out while the play was still in progress—according to Ernest Truex, who played Jerry Frost—was Fitzgerald's close friend Ring Lardner. Accompanying Ring was F. Scott Fitzgerald himself. Some time later when Harold Ober, Fitzgerald's agent, tried to revive interest in the play, the author wrote him: ". . . the whole thing has already cost me about a year and a half of work so I'd rather let it drop. It's honestly no good."[46]

Fitzgerald's dream of the boy from St. Paul who grows up to be the George Bernard Shaw of the American theatre had for the moment proved as futile as dreaming of the Presidency. But Fitzgerald was still in no mood to give up show business. For even as *The Vegetable* was failing, interest in a movie version of *This Side of Paradise* revived, and Fitzgerald was to help write the screenplay. Famous Players paid him ten thousand dollars; for their money they were to receive the rights to *Paradise* and what the author called "a ten-thousand word condensation of my book." "This is not a synopsis," he told a reporter, "but a variation of the story better suited for screening."[47]

The treatment which Fitzgerald wrote for Famous Players began with a discussion of what the author thought the movie should be about. "The theme," he explained, "should be the struggles of the ideals of the young, as exemplified by Amory and Rosalind, against the snobbish and mercenary world into which they were born." "The spirit of the picture," he went on to say, "should be that of the book—the affairs of youth taken seriously."[48] The problem was that in plotting his movie the young author took the affairs of youth a little too seriously—so seriously, in fact, that all loves and hates, happinesses and sorrows, are magnified to the point of melodrama. At one moment the heroine is reduced to tears, at another the hero is elevated to the lofty position of Christ figure.

Scott had not worked out exactly what scenes should be included in the movie, but he did know how he wanted the audience to feel about his hero—sympathetic.

> In order to gain sympathy for Amory at the very start, it would be best to show movie audiences more *obviously* that he is a victim of environment and wrong education. . . . Some nurse might point out St. Francis of Assisi or Sir Galahad to him as a great Saint and Amory might be thrilled, but his mother might angrily snatch him away and point to Lord Chesterfield as a better model for a boy.

By the time Amory arrives at Princeton, "he is a complete product of his environment: arrogant, lazy, selfish—everything that the world wishes onto a child of wealth."

But at the university Amory, by now "an impossible little snob," meets Burne Holiday and "learns that here in college, away from sycophants and snobs, there is such a thing as an honest admiration for nobility of character." Amory has now outgrown Lord Chesterfield; with Holiday as his new saint, he mends his faults so that "the spark of divinity, so nearly extinguished, comes back to life."

Fitzgerald described the two girls in Amory's life in terms of the Jazz Age: Eleanor is "the spirit of wild jazz" and Rosalind "the spirit of, on the whole, good jazz." He went on:

> We could contrast Rosalind and Eleanor not as the bad modern girl and the good, non-existent 1890 girl, but both as Jazz Age girls using the manners of this age in different ways. There is a new generation of movie patrons growing up who never lived in any age but the age of jazz music and wouldn't recognize the innocent country girl if they saw her—or if she existed.

Like many of Scott's later movie ideas, this one would have been hard to photograph, since jazz is invisible, but still the description retains its charm, for the author was reinterpreting his girls in the terms of an age they helped to create.

Amory discovers that he prefers good jazz to wild, but he

also finds that Rosalind sometimes degenerates into cacophony: she has a tendency to be "lazy, mercenary, and selfish, all these qualities being cultivated by a silly, avaricious mother." The girl's "shortcomings . . . strike a sympathetic chord in him, because of their similarity to his own," and soon he "falls deeply in love."

When Amory's mother dies and his fortune is wiped out, however, the blow brings "terror to Rosalind as money is to her a prime requisite." She cannot stop loving Amory, "but heavens! what can she do without money?" She writes in her diary that the only way she could ever bring herself to marry Amory "would be sometime when she is thoroughly tight." She does, of course, get tight, and:

> They go to a dreadful little apartment of a Brooklyn clergyman. . . . The surroundings start to sober her. She realizes that this is the sort of place she will have to live in with Amory. . . . Amory runs down to the florist on the corner to buy Rosalind some flowers. While he is gone Rosalind opens her diary (which she carries everywhere) to the page in which she wrote that the only time she could marry Amory would be when she was tight. She scrawls after it: "I've sobered up. Good-by." Then she hurries home. Amory comes back with a cheap little wedding bouquet . . . and finds her good-by message. It all but kills him, while Rosalind, headed home in a taxi, is weeping.

Fitzgerald must have hoped that his audience would do likewise.

Scott made matters worse—both for Amory and for his movie—by bringing Burne Holiday back into the story. Holiday, now wealthy, begins to court Rosalind, and one night Amory hears that the girl he loves and his former idol have eloped. Too late, he sets out to try to stop them. "Rosalind and Holiday are married . . . they go off through the rain, Holiday driving, and the accident takes place. Holiday is killed. . . . Amory comes upon the accident." In the novel, when Dick Humbird is killed in a car crash, it is the very randomness, the pointlessness, of the death which strikes and frightens us. When Burne Holiday dies a similar death in the movie version, however, we feel that it has all been contrived by the author so that Amory will get the girl.

Now that her husband is dead, "Rosalind's big moment has come . . . She tells Amory that they were not eloping, that Holiday brought her out to talk to her and lecture her on her worthlessness. And so Rosalind gives Amory back his soul." Amory's "Christ vision," which Fitzgerald saw as the "high point" of his picture, is at hand. "He picks up the body of his dead friend and as he stands looking into his face, a look that is Christlike comes over him." In the last scene of the movie treatment, "Amory takes [Rosalind] in his arms and we realize that, at last, he is strong enough to work out the destinies of both of them."

The movie was different from the book: this time the boy was to get the girl. The author, of course, had gotten his girl so why shouldn't his hero get his? Scott would later write of his own courtship of Zelda.

It was one of those tragic loves doomed for lack of money, and one day the girl closed it out on the basis of common sense. During a long summer of despair I wrote a novel instead of letters, so it came out all right, but it came out all right for a different person.[49]

And the same might be said of Amory: the Amory who lost Rosalind in the novel is "a different person" from the Amory who wins her in the movie version of *Paradise*. In the novel, Amory appeared as a kind of "spoiled priest,"[50] but in the movie he is made over into a Savior and the whole story is shifted a little too close to Paradise for comfort.

Back in 1920 Fitzgerald had told a reporter quite prophetically, "I suspect it must be difficult to mold my stuff into the conventional movie form with its creaky mid-Victorian sugar. Personally, when I go to the pictures, I like to see a pleasant flapper like Constance Talmadge or I want to see comedies like those of Chaplin's or Lloyd's. I'm not strong for the uplift stuff. It simply isn't life to me."[51] What better critique of Fitzgerald's own adaptation of *This Side of Paradise* for the movies? The movie industry had come a long way since that night when Edison showed his pictures in Koster and Bial's vaudeville theatre, but Fitzgerald's idea of the movies had not come nearly so far. He took his lifelike modern novel and turned it into a gaslight drama which would have been more at home back in the nineties. Scott and Zelda did not star in *This Side of Paradise* because the picture was never made.

Paradise did not make Fitzgerald's Hollywood fortune, but the young author was not discouraged. Before long he would be on his way to Hollywood in person, not only to try out as a screenwriter but to screen-test as a leading man.

☆ 3 ☆

Beginning in Hollywood

1

Scott knocked while Zelda waited, ladylike, by his side. Carmel Myers, the star, opened the door and welcomed the Fitzgeralds to the party and to Hollywood. Miss Myers led the famous author and his legendary wife into the living room where stars, producers, directors, and even a few screenwriters waited. Graciously, she guided the newcomers from celebrity to celebrity the way Jay Gatsby guided Tom and Daisy when they came to his party.

The Fitzgeralds had earned their invitation several years before in Rome where they met Carmel Myers on the set of *Ben Hur* and watched as cameras recorded her diminutive beauty against a backdrop of "bigger and grander papier-mâché arenas than the real ones."[1] On Miss Myers' bookshelf stood a copy of *The Great Gatsby*, a souvenir of those days in Rome; it was inscribed, "For Carmel Myers from her Corrupter F. Scott Fitzgerald. 'Don't cry, little girl, maybe some day someone will come along who'll make you a dishonest woman.' "[2] The Fitzgeralds had shown the star a good time in Europe and now she wanted them to have a good time in California. She got what she wanted. No one enjoyed her party more than Scott and Zelda, although a good many guests, most of them women, enjoyed it considerably less.

Like two children being shown off by their parents, Scott and Zelda dutifully said how-do-you-do to all of the people to whom they were introduced, then disappeared to carry on with their games. They had heard a lot about this new Babylon, this Hollywood, but it wasn't living up to its reputation—the Fitzgeralds planned to change that. They found the cloak room, filled their arms with ladies' purses and headed for the kitchen.

Miss Myers was one of the first to smell something burning. She joined in the rush to the kitchen to look for the fire. There the hostess and her guests discovered Scott and Zelda, weak with laughter. On the stove stood a giant pot and inside were all the purses, boiling merrily in tomato sauce.

The year was 1927. Fitzgerald had been threatening to come to Hollywood ever since 1925 when he published a book which failed to make him much money. There were those in Hollywood who came to wish that the book had done better.

2

In 1925 Charlie Chaplin appeared on the screen in *The Gold Rush;* René Clair completed his fine picture *Imaginary Voyage;* Sergei M. Eisenstein, the Russian master of montage, won world-wide recognition with his classic *Potemkin* (which Fitzgerald saw and admired)[3]; and Fitzgerald himself published *The Great Gatsby.* In writing his novel, the author drew upon material he had gathered while living in Great Neck, Long Island—a town which he shared with the great Florenz Ziegfeld. Lillian Russell also lived there as did George M. Cohan and many other show people, since the town was only half an hour by Long Island Railroad Express from Broadway. These people had lost little time in making their mark on the village they adopted. Many of their mansions, great white elephants like Gatsby's own, would have been more at home on the Great White Way than they were stuck out on pastoral Long Island. Gene Buck's garish castle was one of these. Buck, Ziegfeld's chief assistant, had had his house decorated by the *Follies'* stage manager, and Ring Lardner said that the living room looked like "the Yale Bowl—with lamps."[4]

In the novel, Gatsby is not legitimately a member of the show-business community in which he lives. He is not a legitimate anything: he is a bootlegger (or so we suspect). Yet he is an actor all the same. "If personality is an unbroken series of successful gestures," Fitzgerald wrote, "then there was something gorgeous about him, some heightened sensitivity to the promise of life, as if he were related to one of those intricate machines that register earthquakes ten thousand miles away."[5] The pose, the act, the personality—they all cohere in the author's mind.

And if Gatsby is something of an actor, he is also something of an inspired Ziegfeld (after all they were neighbors) and P. T. Barnum. In fact, the shadow of show business hovers over all the spectacular parties which Gatsby throws: we come to see them as a sort of Gatsby's Follies. He produces them like a show, not for himself, but for an audience—an audience of one and her name is Daisy Buchanan. The house, the lavish entertainments—they are only the props for the great love story which he hopes to stage.

When Daisy and her husband Tom Buchanan finally do attend one of Gatsby's parties, their host points out a "scarcely human orchid of a woman," a motion-picture star. "The man bending over her," Gatsby tells Daisy, "is her director."[6] Jay has just shown the girl he loves an emblem of what he hopes he and she may become. She is his star, his green light, and he knows that she is a woman who needs a director, one like himself. But Daisy does not see the similarity and admires only the girl, who is in a sense her own reflection. The show has been wasted on her. "She was appalled by West Egg, this unprecedented 'place' that Broadway had begotten upon a Long Island fishing village. . . ."[7] And because she disapproves, the follies close—to be replaced by a tragedy.

Gatsby was followed in February 1926 by the customary collection of stories, this one called *All the Sad Young Men.* In "Rags Martin-Jones and the Pr-nce of W-les," one of the stories in this volume, Gatsby's follies are transformed into John Chestnut's. Heroine Rags has always wanted to meet the Prince of Wales, so, like Toby in "The Offshore Pirate," hero John goes out and hires some actors, one to play the Prince, the rest to make up his entourage. When the party is over and Rags knows that she has been tricked, John tells her what Gatsby might have told Daisy, "Don't you see? I made up the whole thing for you." The evening has given Rags the "second greatest thrill of her life" and she falls in love with the man who staged it for her.[8]

"The Adjuster," tells the story of a spoiled young wife whose husband falls desperately ill and needs her to nurse him. The doctor tells her:

> "We make an agreement with children that they can sit in the audience without helping to make the play . . . but if they still sit in the audience after they're grown, somebody's got to work double time for them, so that they can enjoy the light and glitter of the world. . . . It's your turn to be the center, to give others what was given to you for so long. . . . The light and glitter of the world is in your hands."[9]

The Great Gatsby was adapted for the stage by Owen Davis. When the play opened on Broadway in February 1926, Percy Hammond wrote, "The speech of the characters is retained in much of its clear-cut veracity, and the 'atmosphere' of Long Island's more rakish sectors is pretty well served. . . . *The Great Gatsby* in the theater is at least half as satisfactory an entertainment as it is in the book."[10] The old Triangle Club veteran finally had his Broadway hit, even if it had come to him secondhand. Not long after, the movies bought *Gatsby*. The profits from stage and screen production totaled somewhere between thirty-three thousand and thirty-eight thousand dollars for the author. Fitzgerald was living his own themes—show business and money *were* coming together in support of the author's romantic approach to life. Living in France, he never saw Gatsby on stage, but that summer the author made the rounds of the Paris night spots with James Rennie, the actor who played Jay on Broadway.

Fitzgerald was well versed in night spots by then and must have been a good guide. In fact, through most of 1926 he had done little more than "sit in the audience" watching the workaday world "work double time" for his pleasure. His entire production for the year amounted to only "Your Way and Mine," "The Dance," and "How to Waste Material." Then at the end of the year he stirred. If the "light and glitter of the world" were in his hands, then the biggest show in town was the movies. In Arthur Mizener's words, movies "offered Fitzgerald what always drew him, a Diamond-as-Big-as-the-Ritz scale of operation, a world 'bigger and grander' than the ordinary world."[11] Besides, by the end of 1926, Fitzgerald already needed more money if, like Gatsby, he was to keep up his efforts to live like the very rich. To finance his dreams, Jay had turned to bootlegging; Scott himself chose pictures. He had written Maxwell Perkins in April 1925 that if *Gatsby* "will support me with no more intervals of trash I'll go on as a novelist. If not, I'm going to quit, come home, go to Hollywood and learn the movie business."[12]

Scott received the telegram which allowed him to carry out his threat on the last day of the year 1926. The message came from John W. Considine, a director at First National Pictures, and said:

AM STILL INTERESTED IN GETTING FINE MODERN COLLEGE STORY FOR CONSTANCE TALMADGE AND WOULD LIKE TO HAVE YOU WORK ON STORY WITH ME IN LOS ANGELES STOP IN ORDER TO FAMILIARIZE YOURSELF WITH SCREEN PERSONALITY OF MISS TALMADGE WOULD LIKE YOU TO SEE FOLLOWING PICTURES QUOTE HER NIGHT OF ROMANCE UNQUOTE QUOTE SISTER FROM PARIS UNQUOTE QUOTE DUCHESS OF BUFFALO UNQUOTE . . . FAMILIAR WITH YOUR CAREER AND WORK IN FACT BELIEVE I WAS AT YALE WHILE YOU WERE AT PRINCETON THEREFORE IT OUGHT TO BE EASY FOR US TO UNDERSTAND ONE ANOTHER AND WORK WELL TOGETHER.[13]

So it was that the author of *This Side of Paradise* and *The Great Gatsby* began the new year, 1927, with a new job. He was off to the studios, the back lots and false fronts of the movie world.

3

At first Fitzgerald was so secretive about his trip to Hollywood that one might have thought him a novelist spy on his way to steal the movies' formula for mass entertainment. Perhaps he even thought of himself as an enemy agent: he had an idea for a novel which he wanted to write about Hollywood types, but to bring it off he would need to know more about movieland. On January 4, 1927, just before he left the East, he wired Perkins: GOING TO THE COAST FOR THREE WEEKS CONFIDENTIAL ADDRESS FIRST NATIONAL PICTURES HOLLYWOOD HAPPY NEW YEAR.[14]

Fitzgerald, fresh from ancient Europe and centuries-old New York, was impressed by Los Angeles; the city seemed to have just come from its wrappings. He and Zelda would walk or motor through Beverly Hills and carefully inspect the show-business colony which looked like a bigger and gaudier Great Neck. The author would later describe this star-encrusted community in "Magnetism," a story based on his 1927 trip to Hollywood:

> The pleasant, ostentatious boulevard was lined at prosperous intervals with New England Colonial houses—without ship models in the hall. When the inhabitants moved out here the ship models had at last been given to the children. The next street was a complete exhibit of the Spanish-bungalow phase of West Coast architecture; while two streets over, the cylindrical windows and round towers of 1897—melancholy antiques which sheltered swamis, yogis, fortune tellers, dressmakers, dancing teachers, art academies and chiropractors—looked down upon brisk buses and trolley cars. A little walk around the block could, if you were feeling old that day, be a discouraging affair. . . . Everything in the vicinity—even the March sunlight—was new, fresh, hopeful and thin, as you would expect in a city that had tripled its population in fifteen years.[15]

The Fitzgeralds moved into the fashionable Ambassador Hotel, where they shared a four-apartment bungalow with John Barry-

more, author Carl Van Vechten, and their old friend Carmel
Myers.

The confidential nature of Fitzgerald's visit to Hollywood was
dealt a damaging blow when the author finally reported for
work. He drove out a winding concrete road and discovered in
the emptiness of the hills a group of buildings—a barnlike edifice,
offices all in a row, a commissary, and half a dozen bungalows.
That was the studio, and a big welcome awaited the big-name
author there. First National (later Warner Brothers) did not plan
to make a secret of the fact that they had F. Scott Fitzgerald
working for them. Zelda later recalled:

> We paid homage to the pale aloof concision of Diana Man-
> ners' primitive beauty, and dined at Pickfair to marvel at Mary
> Pickford's dynamic subjugation of life. A thoughtful limousine
> carried us for California hours to be properly moved by the
> fragility of Lillian Gish, too aspiring for life, clinging vine-
> like to occultisms.[16]

And there were parties to which the party couple of the decade
were invited. Parties like those described in "Magnetism," where

> the guests were largely of the old crowd. People who had been
> in the early Griffith pictures, even though they were scarcely
> thirty, were considered to be the old crowd; they were different
> from those coming along now, and they were conscious of it.
> They had a dignity and straightforwardness about them from
> the fact that they had worked in pictures before pictures were
> bathed in a golden haze of success. They were still rather
> humble before their amazing triumph, and thus, unlike the
> new generation who took it all for granted, they were con-
> stantly in touch with reality.[17]

Sometimes, however, Fitzgerald himself seemed to catch the
disease of those who took success for granted. The movies and
wealth were locked up in the same purse in his imagination, the
one implying the other, and so one night Scott made the Hollywood skies literally rain down money in silver puddles. "Scott
asked the clerk of the Ambassador Hotel for one hundred dollars

in coins," remembers H. N. Swanson, who would act as the writers' Hollywood agent a decade later. "Then he started throwing handfuls of silver up against the hotel windows, shouting, 'It's money, it's money, it's money! It's free!'"

Soon the Fitzgeralds were not only no longer secretive—at some parties they even, in the words of one columnist, made themselves "conspicuous by [their] presence."[18] The night the columnist had in mind was the one when Scott and Zelda boiled the ladies' purses. Later that same night, the couple retreated to the parking lot of the Ambassador, their spirits still high. With them were Reginald Simpson and James Montgomery Flagg, a man who looked something like Uncle Sam in the I WANT YOU poster. The resemblance may not have been accidental. Flagg, an illustrator, drew the wizened gent for what he used to refer to as the most famous poster in the world. Zelda was serenading the long-faced old man, singing a ballad about a *maison de joie*. When they grew restless, Scott gave the hotel clerk a fifty-dollar bribe to cash a check; then they hired a car. At four o'clock in the morning, the quartet started off in search of writer John Monk Saunders. Zelda said that he was too successful with women and that they should do something about it. She had some drastic measures in mind.

In his autobiography Flagg remembered the rest of the evening this way:

At last we stopped at the foot of a tall hill and Reg and I decided to let the Fitzgeralds get out and climb up to see if it really happened to be the right place. We thought we'd prefer having the pants bitten off the Fitzgeralds by a possible bulldog. They found Saunders in and called down to us. It was okay and we climbed up through the Jap garden to the house where Saunders was in his pajamas and a Sulka dressing robe and sandals; smiling imperturbably and getting drinks as if nothing surprised him. He turned on his phonograph and we set about chatting, with the exception of Mrs. F., who in prowling around found a pair of editor's shears and then sat down next to Saunders on a lounge, pulled open his robe and took a deep inhalation, then called:

"Scott, come here. John smells lovely!"

Scott went over and sat on the other side of Saunders and they buried their noses in his manly chest. They sighed luxuriously. Nothing fazed Saunders. Then Mrs. F. remembered the shears and began gently urging her host to let her perform a quick operation on him, explaining with quiet eloquence that his earthly troubles would be over if he would submit.

Saunders "firmly but politely" declined emasculation.

On the way back to the Ambassador, Fitzgerald turned around from time to time to peer at Flagg in the back seat. Disgusted, Scott would say, "God! But you look old!"

When the illustrator finally extricated himself safely from the Fitzgeralds' lives, he vowed not to get to know them better. "If I had ever seen them again," Flagg wrote, "it would have been too soon. . . . These charming young people."[19]

But if Fitzgerald made some enemies on his first tour in Hollywood, he also made some friends. As he later wrote his daughter, "Hollywood made a big fuss over us and the ladies all looked very beautiful to a man of thirty." To one of his cousins, Scott wrote, "This is a tragic city of beautiful girls— the girls who mop the floor are beautiful, the waitresses, the shop ladies."[20]

One of the ladies who looked the most beautiful was a young actress named Lois Moran. Miss Moran wanted Fitzgerald to be her leading man in a film and he seems to have wanted the same thing, so she arranged a screen test for him just as Rosemary Hoyt would later arrange one for Dick Diver in *Tender Is the Night*. Dick, profiting from his creator's hindsight, is allowed to take a superior attitude, but Fitzgerald himself went before the cameras. The studio, however, decided not to make him a star. The old dream of the drama of love and show-business drama actually coalescing into one and the same thing had to be put off once again. But like all things which might have been, it was easily imagined: so Fitzgerald wrote in "Magnetism" about an actor much like himself who plays opposite a young actress much like Miss Moran.

He gave the actress the name Helen Avery and described her as "a dark, pretty girl with a figure that would be full-blown sooner than she wished. She was just eighteen." The actor, age thirty, is called George Hanaford, and we are told that "he had determined, when he saw Helen Avery's first release, that she should play opposite him."

> He hadn't said a word to Helen Avery that Kay [his wife] could have objected to, but something had begun between them on the second day of this picture that Kay had felt in the air. . . . He had felt that they both tolerated something, that each knew half of some secret about people and life, and that if they rushed toward each other there would be a romantic communion of almost unbelievable intensity. It was this element of promise and possibility that had haunted him for a fortnight and was now dying away.[21]

But even as the feeling died, Fitzgerald's hero was still absorbed by the memory of it.

> There was in his mind, first, a horror that anyone should come between him and Kay, and second, a regret that he no longer carried that possibility in the forefront of his mind. It had given him a tremendous pleasure, like the things that had happened to him during his first big success, before he was so "made" that there was scarcely anything better ahead; it was something to take out and look at—a new and still mysterious joy.[22]

4

Sometimes Fitzgerald was a little overly secretive about his screenplay. One morning Carl Van Vechten saw him walking up and down in front of his bungalow, trying to compose in his head.

"Scott, come here!" Van Vechten called, meaning to be friendly. "I can't," Fitzgerald shouted back, "I've got scarlet fever."[23]

Why was the project so secret? Appropriately, it did have to do with a small, bomb-shaped object which could have been dangerous. That is, it had to do with a stick of magic lipstick, one guaranteed to draw men, guaranteed to make a girl magnetic. In "Magnetism," the story about Hollywood which Fitzgerald later wrote, George Hanaford discovers that to possess a magnetic personality is to be faced with special, ironic responsibilities. Later, some of this same magnetism—along with much of the prose in the story—would be carried over into *Tender Is the Night*, where Dick Diver's charm would draw many into his circle. But that was literature. *Lipstick* was only a movie and Fitzgerald was not yet ready to take movies seriously, so the magnetism here is simply exploited as a gimmick, a magician's trick.

Nineteen twenty-seven was the year of the spectacular: Metro's *Ben Hur* and Cecil B. De Mille's *The King of Kings* were drawing big audiences all across the country and Carl Dreyer was just completing *The Passion of Joan of Arc*. It was also the year of sound! *The Jazz Singer* would have its premier in October and revolutionize the industry. But for Fitzgerald it was the year of *Lipstick*. He was still thinking like a latter-day Georges Méliès, the French magician who created film sleight of hand with his *Little Red Ridinghood* and *A Trip to the Moon* in 1901 and 1902.

First National paid Fitzgerald thirty-five hundred dollars down on *Lipstick;* another twelve thousand five hundred was to follow if the studio accepted the finished script. The man who was to pass on the script was John Considine, who had a bad reputation among writers. "He was a college graduate," says Edwin Knopf, "but that doesn't mean too much." Frances and Albert Hackett remember Considine this way: "He was our first producer—he didn't know anything. Oh that dreadful man! For Scott to be linked with him . . . ! He read with a blue pencil in his hand ready to mark up the script. One day he was reading one of our scripts and he crossed out a line. 'That's not necessary,' he said. We said, 'Wait until you read the next page.' He had no

conception of setting something up on one page that wouldn't
be developed until a page or two later." Nor was the producer
a particularly keen judge of new talent, according to the
Hacketts. "We suggested Fred Astaire to him," they recall. "We
had worked with Fred in New York. When Considine saw Fred's
test, he thought that Fred was the most awful thing that he had
ever seen."

In short, Fitzgerald already had problems even before he
started writing. After he started, he had even more.

The picture was to star Constance Talmadge, a film flapper
whom Fitzgerald admired. In *Tender Is the Night* the director
Earl Brady would tell Rosemary, "Rather make a picture with
you than any girl since Connie Talmadge was a kid."[24]

The screenplay which Fitzgerald wrote for Miss Talmadge
was essentially a Cinderella story, but heroine Dolly Carroll is
more than a prisoner of circumstance, figuratively chained to the
fireplace—she is really in jail. She has no stepsisters, but she
does have pictures of debutantes and movie stars pinned up
around her cell to make her feel like a nobody. The captions
beneath the pictures read: "Miss Mimi Haughton Presented to
Society at Dinner Dance at the Plaza" : "Flapper Army Besieges
Mayor for Mother's Relief" : " 'Necking Parties on Wane' Say
Club Women." Fitzgerald wrote, "These are life to her—the
world outside."[25] But for Dolly, as for many others less literally
imprisoned by American society, pictures in a newspaper seem
to be about as close as she will ever get to the Roaring Twenties
or the American Dream.

Then one day a group of visitors from an unnamed university
(one much like Princeton) come to see Dolly and all the other
specimens locked behind Hamlin Prison's bars. Among them is
Ben Manny, who is described as

> what used to be known as a "superior person"—that is he is
> sure of himself, he knows that his position in this world is
> based on solid rock of confidence and plenty and this has
> given him an air of "Who are you, anyhow?" toward those

whose breeding he suspects. . . . In a way he is like this university—a symbol of its type.

When Ben sees Dolly, he grumbles to his instructor, "Bunch of
degenerates, Professor." When Dolly sees Ben, she falls in love.
As Ben leaves the prison, Dolly goes up and stares into the news-
print eyes of one of the debutantes gracing her cell wall. "You
wait," she promises Mimi Haughton's picture. "I'll catch up with
you."[26]

The rest of the script details Dolly's race to overtake the
privileged class. She is freed from prison, inherits money, and is
given a stick of magnetic lipstick—the latter evidently proving
that magic is the great leveler in society. Dolly even gets an
invitation to the university prom, but it comes not from Ben
but from his professor.

Fitzgerald's best comic scene takes place at a faculty banquet
to which this academician drags Dolly. All of the deans, professors, assistant professors, and instructors are shrouded in black
robes and mortarboards. It is the kind of banquet where the dinner
music should be "Pomp and Circumstance"—except for one thing:
someone has stolen all of the silverware, and the distinguished
pedagogues are reduced to eating with "half-pint spoons of tin
or wood, toasting forks with two prongs, carving knives, pancake
turners, cleavers, even an egg beater." The novelist of manners
had produced a convincing slapstick of manners which depended
for its effect on the decorum expected of university professors
who even as they dine throw "horrified glances at one another."[27]

In *Lipstick* Fitzgerald set out to show that the universities
have a lot in common with prisons, and that debutantes and
undergraduates could be as dishonest as thieves. The final scenes
leading up to the climactic larceny take place at the prom itself
where Dolly, wearing the magic lipstick, attracts dance partners
the way an heiress attracts proposals. Among her admirers is the
same haughty Ben Manny who called Dolly a "degenerate" when
he saw her in prison. Ben's date is Mimi Haughton, the news-

paper debutante, who soon grows criminally jealous of the magnetic ex-con. The plot develops as many twists and turns as the university's Wedding Stair, with chases, locked doors, and, in the end, theft: Mimi steals Dolly's lipstick, but it is all to no avail and she almost winds up in jail herself. The girl with the prison record wins Ben; the debutante with the pedigree comes up empty-handed.

Fitzgerald came up empty-handed, too: he never got the twelve thousand five hundred which was to be paid on acceptance of his script. In the year of the spectacular, *Lipstick* must have seemed too rickety a vehicle to enter against *Ben Hur*'s chariots at the box office. In April, long after Scott had left Hollywood, he received a wire from Considine:

> DEAR SCOTT VERY SORRY TO HAVE NEGLECTED YOU SO LONG STOP WE HAVE DECIDED NOT TO PRODUCE PICTURE BASED ON YOUR STORY STOP EVERYONE THINKS THE BEGINNING OR PREMISE CONTAINS EXCEPTIONALLY FINE MATERIAL BUT THAT REST OF STORY IS WEAK STOP . . . SUGGEST YOU SUBMIT STORY TO B P SCHULBERG ASSOCIATE PRODUCER FAMOUS PLAYERS LASKY CORPORATION LOS ANGELES AND ASK HIM TO CONSIDER SAME FOR BEBE DANIELS STOP BELIEVE IT INADVISABLE FOR YOU TO MENTION MY NAME IN THIS CONNECTION STOP.[28]

The author later explained his Hollywood failure this way:

> At that time I had been generally acknowledged for several years as the top American writer both seriously and, as far as prices went, popularly. I . . . was confident to the point of conceit. . . . I honestly believed that *with no effort on my part* I was a sort of magician with words—an odd delusion on my part when I had worked so desperately hard to develop a hard, colorful prose style.[29]

And there perhaps lies *Lipstick*'s comic flaw—not in the conceit but in the belief that a "hard, colorful prose style" had anything to do with writing a good silent picture. For what Fitzgerald wrote for the studio was not so much a scenario as a short story. It begins:

School was over. The happy children, their books swinging carelessly at a strap's end, tripped out into the Spring fields—Wait a minute, that's the wrong story.

It was the wrong story—yes, also the wrong medium. We can almost hear the Hollywood pro saying *How do you photograph that?* In fact, from beginning to end we find ideas and emotions which could never be photographed. For instance, at one point we are told that Dolly is "so lonesome that she [tries] to look as if she hopes no one will speak to her."[30] If an actress followed these instructions, however, we would probably take her act at face value and miss the loneliness behind the mask.

But if much of *Lipstick* is inept and some of it simply old-fashioned, there are at the same time flashes of prophecy. For one thing, Fitzgerald's prom scenes were far ahead of their time. "Looked at from above," he wrote, "the prom resolved itself into a central circle of closely packed stags around which hub revolved the varicolored wheel of dancers."[31] Three years later Busby Berkeley came to Hollywood to make *Whoopee* with an idea much like Fitzgerald's: since he saw no reason why screen dance numbers should be mere reprints of stage numbers, he put a camera up in the flies, shot straight down on the dancers, and with this trick made his fortune.

Fitzgerald's choice of heroine in *Lipstick* also affords a glimpse of things to come. When the author first arrived in Hollywood, a reporter asked him how the flappers of the screen differed from the ones he had popularized in his fiction. Fitzgerald said that he would rather talk about Tom Mix. Evidently he was tired of his name being associated with wild debutantes. In *Lipstick*, therefore, he showed the flapper fallen from innocence and comically involved in a life of crime, purse snatching, and husband snaring. With the elevation of a girl like Dolly Carroll to heroine we are already pointed in the direction of Kathleen, heroine of *The Last Tycoon*. In his notes for that last unfinished novel, Fitzgerald says of his heroine what he might well have said of Dolly: "People simply do not sympathize deeply with those who have had *all* the breaks, and I am going to dower this girl, like Rosalba in Thackeray's *Rose and the Ring*, with 'a little misfortune.' "[32]

Fitzgerald went away without the big money, but perhaps one afternoon spent in the MGM commissary made the whole adventure worthwhile. It was there that the author who wrote, "Show me a hero and I'll write you a tragedy,"[33] got acquainted with Irving Thalberg. Thalberg, who was head of production at Metro, was then dating the girl who was to have starred in *Lipstick*, Constance Talmadge. Since both men were in a sense courting her—the one professionally, the other romantically—they were thrown together. One day they met over lunch in Metro's Lion's Den. It was the first time Fitzgerald had ever been alone with Hollywood's wonder boy and he listened closely to what the other man said. Years later he would recall the conversation as follows:

> . . . he said, "Scottie, supposing there's got to be a road through a mountain—a railroad, and two or three surveyors and people come to you and you believe some of them and some of them you don't believe, but all in all, there seem to be half a dozen possible roads through those mountains, each one of which, so far as you can determine, is as good as the other. Now suppose you happen to be the top man, there's a point where you don't exercise the faculty of judgment in the ordinary way, but simply the faculty of arbitrary decision. You say, 'Well, I think we will put the road there,' and you trace it with your finger and you know in your secret heart, and no one else knows that you have no reason for putting the road there rather than in several other different courses, but you're the only person that knows that you don't know why you're doing it and you've got to stick to that and you've got to pretend that you know and that you did it for specific reasons, even though you're utterly assailed by doubts at the time as to the wisdom of your decision, because all these other possible decisions keep echoing in your ear. But when you're planning a new enterprise on a grand scale, the people under you mustn't ever know or guess that you're in any doubt,

because they've all got to have something to look up to and they mustn't ever dream that you're in doubt about any decision. Those things keep occurring."

At that point, some other people came into the commissary and sat down, and the first thing I knew there was a group of four and the intimacy of the conversation was broken, but I was very much impressed by the shrewdness of what he had said—something more than shrewdness—by the largeness of what he thought and how he reached it at the age of twenty-six, which he was then.[34]

Thalberg had already been running a major studio for six years.

In 1927 the Fitzgeralds' road lay east through the mountains to Wilmington, Delaware, and a house called Ellerslie. As their last Hollywood gesture, they stacked all the furniture in the center of their Ambassador Hotel room, and at the top of this impromptu altar they placed all their unpaid bills. Then they left and Scott pronounced the movie capital a town of "almost hysterical egotism and excitability hidden under an extremely thin veil of elaborate good-fellowship."[35] Lois Moran wired them: BOOTLEGGERS GONE OUT OF BUSINESS COTTON CLUB CLOSED ALL FLAGS AT HALF MAST . . . BOTTLES OF LOVE TO YOU BOTH.[36]

But four years later Scott Fitzgerald was back on the Hollywood road once again. This time when he arrived, his boss was the young man who had talked to him about roads in the commissary that day. Thalberg himself handed the author his new assignment: make Jean Harlow a star.

The Wrong Kind of Picture

1

The title marker, a small hand-held blackboard with a hinged arm on top, flashed onto the screen. It was there to announce in crooked, chalked letters that the strip of film about to be shown was THE REDHEADED WOMAN, TAKE ONE. Marker arm up, *whack!* The blackboard came away like a curtain rising and there she was—Jean Harlow. Her career had moved ahead in fits and starts until now, but after this movie she would be the new Clara Bow and Pola Negri rolled into one.

The rushes were being reviewed in one of MGM's many projection rooms, very likely Irving Thalberg's own. Fitzgerald later described that room in *The Last Tycoon:*

> [It] was a miniature picture theatre with four rows of over-stuffed chairs. In front of the front row ran long tables with dim lamps, buzzers, and telephones. Against the wall was an upright piano, left there since the early days of sound. The room had been redecorated and reupholstered only a year before, but already it was ragged again with work and hours.[1]

Gathered in that room to see the new star rising were representatives of all technical departments along with supervisors and unit managers. Since it was an important picture, Eddie Mannix was present. (Eddie, a former bouncer at Palisades Amusement Park and now a special aid to L. B. Mayer, was one executive who gave Fitzgerald trouble from the moment he entered MGM in 1931 to the moment he left for good in 1938.) Ruling over the assembly, his thin knees drawn up beside him in his chair, was Thalberg himself. Everyone was there, in fact, except Jack Conway, the film's director. "The directors did not appear at these showings," Fitzgerald would later explain in *Tycoon*. "—officially because their work was considered done, actually because few punches were pulled here as money ran out in silver spools. There had evolved a delicate staying away."[2]

On the screen: Harlow had just come home to an apartment which she shared with her girl friend.

"Going out with Sol tonight?" the girl friend asked (or words to that effect).

"I certainly am not," Harlow declared, as if she had just been offered sardines when she was expecting filet of sole.

"Why not?" the girl friend wanted to know.

"I met a banker."

"So suddenly Sol isn't Prince Charming."

"That bum!" Harlow exploded and pointed with disgust to the "bum's" picture on her dressing table.

The camera panned to the picture and everyone broke up with laughter. Everyone, that is, except Eddie Mannix, for the bum in the picture was Eddie himself. He was furious! Where was the director? Who was the smarty playing expensive tricks, anyway? And he wanted the footage shot over again tomorrow, *first thing*. Unfortunately, Fitzgerald missed the fun. A joke of his own, a well-meant prank, had already cost him his job at the studio.[3]

2

Fitzgerald had returned to California in November 1931, this time alone. His wife was now at the edge of insanity and much too ill to risk a trip to madcap Hollywood; he left her with her parents in Alabama when he headed west. The author needed money and that had helped him make up his mind to try the movies once again. In the old days he had once locked himself up for ten days, written four short stories, sold them, and used the money to rent a yacht he needed for a party he was giving. But in 1931 there were other bills to pay—bills for his daughter's schools, bills for his wife's sanitariums. Yet as badly as he needed the money, he had not come back to pictures for the high salary alone. Perhaps even more important was the novelist's fear of becoming a museum piece. "As long past as 1930," he later wrote in his *Crack-Up* essays, "I had a hunch that the talkies would make even the best-selling novelist as archaic as silent pictures."[4]

When he arrived, movieland once again "made a big fuss" over him. "Scott Fitzgerald is almost the only writer who never has cause to complain of his Hollywood welcome," Dorothy Speare observed at the time. "He is famous even in Hollywood, where his meteoric arrivals and departures are discussed in film circles as avidly as they discuss themselves."[5]

The Glamour Figure of the twenties at first found the Glamour Capital a very comfortable place to be. "The American Riviera and all that,"[6] Fitzgerald called it. In fact, he made himself so much at home that Miss Speare had trouble meeting him. In a *Saturday Evening Post* article she wrote:

> Coming in one night to a party at Carmel Myers', I find everybody in a state of feverish anticipation. Scott Fitzgerald is here. "All right," I said, "where is he?"
> "Sh, darling!" I'm informed. "He's taking a bath."
> He takes so long over it that I have to leave before he appears, as we are going to some other castle.

When Miss Speare and Fitzgerald finally did come together, he told her, "You were the last person on earth I wanted to meet after the way we used to slam each other's work every time we had a chance to be quoted!" In the twenties the two had been pictured in a *New York Tribune* cartoon quarreling over the role of the Modern Girl, but now the modernity had rubbed off both of them. Besides, heroes of the 1920s had to band together for their mutual protection now that a new decade had come. So Speare and Fitzgerald took a sentimental journey from night club to night club.

At a little restaurant where "an old man plays old tunes upon a xylophone," Fitzgerald asked to hear "all the songs to which the generation that he immortalized once danced—'Babes in the Wood'; 'The Crickets Are Calling'; 'Japanese Sandman.'" "So nostalgic," he said. The twenties were only two years in their grave, and already the music made the man and woman feel like ghosts as the xylophone played:

> The crickets are calling, "Enjoy today;
> Never mind what comes after."[7]

At MGM Fitzgerald was working for Thalberg, the man about whom he would later write *The Last Tycoon*. He had a five-week contract at twelve hundred a week, so this time he would get the money whether they made his movie or not. But on this second trip to Hollywood Fitzgerald was not being asked to do an original—every screenwriter's ambition. Instead he was supposed to work on a story by an author who was not even an original herself. That is, he was hired to help write a screen adaptation of *The Redheaded Woman,* a novel by his imitator Katharine Brush. Fitzgerald was faced with the problem of trying to write like a copy of himself, and it showed.

There were other problems, too. As Fitzgerald later explained to his daughter:

> Life had gotten in some hard socks and while all was serene on top, with your mother apparently recovered in Montgomery, I was jittery underneath and beginning to drink more than I ought to. Far from approaching it too confidently I was far too humble. I ran afoul of a bastard named [Marcel] de Sano, since a suicide, and let myself be gypped out of command. I wrote the picture and he changed as I wrote. I

tried to get at Thalberg but was erroneously warned against it as "bad taste." Result—a bad script.[8]

Of course, had Fitzgerald been willing to risk "bad taste" in his fight to see Thalberg, he might have found that the undertaking was also a bad bet. Metro's head of production was an extremely hard-to-see man. Once Thalberg kept Groucho, Harpo, and Chico Marx waiting so long that they got a pan, started a fire in it, and then fanned the smoke under his door. When the great man came bursting out, they met him at the threshold. Fitzgerald did eventually see Thalberg, but it was at Thalberg's request rather than vice versa; he had just read what Fitzgerald and his collaborator were preparing for Harlow, and he evidently smelled smoke once again.

All that remains of the work which Fitzgerald did for Thalberg is an unfinished seventy-six page script, the one de Sano reworked. (A few years later the studios began preserving copies of all drafts by all writers; not one word written on studio time was to be lost. Not so in the early days; they didn't hoard and consequently much disappeared, including the Fitzgerald script as it existed before de Sano got his pencil on it.) Fitzgerald later wrote a story about the problems of collaborating. It was called "Teamed with Genius" (1940) and in it the collaborator is seen "working frantically, [making] several dozen small changes. He substituted the word 'Scram!' for 'Get out of my sight,' he put 'Behind the eightball' instead of 'In trouble,' and replaced 'You'll be sorry' with the apt coinage 'Or else!' "[9] With help like that it did not take long for Fitzgerald to find himself "behind the eightball" at the studio.

The collaborators' unfinished screenplay opens in a roadhouse where we are introduced to the ways of the Redhead. Lily Andrews leaves her date waiting at a table while she goes to the ladies' powder room. She then exits through the powder room's back door to meet one of the richest boys in town for a rendezvous in the woods.

A movie which begins in a rest room is not likely to offer the usual Fitzgerald charm. Yet the philosophical terrain in the screenplay, if sometimes rough, is at least familiar. As Malcolm Cowley once wrote, "It was as if all [Fitzgerald's] novels described a big dance to which he had taken . . . the prettiest girl . . . and as if at the same time he stood outside the ballroom, a little Midwestern boy with his nose to the glass, wondering how much the tickets cost and who paid for the music."[10] Lily Andrews is another character in this tradition. Walking through the forest with the rich boy, she asks if he will take her to the country club someday. He promises that he will. Then the dialogue descends to:

> LILY: Would you?—oh really—please—I—I bet you got lipstick all over you—[11]

After this woodland adventure, Lily seems to forget all about the boy who has promised her the country club, getting down instead to more serious business, the seduction of her married boss. It should be remembered that such stories were common at the time: gangsters and fallen women were the screen heroes and heroines of the early years of the Great Depression. Edward G. Robinson and others muscled their way into the theatres with titles like *The Big House* (1930), *Little Caesar* (1930), *The Public Enemy* (1931), *The Secret Six* (1931), and *Scarface* (1932). And while the guys were busy climbing out of poverty into gangland, the molls were moving up from the slums to brothels. A prostitute was the heroine in *Susan Lenox* (1931), followed by *Blonde Venus* (1932) and *Letty Lynton* (1932). Like the gangsters, the whores told their audiences that the only way to beat the Depression was to beat middle-class standards. In short, Fitzgerald and de Sano had the right formula in *The Redheaded Woman:* a girl who does her social climbing in bed. But perhaps they overdid it.

All the while Lily is setting her boss up for the kill, the screenwriters were setting her up for the same thing. By the time they finished with her, she was hardly a sympathetic whore. They had her enter her boss's wife's bedroom, where she fingers the wife's clothes and steals her "Gardenia" perfume. They had her accidentally drop an ice cube down the back of her own dress and scream for her boss to get it. He retrieves the cube and is surprised to find that it is mostly melted. Hot little Lily asks flatly, "What do you expect?"[12]

The last words in the unfinished Fitzgerald–de Sano script were: "You're not so bad yourself, Big Boy." Their collaboration had ended as it had begun, with a heavy hand and a cliché. Had the screenplay gone on past page seventy-six, the plans were for Lily to continue her travels from bed to bed—but she was taken out of the writers' hands before they could finish her nocturnal Odyssey.

It did not take Irving Thalberg long to see that the script on which Fitzgerald and his collaborator were working did not represent the kind of picture he had had in mind. So he called a meeting. Since Bess Meredyth and C. Gardner Sullivan had worked on the project before Fitzgerald and de Sano took it over, they were summoned, too. To begin with, Thalberg didn't like that opening sequence with Lily in the roadhouse.

"I'd rather assume she'd had some hell-raising doings," he explained, ". . . than just see them in a dive together. Your audience['s] imagination is working for you here if you let it."

Someone nodded.

"It seemed tacked on," one of the writers said—or at least that is how the conversation is recorded in an unpublished draft of Fitzgerald's *The Last Tycoon.*

This scene may be pure fiction, but it probably isn't. *The Redheaded Woman* was the only picture Fitzgerald ever worked on with Thalberg; moreover, the movie the writers and the producer are sweating over in the novel is very like Fitzgerald's script about that Redhead.

In the unpublished *Tycoon* draft, what happens is this: Stahr has summoned supervisor Reiny Reinmund, director John Broaca, and writers Wylie White and Jane Meloney for a story conference. After he tells them that he does not like their opening and gets them to admit that it seems "tacked on," he says, "We've had that problem before with stage plays." (Of course in real life *The Redheaded Woman* was based on a novel rather than a play, so some fictionalizing has been done here.)

> "In *Tattersall* [Stahr explains] we took all the hints of what had gone before and even shot two thousand feet of it. Finally we cut it all—that's why it was such a short picture. Sherwood knew when he wanted to start his play and he was right. Don't you think so, Johnny?"
>
> Broaca nodded.
>
> "If you say so, Monroe."
>
> "I do say so, Johnny. And I'd say so even if something developed out of your scene—if it had action instead of just motion. When you extend a play with a prelude you're asking for it—you're including a lot of situations the playwright has already rejected. That's why he's reduced them to a mention. Why should we take that mention like one of those dried fish from Ireland and dip in water. You can make it swell but you can't bring it to life."

Why Edmund Wilson decided not to include this conversation in his edition of *The Last Tycoon* is not clear, for it belongs to a scene which he does print. The scene in question appears in Chapter Three, where Stahr goes on to say:

> "Ten million Americans would put thumbs down on that girl if she walked on the screen. We've got an hour and twenty-five minutes on the screen—you show a woman being unfaithful to a man for one-third of that time and you've given the impression that she's one-third whore."
>
> "Is that a big proportion?" asked Jane slyly, and they laughed.
>
> "It is for me," said Stahr thoughtfully, "even if it wasn't for the Hays Office. If you want to paint a scarlet letter on her back, it's all right, but that's another story. Not this story. This is a future wife and mother."

What kind of girl did Stahr approve of in a picture like this one? Answer:

"At all times, at all moments when she is on the screen in our sight, she wants to sleep with Ken Willard. Is that plain, Wylie?"

"Passionately plain."

"Whatever she does, it is in place of sleeping with Ken Willard. If she walks down the street she is walking to sleep with Ken Willard, if she eats her food it is to give her strength to sleep with Ken Willard. *But* at no time do you give the impression that she would even consider sleeping with Ken Willard unless they were properly sanctified. I'm ashamed of having to tell you these kindergarten facts, but they have somehow leaked out of the story."[13]

Fitzgerald may have made up this speech from beginning to end, but it *does* have a Thalberg ring to it. Thalberg's widow Norma Shearer would later turn down a chance to play Scarlett O'Hara because her fans wrote begging her not to portray a "bad woman."

In the face of Stahr's criticism, Reinmund insists, "This is the structure we agreed on—" "But it's not the story," Stahr interrupts. "Remember this in the future—if I order a limousine, I want that kind of car. And the fastest midget racer you ever saw wouldn't do." The Harlow vehicle manufactured by Fitzgerald (as reworked by de Sano) was a racy midget.

It would be a mistake, of course, to take too literally a conversation written in a novel. For one thing, much of what Stahr is given to say must have reflected Fitzgerald's own ideas about pictures rather than Thalberg's—after all, he had learned a lot in his years in Hollywood and he was anxious to prove it. Once all reservations have been registered, however, it is still not hard to imagine that a confrontation much like that described in *The Last Tycoon* actually occurred when Scott Fitzgerald, the boy luminary risen in the East, finally met Irving Thalberg, the young sun risen in the West.

3

Perhaps Fitzgerald lost his job at MGM simply because he had written the wrong kind of picture for Thalberg. But he more than

likely lost it not for his performance as a writer but for his performance as a performer. It happened one "crazy Sunday." In a
story of that name he wrote:

> Behind, for all of them, lay sets and sequences, the long waits
> under the crane that swung the microphone, the hundred miles
> a day by automobiles to and fro across a county, the struggles
> of rival ingenuities in the conference rooms, the ceaseless com-
> promise, the clash and strain of many personalities fighting for
> their lives.

And now Sunday, a day for rest and tea at the Thalbergs'.

> It would be a party out of the top drawer. It was a tribute to
> himself as a young man of promise. The Marion Davies crowd,
> the high-hats, the big currency numbers, perhaps even Dietrich
> and Garbo and the Marquise, people who were not seen
> everywhere.[14]

Fitzgerald drove out to the Thalbergs' with Dwight Taylor, the
only other writer from the studio invited to the tea. After ringing
all the right bells and having a series of doors unlocked before
them, they were shown into a large living room. "I could see at
once that we had landed on our feet," Taylor remembers. "Everybody who *was* anybody in the picture colony was there. . . . The
room was restless and exciting, with all the glamour of a fair."[15]
Fitzgerald looked about him and decided that the Thalberg
home "was built for great emotional moments—there was an air
of listening, as if the far silences of its vistas hid an audience,
but this afternoon it was thronged, as though people had been
bidden rather than asked."[16]
Over to one side of the living room stood Thalberg with a
group of people who seemed to be standing in line awaiting their
turn to try and impress him. Fitzgerald knew that one way to
make a bad impression was to look like a "rummie" and so he had
decided to stay away from cocktails. But before long someone
slid a glass into his hand.
Robert Montgomery was the first to turn against Fitzgerald. At
the beginning of the party the actor had wanted to meet the

author whom he had long admired; then he did meet him and all that changed. Montgomery had come to the tea in white riding breeches and black boots, looking a little like a penguin. Suddenly Fitzgerald approached him, looked at him queerly as if he really were a relative of that bird, and asked, "Why didn't you bring your horse in?" The author's face said that the question was not a joke. The actor turned and walked away.

Then, his "blood throbbing with the scarlet corpuscles of exhibitionism,"[17] Fitzgerald announced to the crowd at large that he wanted to sing. Norma Shearer (Mrs. Thalberg) politely asked what it was that he wanted to sing. A song about a dog, he said, and the maid was dispatched upstairs to get her mistress' poodle. Ramon Novarro, who played the title role in *Ben Hur,* was selected to improvise a piano accompaniment. "The others gathered in a half circle near the piano," Dwight Taylor recalls, "but not too near, their faces devoid of expression, like people gathered at the scene of an accident."[18]

Cradling the dog like a baby in the crook of his arm, the great author sang his lullaby:

> In Spain, they have the donkey
> In Australia, the kangaroo,
> In Africa, they have the zebra,
> In Switzerland, the zoo.
> But in America we have the dog—
> And he's a man's best friend.

While the crowd of professional entertainers smiled and waited indulgently for the punch line, the singer launched into his second verse, one much like the first except with different animals annexed to different countries. And then the big chorus again:

> But in America we have the dog—
> And he's a man's best friend.

Slowly it began to dawn on the restless crowd that that *was* the punch line. Directly in front of him, Fitzgerald saw "the Great Lover of the screen [glare] at him with an eye as keen as the eye of a potato."[19] The Great Lover's name was John Gilbert and he had been known to wear a loaded six gun to such parties.

"A sharp pang of doubt" went through the singer but he could no more stop himself from singing a third and fourth verse than he could stop himself from drinking. As Fitzgerald wrote of his hero in "Crazy Sunday":

> . . . as he finished he had the sickening realization that he had made a fool of himself in view of an important section of the picture world, upon whose favor depended his career. . . . He felt the undercurrent of derision that rolled through the gossip; then—all this was in the space of ten seconds—the Great Lover, his eye hard and empty as the eye of a needle, shouted "Boo! Boo!" voicing in an overtone what he felt was the mood of the crowd. It was the resentment of the professional toward the amateur, of the community toward the stranger, the thumbs-down of the clan.[20]

The next day Fitzgerald dropped by Dwight Taylor's office, a glass cubicle which held the writer like a cellophane bag. When he walked in he was wearing that funny half-smile that he must have worn in Paris when he chewed up twenty-dollar bills and spat them out a taxicab window. It was the smile of the practical joker who had scandalized Hollywood in 1927 and the smile of the man who had just recently gone to Carmel Myers' to take a bath.

"Nice party," he observed to Taylor.

Taylor nodded.

"How was I?"

"Not so good," Taylor told him.

The smile and the face changed. _You don't really want to see me, you're only being polite_. It was an old face now; its lines had re-formed themselves into the mask which Fitzgerald would show to Hollywood when he returned for the last time in 1937.

"This job means a lot to me. I hope I didn't make too much of a jackass of myself," he said. He talked about the bills for Scottie's schooling and the bills for setting props under Zelda's mind. "I don't know why I chose yesterday of all days to go off," he told Taylor. "I always do that—at just the wrong time. I've been under quite a strain."[21]

Fitzgerald went off to the commissary for a Coke and a chance to think over Taylor's disapproval. The big room was crowded and looked like a circus side show. Mixed in with the stars, secretaries, and carpenters were tables where sat sad, lovely Siamese twins, mean-faced dwarfs, and one proud giant—the studio was shooting a movie called *The Freaks*. Scott sat down at a table near some of the deformed and they deepened his somber mood, but when he returned to his office, he found good news waiting. Fitzgerald hurried off to tell Taylor. His face had found its strength once again as he read aloud the telegram he had just received from Norma Shearer: I THOUGHT YOU WERE ONE OF THE MOST AGREEABLE PERSONS AT OUR TEA.[22] Scott thought the gesture was "the sweetest thing I ever heard of in my life!"[23] He relaxed. At the end of the week they fired him.

A box of gardenias and a card signed F. Scott Fitzgerald were delivered to Dorothy Speare the day after the author got sacked. The flowers touched her—a funeral wreath for the hatchet they had buried and all that. For a moment she even wondered if the old feud might not turn the corner into romance. Then the phone rang and Miss Speare heard the voice of a girl who wrote for one of the fan magazines. Did Miss Speare like the flowers? Yes. "You see, Scotty left in such a hurry, darling," the voice explained, "he just asked me to take care of you and all the others who were so nice to him. I'm *so* glad you liked them."[24] Perhaps Miss Shearer received flowers, too.

Fitzgerald's old friend Anita Loos was called in to rewrite Scott's script and she did a spicy job. Her Lily was still hot enough to melt ice cubes, but the new screenplay was more than a scorcher—it was a funny scorcher. Miss Loos hoped that if you kept people holding their sides, they wouldn't have time to wag a finger. Still, some people did object to the picture, among them the film's own director. Thalberg had assigned Jack Conway to do *The Redhead*, but after Conway read the script he no longer wanted the job. He said that he had known women like Lily and that they hurt too many people. But Thalberg insisted and Conway acquiesced, all except for one scene. The director said that Miss Loos would either have to rewrite it or direct it herself. Thalberg called his lady screenwriter and told her about Conway's ultimatum. She powdered her nose and then headed for the set. To direct.

Meanwhile, Fitzgerald was on his way back east, back to his wife and back to the novel. "I left with the money," he later wrote, "for this was a contract for weekly payments, but disillusioned and disgusted, vowing never to go back. . . ."[25] And yet the last line of his story "Crazy Sunday" vowed "with a certain bitterness" something else. "Oh, yes, I'll be back," the hero thinks, "—I'll be back!" He had failed this time, a second time, but he would keep his promise. "Oh, yes."[26]

In fact, once he finished *Tender Is the Night* as a novel, he began immediately trying to turn it into a movie. He even decided who should be in it. As Dick Diver he wanted the man whom he had insulted at the Thalbergs' party: Robert Montgomery.

☆ 5 ☆

Tender Is the Night
and the Movies

1

It was four o'clock in the morning when Bill Warren's phone rang.

"Get over here and straighten this out," said a man with a thick voice at the other end. He meant straighten out *Tender Is the Night.*

The seventeen-year-old never protested. He dressed in his dark Baltimore home at 605 North Charles Street, then headed for 1307 Park Avenue. He found the author standing at a high, old-fashioned desk. Scott had taken to doing all his writing on his feet, but if this eccentricity made him look like a pastor at his pulpit, he was one with liquor on his breath. Bill walked over and stood beside him, and they both looked down at the new pages covered with handwriting which could not walk a straight line. "He wanted me to make sense out of what he had written," Warren remembers, "but sometimes I couldn't even figure out the words."

Bill went to work editing, rewriting, changing, while Scott looked on, growing more and more impatient. The boy crossed out "he expostulated" and wrote in "he said." Scott put his arm around Bill, whom he had already taken as his godson.

"Don't change that," he said. "That's why I'm who I am. Who the hell are you?"

The unpublished beginner and the recognized author had the same argument almost every day. "I always thought that dialogue was very well contained if you used 'he said,' 'she said,'" Warren explains. "Scott would write, 'he expostulated,' 'he ejaculated,' '"Ah," he complained.'"

When they weren't fighting about how to write dialogue, they fought about how to open chapters. "Scott always wanted to begin chapters with 'The moon shone thinly over the city,'" Warren remembers. "I would begin, 'The trains from the South arrived three times a day. She was on one of them.'"

"How dare you rewrite me?" was Fitzgerald's standard protest. "How do you know the trains arrived three times a day?"

Warren had an answer: "You told me."

One night while Scott stood at his desk with his arm around Bill's shoulder, asking, "Don't you know the difference between a vowel and a consonant?" Zelda crept into the room. She came up behind Bill and reached around him with both hands as if to cover his eyes to play "Guess who?" But Zelda was not playing. She dug her fingernails into the skin at the rims of the boy's eyes, then raked the sharp points down over his cheeks and chin, laying open wounds the length of his face. They rushed Warren to the hospital. Fitzgerald had once written, "I left my capacity for hoping on the little roads that led to Zelda's sanitarium," and now Bill's face looked like a map of those roads.

Fitzgerald had begun *Tender Is the Night* in France eight years before, when Bill Warren was nine years old and Zelda was whole. No mental illness clouded those first drafts: the novel was originally conceived as a story about the movies. Scott called his hero Francis Melarky, made him a motion-picture cameraman, and placed him in Europe.

At first Francis is bored with the whole expatriate merry-go-round. Then he discovers that Earl Brady has come over and is making a picture in Monte Carlo. Tired of doing nothing, Francis drives to Brady's studio, a little Hollywood marooned on the

Riviera, where he hopes to get back into pictures. Making his way across a darkened stage, Francis notices (as George Hanaford in "Magnetism" and Rosemary Hoyt in *Tender* would after him) that "here and there figures spotted the twilight, figures that turned up ashen faces to him, like souls in purgatory watching the passage of a mortal through." When the unemployed cameraman finally finds the man he is looking for, the director Brady, he stands in the shadow watching him work, and is thrown "into a sympathetic and approving trance."[1] Soon Francis, like Gatsby, begins to dream, but he dreams not of a girl like Daisy, nor of a green light across the bay. His dreams are movie dreams:

> More than anything in the world he wanted to make pictures. He knew exactly what it was like to carry a picture in his head as a director did and it seemed to him infinitely romantic. Watching, he felt simply enormous promise, an unrolling of infinite possibilities in himself. He felt closer to Brady, murmuring on in his quiet deep-seated voice, than he had to anyone for months.

Moved by his desire to make movies, Francis goes up to Brady and introduces himself. Brady remembers the young cameraman from Hollywood and so offers him some backhanded flattery. "You've got ideas," the producer says. "You're sort of a stimulating kid. Take for instance authors—I've never been able to use their God damn stories, but I kept bringing them out to the coast because they're stimulating to have around." Fitzgerald, who would soon be on his way to the coast to write *Lipstick,* could not have known how prophetic these words would prove to be.

When Francis tells his mother—whom he was to kill later in the story—that he plans a comeback as a cameraman, she reminds her son:

> "You told me all they did was make you wait. You said you sat around one whole morning waiting."
> "I did say that, but I explained to you that waiting is just part of the picture business. Everybody's so much overpaid that when something finally happens you realize that you were

making money all the time. The reason it's slow is because one
man's keeping it all in his head, and fighting the weather and
the accidents—"

"Let's not go over all that again, dear."

Even before his trip to Hollywood, Fitzgerald already knew what
kind of world he would find there.

Mrs. Melarky does not know much about the movies, but like
any American mother she does know enough to put Hollywood
and drugs together. She calls Brady her son's "drug-taking friend
in Monte Carlo." Francis tells her, "It's not everyone who can
get the dope habit from a prominent moving-picture director."
Twenty years later Fitzgerald would not be able to dismiss the
Hollywood drugs so easily. One of his producers at MGM was
hooked.

Brushing aside his mother's worries, Francis jumps back into
pictures. Like his creator, Francis had been away from his art
for a long time, but thanks to Brady he sees his direction once
again—just as Fitzgerald, writing the story, must have thought
that he saw his:

> Walking out on the beach for a swim before dinner, Francis
> evoked from the day's hope and from the health in his brown-
> ing body, a robust old thought that work was more fun than
> anything. He felt that he was a good man and could do things
> no one else could. The few strangers left on the beach realized
> this and swaying together clinked glasses to him. "Hurray for
> Francis Melarky!" He resolved to cut out the beer he drank
> with his meals, for how could he be at his best when he was
> short-winded? On the other hand, so he thought perversely, if
> he became an athlete in perfect trim, how could he respond to
> such toasts as they had just given him here? To achieve and to
> enjoy, to be prodigal and openhearted and yet ambitious and
> wise, to be strong and self-controlled, yet to miss nothing—to
> do and yet to symbolize . . . to be both light and dark.

In articulating the aspiring young movie maker's dilemma—*to
do and yet symbolize*—Fitzgerald had set down his own. On the
one hand he wanted to prove that he was a better writer "than

any of the young Americans *without exception*."[2] On the other hand he wanted to have more fun than anyone else in France. He even took time away from his novel to try to become the man he was writing about—time to sight through a whirring camera, time to make an amateur film. His production crew consisted of Ben Finney and Charles MacArthur, his stars Ruth Goldbeck and Grace Moore. They did most of their shooting on location in Monte Carlo with the Mediterranean stretching about them; up and down the coast the eggshell walls of the beach houses gleamed in the sun; and the Casino, richer than any Diamond as Big as the Ritz, loomed in the background. "Just a real place to rough it,"[3] was Fitzgerald's description.

Fitzgerald was behaving as though he actually knew how to carry a picture in his head, fighting weather, actors, and accidents. His romantic illusions were fulfilling themselves as the camera zoomed in on . . . *dirty words*. It was like photographing a well-inscribed bathroom wall, except that it was really the pink wall of Grace Moore's villa.

Miss Moore, star of musical comedies, operas, and later the movie *One Night of Love*, remembered those unprintable words in her autobiography:

> One of the devices of the script was to write the titles on the outside walls of my pink villa and photograph them that way. But during the night the collaborators would always think up a few new unprintable titles, and I never knew, when I looked out in the morning, what new four-letter horror would be chalked up on my house to throw into a dither the tourist schoolmarms who might be passing by. I complained and scrubbed once or twice, but the new captions that then appeared were so much worse than the old that it seemed better to do with the four-letter words one knew than those one knew not of.[4]

In their movie, Miss Moore played Princess Alluria, the wickedest woman in Europe, and Miss Goldbeck was cast in a supporting role as the farmer's daughter. Several of the action shots were filmed on the grounds of the fashionable Hotel de Cap.

When Fitzgerald was not playing cameraman himself, he went on with his story of Francis Melarky, but as he wrote, his hero began to twist beneath his pencil. "About this time a change began to come over Francis," Fitzgerald put down. "He began to see himself as a more powerful person. . . . The symbol of his power became Earl [Brady]." Francis wanted a director's privileges not only at the studio but in society; he began to believe that "it needed only a word from him to change entire relations." To detach a wife from a husband would be as easy as ordering an actress to walk across the stage, or so Francis believed, and he set out to prove that he was right.

As important as the change which came over Francis, however, was a change coming over Fitzgerald himself. Once he became preoccupied with a director—once the director became for him "the symbol of . . . power"—the author began to lose interest in Francis. Why write a story about a man who ran a camera when he could write about a man who ran the whole show? The year was probably 1927, a time for upheavals. Francis Melarky, like the silent movies, was about to be replaced.

At this point, Fitzgerald broke off working on the Melarky story. Perhaps he, like Francis, felt that "more than anything in the world he wanted to make pictures," so he took a job in Hollywood. The result was *Lipstick*. Failing to strike gold in California, the author left the West and moved to Ellerslie, just outside Wilmington, Delaware, where he took up his novel again, but he did not take it up where he had left off. Rather, he decided to scrap Francis and start over. This time he chose as his hero Lew Kelly, a brilliant young director of motion pictures. Kelly's mind was described as "made up of all tawdry souvenirs of his time, things given away, unearned, like the pictures of celebrities he had once collected from cigarette packages. Somewhere in the littered five-and-ten glowed the low, painful fire of his talent." We are first introduced to Kelly and his wife Nicole on board a ship bound for Europe. A young actress named Rosemary is also making the crossing. Her ambitious mother persuades her to sneak across from tourist class into first class so that she can meet the prominent movie maker. In this early version of the story, she is literally looking for a director. In the final version, she would find her director, symbolically, in Dick Diver.

In 1931 the author decided to make his second raid on Hollywood. His script for *The Redheaded Woman,* of course, failed to make his fortune; banished from Metro, he headed back east and back to his novel. He rented a house in Baltimore and there, far from the Riviera, took up the story of his American expatriates.

2

Charles (Bill) Warren met Scott Fitzgerald in Baltimore's Vagabond Theatre. "I was doing a musical called *So What* with Gary Moore," Warren remembers. "I had written the book and the music. We were rehearsing one afternoon very late—all of the chorus girls and skit girls had gone home. I was at the piano playing 'Our Life Will Be a Wow' and telling this one girl to make the song light, airy, when out of the dark came this great big fedora. I saw a man dressed for winter, overcoat and all, and here it was the dead of summer. The man introduced himself and said, 'I'd like to work with you.' With youth's arrogance, I thought, 'Who the hell wouldn't?' When he left, everyone asked me, 'Do you know who that was?' But I didn't know F. Scott Fitzgerald. Hell, I didn't know Ernest Hemingway. I was a fast seventeen. After I found out that he wasn't a ragpicker, no matter what he dressed like, I went to see him."

Fitzgerald liked Warren because the boy combined two of his dreams: he was in the theatre and he played football. When Scott and Bill first met, Warren was a prep-school star who had just been named All-Maryland. (Later Bill won a football scholarship to Princeton, which pleased Scott, but when he arrived to try out for the varsity, he lasted about as long as had the author of *This Side of Paradise*—ten days.) One morning Scott woke Bill at two a.m. He also woke a priest. At a nearby church Bill Warren, whose real name was Charles Marquis Warren, was baptized, while Fitzgerald stood as godfather. The godson remembers feeling foolish "getting water sprinkled on my head like a baby."

During those years Zelda was in and out of the Shepherd Pratt Clinic. Scott would visit her there and the couple, who always competed against one another, would go out to the courts and play tennis. One afternoon Scott took Bill along and insisted that Zelda play the boy. The wife acted as if her husband were backing out of the honeymoon, but Scott ignored her, climbing up into the high judge's chair to referee the match. The two reluctant players took their places and began to rally. After the first point, Zelda took off her sweater. The judge high up over her head said nothing. After the second point, she reached behind her back, unhooked her bra and tossed it away. Still Scott remained silent. After the third point, Zelda's short white tennis skirt dropped like a hoop at her feet. After the fourth, she freed herself from her panties.

"I was playing with a stark naked woman," Warren remembers. "She had a gorgeous body—it was the first time I noticed that a woman could be brown all over. But when you are playing tennis with a naked woman whose husband is watching, you try not to look. I was having a terrible time returning her shots."

Warren believes that if Scott had told Zelda to stop, she would have, but the author sat up in his chair looking on as if the only bounds being overstepped were the white lines drawn on the courts. The game ended when the clinic attendants brought damp sheets, wrapped them around Zelda, and carried her away. "She didn't go docilely," remembers Warren. "She was screaming at Scott."

Zelda was teaching Scott lessons about tragedy which Aristotle had left out. He retained the young actress Rosemary in his story, but changed his hero from a director to a doctor. The doctor, however, was to be something of a showman. He was not descended from actor George Hanaford ("Magnetism"), cameraman Melarky, and director Kelly for nothing.

Warren worked with Fitzgerald on the final drafts of *Tender Is the Night*, then they collaborated on a motion-picture treatment of the novel. Some days Bill simply acted as a kind of stenographer. Other days he would take pages covered with

Scott's sprawling handwriting, sit down with a legal pad, and rewrite whole scenes. He remembers especially the shooting episode at the railroad station in Paris, which he reworked, trying to give it a more dramatic structure. In recognition of Bill's efforts, Scott put him in the book: the author named Nicole's father Charles Marquis Warren in the first edition of the novel, then changed it to Devereux Warren in later printings. "It was our hidden symbol," remembers the man who gave his name.

"If I tell you that I wrote part of *Tender Is the Night,* then you'll tell me that you wrote *The Sun Also Rises,*" says Warren. But when the novel was published, eight years after it was begun, Fitzgerald inscribed a copy to his "godson" as follows: "For Charles (Bill) Warren with the hope that our co-operation will show us to prosperity. April 1st (fool's day 1934)."

In that book Rosemary Hoyt, the young actress, meets Dick Diver on the Riviera and, as she falls in love, realizes that this will be "one of her greatest roles." Rosemary is the kind of girl who during moments of emotional strain finds herself "wishing the director would come." And so Dick is perfect for her: he is the most skilled director she has ever known and she wants to submit to him completely. We are told that the "most sincere thing" that she ever said to him was, "Oh, we're such *actors*—you and I."[5] Which happens to be precisely what Helen Avery says to George Hanaford, a professional actor, in "Magnetism."[6] Rosemary wants Dick to be in a screen test, explaining, "I thought if the test turned out to be good I could take it to California with me. And then maybe if they liked it you'd come out and be my leading man in a picture."[7] Dick takes a superior attitude. He refuses the test and refuses to be Rosemary's leading man either in pictures or in private.

Still, Dick is drawn to this actress, this pretty, uncomplicated dream girl so different from his own wife. And his view of her is in many ways tied up in the dreams which the movies have transmitted to us all. Fitzgerald writes of "the current youth worship, the moving pictures with their myriad faces of girl-children, blandly represented as carrying on the work and wisdom of the

world." Rosemary is such a girl-child, the model for the mold.
When she leaves France and Dick's life, he, like so many
dreamers, is reduced to going to the movies to see his girl. "I've
seen you here and there in pictures," he tells Rosemary when
they meet much later. "Once I had *Daddy's Girl* run off just for
myself!"[8]

Dick Diver is an actor, but only as Gatsby is—perforce and as
a layman. His charm, like Gatsby's personality, is partially based
on "an unbroken series of successful gestures." It is an act, and
that is why it is not enough for him. In a passage later cut from
the novel, Dick asks Rosemary, "Do you remember you said once,
'Oh, Dick, we're both such actors'? Well, I've more or less retired
from that. I expect a good deal of nourishment from people, or
else old Diver doesn't give any out." Dick Diver had been like
the director whom Francis Melarky admired, for "it needed only
a word of his to change . . . relations." When he stops acting,
stops directing, he is already on the road to exile in Hornell, New
York. There is something gained: he may be a better doctor now.
But there is loss too, enough loss to make the story a tragedy.
Before he gave up the act, "the light and glitter of the world"
had been in his hands. Now it is dashed and the players scattered.

3

In 1934, when *Tender Is the Night* appeared in the bookstores,
the Depression was hurting book sales much more than the picture business. A few farmers might escape the Oklahoma Dust
Bowl by piling into an old Ford and heading for California, but
most Americans sought escape from hard times by piling into
movie houses. They lost themselves in films like John Ford's *Lost
Patrol;* went to Frank Capra's *It Happened One Night* to see
long-legged Claudette Colbert trounce Clark Gable in a hitch-
hiking contest; fell in love with the man who hated dogs and
small children, old bulb-nosed W. C. Fields, star of *It's a Gift.*
That was stern competition, especially for a book like Fitzgerald's
which offered no refuge—a book which was, in fact, about de-
terioration. *Tender Is the Night* sold only thirteen thousand

copies—*This Side of Paradise* had sold twice as many the first week—and left Fitzgerald in financial quicksand.

It did not take long for Scott to see that the lines were forming in front of the theatres, not the bookstalls, and so once again he began to think about show business. After all, the movies had haunted the author and his novel ever since those early chapters about Francis Melarky, the man who wanted to make movies more than anything. Scott decided that he and Warren should write a movie treatment of *Tender Is the Night* which they would sell to Hollywood. They began by thinking up a dream cast which included Ina Claire, the actress Scott had seen in *The Quaker Girl* when he was a schoolboy at Newman, and Robert Montgomery, the man he had insulted at the Thalbergs'. The full list of stars considered worthy of the novel's characters read as follows:

> Nicole Diver—Katharine Hepburn
> Miriam Hopkins
> Helen Hayes
> Ann Harding
> Myrna Loy
> Dolores del Rio

> Dick Diver—Fredric March
> Herbert Marshall
> Robert Montgomery
> Richard Barthelmess
> Paul Lukas
> Douglas Fairbanks, Jr.
> Ronald Colman

> Baby Warren—Kay Francis
> Ina Claire

> Paklin Troubetskoi—George Raft
> Ronald Colman
> Charles Bickford
> Douglas Fairbanks, Jr.[9]

"Scott didn't know anything about adaptations," Warren says. The *Tender Is the Night* which the author and his young collaborator knocked out in a few weeks for the screen was very different from the novel which had cost eight years. "I would tell him," Warren remembers, " 'If you're going to do the book, do the book.' He wouldn't pay any attention to me. He was going to show them, going to prove that he knew movies."

The two amateurs opened their story in classic melodramatic form with an accident which brings the hero and heroine together. The mishap takes place during a "short, hilarious gallop" led by Prince Paklin Troubetskoi, an "exiled Russian nobleman and ex-Cossack" who runs a "fashionable girls' riding school on the shores of Lake Geneva in Switzerland." A seventeen-year-old American heiress named Nicole Warren, "Troubetskoi's pet," "is thrown in a nasty fall and dashed against the base of a tree." The riding master dispatches one of his pupils to a nearby charity hospital where "Richard Diver, . . . promising young brain surgeon and psychiatrist, is just completing a delicate operation."[10] Dr. Diver takes a horse and hurries to the scene of the injury.

Life, when taken in at the local Bijou, was evidently a much simpler puzzle than when confronted in a novel. In the book Nicole has been raped by her father, a rich capitalist, and his act becomes a metaphor for capitalism's original sin; the "winding mossy ways"[11] of her own mind become her purgatory as she atones for her father's guilt by going insane. In the movie treatment she simply gets a bump on the head.

At first Dr. Diver thinks of Nicole as just another patient, but eventually they are literally thrown together on a mountainside. "By coincidence," Dick meets Baby and Nicole in a funicular making a trip up a mountain:

> A casual conversation between two of the passengers about the possibilities of the cable that pulls the car breaking seems to upset Nicole. . . . The car begins to tremble and amid the terror of the passengers, Dick's one thought is for Nicole's safety. The cable splits and the funicular is precipitated down the incline for a horrible moment, then derailed. It crashes over on its side and amid the confusion that follows, Dick clutches Nicole tightly to his heart. Thankful that she is safe, and realiz-

ing that this girl and her future mean everything to him, he . . .
realizes . . . that he is to be her husband and private doctor for
life.[12]

After Dick and Nicole's marriage, a melody is introduced into
the story. The collaborators explained:

> In the book, *Tender Is the Night,* there is much emphasis on
> the personal charm of the two Divers and on the charming
> manner in which they're able to live. In the book this was con-
> veyed largely in description, "fine writing," poetic passages, etc.
> It has occurred to us that a similar effect can be transferred to
> the spectator by means of music, and to accomplish this we
> have interpolated . . . a melody written . . . by Charles W.
> Warren.[13]

Warren says that he told Fitzgerald, "You don't insert music. The
studios have their own music departments." But if Scott had a
fuzzy understanding of how to write movie treatments, he saw
his own art with considerable clarity. He knew that in *Tender Is
the Night* he had told his readers about Dick Diver's "extraordi-
nary virtuosity with people"[14] without really demonstrating that
charm dramatically. In fact, in an early draft of the book he had
written: "The shadow of his charm plays about me still, as if to
warn me, frighten me away from my story. And it's the one thing
I can never capture—never though I press this lead till it crum-
bles. You may look through this book for it but you will not
find it." In the novel, we are told almost nothing of the specific
acts of charm performed by Dick but rather how he made others
feel, and these feelings would have been hard to film.

The camera was to have shown the Divers' luxurious "Villa
Diana" at the top of a steep cliff, and a piano at the bottom.
Several workmen are preparing to haul the instrument up the
face of the cliff with a rope which is hitched to a team of horses
on top. One workman is sitting on the piano, leaning over so that
he can reach the keyboard, pecking out the melody to "Our Life
Will Be a Wow," the number Warren was playing when Fitzgerald walked into his life. Suddenly the man and the piano are

hoisted into the air as a "fellow workman runs up a zigzag stair-case, cut on the side of the stone hill, crying . . . 'Stop the horses!' " The piano settles safely to the ground once again and the man who had risen with it resumes his melody. Nicole, looking "happy and the picture of health," appears and goes to the piano where she plays "the tune more fully than the workman." When Baby Warren enters with her boy friend, "a Prince Somebody from the Balkans," the music changes: the prince "plays a repetition of the previous melody but now comically in the highest octave on the piano." Baby herself takes over and "again there is an ominous note in the score as [she] finishes the tune in the bass cleff."[15]

The use of music in a motion picture to create a kind of poetic emotional state was a commendable idea. It was not, however, a particularly new one; even before the old movie houses were wired for talkies, they all had pianos. Still, Fitzgerald was onto something. His use of music in *Tender Is the Night* seems a little contrived, but much later, as he worked on *Madame Curie* at MGM, he would revive his ideas about melody and handle them more skillfully. In Fitzgerald's script for that film, an exiled Polish pianist sits alone in a shabby Paris hotel room and sere-nades his lost country.

While their marriage is still new, the Divers are happy, but "the luxury and ample supply of the Warrens' money" begin to rust Dick's more important talents. His "charm and ability to stage-manage his parties" become a substitute for his profession. The problem is that the Warrens have made him a showman when what he wanted to be was a doctor, and "inwardly there have been longings and old regrets . . ."[16]

Soon jealousy makes an already tense situation even worse. One day, in the same way that Dick and Nicole were thrown to-gether in the cable-car crash, Dick and the young actress Rose-mary are thrown at one another in an automobile:

> Bewildered and uncertain, Nicole sits next to Dick who is driving. It is when Dick has stepped on the accelerator for a short straightaway run that Nicole, laughing hysterically,

clutches the steering wheel and swerves the car off the road, down a little incline at the bottom of which it rolls over on its side. Dick's leg, unknown to the others, is pinned agonizingly under the side of the car. Rosemary is thrown against him in such a way that it looks as though he might have crawled over to her.[17]

In the next weeks, suspicion and irritation mount until Dick and Nicole separate. "Perhaps I won't make such a mess of things alone," Dick vows.

Nicole and her former riding teacher Paklin Troubetskoi begin a flirtation—just as Nicole and Tommy Barban do in the novel. The motion-picture treatment is true to the book up to the point where Nicole's virtue is tested:

> Driving through the pleasant countryside Nicole does not object when Paklin turns the car into a drive that leads to a small mountain hotel. She hovers, outwardly tranquil, as Paklin fills out the police blanks and registers the names—his real, hers false. Their room is simple, almost ascetic. . . .
>
> Moment by moment all that Dick has taught her, all that he has grown to mean to her, comes back. Realizing that she cannot go through with her "affair," she tells Paklin so, as gently as she can. . . .
>
> "You don't know what a really good time is," Paklin says angrily. "You've never had one. You couldn't be gay—really gay, with a psychiatrist nagging you all the time. Now you're throwing over what could be the happiest part of your life—"
>
> "Because I love Dick."[18]

In real life Zelda had had an affair with an "officer of aviation" who wore a white uniform and talked "romantically [of] how he want[ed] to smoke opium in Peking."[19] The novel recorded the wife's unfaithfulness, but on the screen husbands and wives were different—they were faithful. Or so Fitzgerald thought in 1934. In 1938, he would think differently, calling one of his best screenplays *Infidelity*.

One of the most moving scenes in the novel describes the way

Dick Diver is beaten up first by Italian cab drivers and then by Italian cops. Fitzgerald had actually received such a beating himself while in Rome, and ever after he had hated all of Italy for it. In the movie treatment, however, wish fulfillment seems to take over, so that it is not Dick but his rival Troubetskoi who is beaten. Nicole tries to rescue the riding master but, at the sight of his hamburger face, she dissolves into hysteria. Luckily, that "promising young brain surgeon and psychiatrist" Dick Diver once again is waiting in the wings to save her. Nicole is taken to a hospital and Dick is called in to operate:

> Whether he is operating on Nicole to save her for Paklin, Dick doesn't know, but he is making the attempt regardless.
> In the quiet, mechanical smoothness of the operating room, in the midst of his delicate work—with the newness and mystery of this particular operation—and the burning sensation that he is trying to save Nicole for another man, Dick's nerve fails.
> But Nicole, deep in the oblivion of the anesthetic, murmurs once "Dick" and his hand does not falter after that.[20]

By the end of the movie, Dick Diver has become not a symbol of self-destructive charm but simply one more Prince Charming.

When the movie treatment was finished, Fitzgerald staked his collaborator to a trip to Hollywood. Scott hoped that Warren, besides selling himself to the studios, might be able to sell *Tender Is the Night*. Fitzgerald gave Warren several letters of introduction which were supposed to unlock the movie world for him. He wrote Bess Meredyth, a writer who had shared his own unfortunate entanglement with *The Redheaded Woman:*

> Between your amours, intrigues, affairs, your coquetries, oglings and pawings, triumphs and frustrations, between your bootlegging perfumes over the border and your politeness to Marcel de Sano, most of all for the sake of my love I ask you to find a few minutes to give to the young man, Charles Warren, who presents this letter, a few wise words from a girl who was on the set when Griffith invented the close-up and Cedric

Gibbons invented the clothes hanger. . . . Let him sit in your office for a moment, will you, dearie, and inhale the stale but sacred Chesterfield smoke.

Fitzgerald explained that Warren had helped him with a treatment of *Tender,* but added, "My God, it is third best seller in the country and seems to be about as inadaptable to treatment as was the carrot-topped tart of three years ago."[21]

Scott wrote to Warburton Guilbert, who was then in Hollywood writing scores:

I saw your show in New York and thought it great stuff and all your promise fulfilled and was delighted to see an old Triangle friend come through. Incidentally, working with this man, Warren, has taken me back to those days of pounding out lyrics to "Puccini Cowboy" and "The Beautiful Chord Come True" and my real favorite of all your early songs—"The Land of the Never Never."[22]

Fitzgerald wrote George Cukor that Warren "seems to have more stuff than any young man I've met since Hemingway, though his specialty is a gift for the theatre rather than for literature."[23]

Soon Warren was sending Fitzgerald letters from the coast. One informed Scott: "Your name is big and hellishly well known in the studios. You rate out here as a highbrow writer but you rate as a thoroughbred novelist and not a talkie hack and therefore these people look up to you." The letter went on to suggest, however, that being looked up to was no way to get rich. "Lower your highbrow & help on some trash," he advised the author of *The Great Gatsby* and *Tender Is the Night.* "They buy trash here —they're quite willing to pay high for it. . . . If you would forget originality and finesse and think in terms of cheap melo theatrics you would probably have made a howling success of your visits here and would likewise have no financial worries now."[24] (Much later, Warren would follow his own advice and create the world's most successful television show, *Gunsmoke.*)

It evidently occurred to Scott that perhaps the young man was right. On a single page he wrote out an outline for a story and sent it off to Warren offering to "go 50–50" if he sold it to a studio. His cast of characters included an "old-fashioned ham actor," "typical flapper," "woman who took fan letter answer seriously, and who believed all sorts of junk," and a "Big Shot writer trying to get in studio." The story which the writer hoped would end his financial worries went as follows:

> Row between extras.
> Some of the big stars walk through.
> The Big Shot who has been reverently mentioned the entire time finally makes appearance and is insignificant little boob.
> Pathetic appeal of extra person or persons who need work desperately and the job is landed by boob who doesn't need it. . . .
> One of the directors commits suicide and someone phones it in immediately and "yes man" who comes out is more interested in who's gonna take over the picture than the suicide.
> Shot of extras with jobs coming off the lot or sets with their make-up and costumes on and their cheeriness and flippancy compared with the ones in the room and how they accept the luck of their fellows.

Fitzgerald closed by saying, "Can't co-operate at the moment but would if it isn't too like *Merton of the Movies!*"[25]

Despite his high hopes and fine understanding of melo Hollywood, Bill Warren could not find a studio job or interest anyone in *Tender Is the Night;* he returned to New York and went to work writing detective stories for the pulps. Fitzgerald wrote Maxwell Perkins that "for a whole year" he had hoped for a financial "break in the shape of either Hollywood buying *Tender* or else . . . getting . . . someone else to do an efficient dramatization." But the break had not come and the author thought that he knew why.

> I know I would not like the job, and I know that [Owen] Davis who had every reason to undertake it after the success of [his Broadway version of] *Gatsby* simply turned thumbs down from his dramatist's instinct that the story was not con-

structed as dramatically as *Gatsby* and did not readily lend itself to dramatization.[26]

Perhaps Fitzgerald was remembering the problems he had had turning *Tender Is the Night* into a movie when he wrote in a short story called "Financing Finnegan":

> It was only when I met some poor devil of a screenwriter who had been trying to make a logical story out of one of his books that I realized he had his enemies.
> "It's all beautiful when you read it," this man said disgustedly, "but when you write it down plain it's like a week in the nuthouse."[27]

At one point in *Tender Is the Night*, Nicole looks at Dick and thinks, "It was as though an incalculable story was telling itself inside him, about which she could only guess at in the moments when it broke through the surface."[28] The movie camera and the movie audience would have been in a position much like Nicole's: they would have missed the "incalculable story" because the camera, unlike the novelist, cannot probe inside the mind. But if the job of adapting *Tender* for the screen was likely to drive one crazy, it was not because of some flaw in the "fine writing" of the novel. *Tender* had never been intended as a dramatic novel; Fitzgerald was experimenting with something very different— the "psychological novel."[29]

The camera could not show the mind, but it had nonetheless to show something. So the collaborators, Fitzgerald and Warren, manufactured what they must have thought of as "movie action." A lecture which Stahr gives the writer Boxley in *The Last Tycoon* more or less sums up what went wrong. Boxley had written a scene which began with a duel and ended with one man falling into a well so that he "has to be hauled up in a bucket."

> "Would you write that in a book of your own, Mr. Boxley?"
> "What? Naturally not."
> "You'd consider it too cheap."
> "Movie standards are different," said Boxley, hedging.
> "Do you ever go to them?"

"No—almost never."

"Isn't it because people are always duelling and falling down wells?"[30]

Yes, and falling off horses and tumbling down mountains in funiculars.

In 1938 a New York dramatist named Mrs. Edwin Jarrett wrote a dramatic version of *Tender Is the Night* which she hoped to see staged on Broadway. A carbon of her adaptation reached Fitzgerald in Hollywood shortly after a producer had rewritten a screenplay on which Scott had worked for months. "I want especially to congratulate you," Scott wrote Mrs. Jarrett, ". . . on the multiple feats of ingenuity with which you've handled the difficult geography and chronology so that it has a unity which, God help me, I wasn't able to give it." Fitzgerald worried, however, about the handling of Dick Diver in the play. "I did not manage, I think in retrospect, to give Dick the cohesion I aimed at," the author confessed, "but in your dramatic interpretation I beg you to guard me from the exposal of this. I wonder what the hell the first actor who played Hamlet thought of the part? I can hear him say, 'The guy's a nut, isn't he?' (We can always find great consolation in Shakespeare.)"[31] Fitzgerald noted that the play would have to "get by Broadway first," but if it did, he assured the playwright that Robert Montgomery wanted to play Dick Diver in a film version. But the play never did get by Broadway—it never even got to it.

It was not until 1962, twenty-two years after Fitzgerald died a Hollywood failure, that his novel was finally made into a movie. It was released by 20th Century–Fox, for whom the author had once worked (they had fired him after a few weeks). *Tender Is the Night* starred Jennifer Jones as Nicole and Jason Robards, Jr., as Dick Diver. Jill St. John was Rosemary and Joan Fontaine played Baby.

In 1936 Edwin Knopf heard that Fitzgerald had fallen on what he calls "very evil days." Since he wanted to help the author, whom he had met in France during the twenties, Knopf contacted

Fitzgerald through H. N. Swanson, a Hollywood agent. That year the author's income had fallen to a new low—$10,180. Moreover, his debts amounted to forty thousand. But when Knopf offered to pay Fitzgerald a thousand dollars a week to come to Hollywood as a screenwriter, Swanson said that he wouldn't insult his client with peanuts.

A Yank at Oxford:
Pictures of Words

1

F. Scott Fitzgerald looked down from the silver screen at his
Baltimore audience. Once again he was so successful that he
made you feel dirty. On his desk lay the manuscript of the best
book he had ever written. And at his side as a kind of reward—
a golden loving cup for the champion—sat a beautiful woman.
She wore a dark shawl over her golden head and a heavy coat
with a big floppy collar. She looked at the writer, very serious,
through heavily made-up eyes. "I wonder what you were when
you were a little boy," she said through the then fashionable
apple-red lips; she had a romantic Russian accent. People were
already comparing her to Garbo and Dietrich, and she was all
his. "Life *was* like that, after all . . ."[1]

In the audience, sitting toward the back of the house and
hunched down in his seat, sat a little man with a gray face. The
brightly lit author on the screen made the shadow which hung
over this man seem all the darker. While the man up there was
writing at the top of his talent, the man in the audience thought
that his writing career was over.

"I have asked a lot of my emotions," he had written in his

notebooks, "—one hundred and twenty stories. The price was
high . . . because there was one little drop of something—not
blood, not a tear, not my seed, but me more intimately than
these, in every story, it was the extra I had. Now it has gone and
I am just like you now. Once the phial was full—here is the
bottle it came in."[2]

And for a writer who could no longer write there would be
no badges, no medals, no beautiful women—only memories and
a mad wife convalescing in a sanitarium. While the author on
the screen solved his problems, life was more a puzzle than ever
to the author in the audience. The Fitzgerald in the audience
could look up at the Fitzgerald on the screen, but did he
recognize the man he saw there? No, the real Fitzgerald was not
like that anymore. He was cracking up.

The year was 1935. "One harassed and despairing night" only
a few weeks back, Fitzgerald had "packed a briefcase and [gone]
off a thousand miles to think it over." He later wrote in his
Crack-Up essays: "I took a dollar room in a drab little town where
I knew no one and sunk all the money I had with me in a stock
of potted meat, crackers, and apples." The town was Hendersonville, North Carolina, and the author was amused by "the very
deferential clerk not knowing that I was not only thousands,
nay tens of thousands in debt, but had less than forty cents cash
in the world and probably a deficit at my bank." The only underwear Scott took "was a pair of pajama pants" which after several
days of constant wear he thought worthy of "presenting . . . to
the Hendersonville Museum."[3]

After Hendersonville, Fitzgerald at first seemed to get better,
then worse. Years later, while killing time between pictures in
Hollywood, Scott scribbled on a scrap of paper a short scene
which tried to show the way his crack-up came over him:

A RAILROAD SIDING . . .

Begin with a montage of the actual crash of a great wreck. . . .
GIRL: Seems to be a general breakdown.

BARNABY: Do I show it that bad?

GIRL: Show what?

BARNABY: The breakdown. I haven't had it yet.

GIRL: I mean the wreck.[4]

"And then suddenly, surprisingly, I got better," Fitzgerald wrote in "The Crack-Up," "and cracked like an old plate as soon as I heard the news."[5]

Hendersonville, at least, was behind Fitzgerald now, but as he looked up at the author in the movie who lived in a big house in Connecticut, a kind of feudal lord among the immigrants who worked the tobacco fields, his own Baltimore apartment must have seemed small. It was located across the street from the Johns Hopkins University; since Fitzgerald was alone there much of the time, he developed the habit of going days at a time without bothering to change out of his pajamas.

In "The Crack-Up" Fitzgerald wrote that he "liked doctors, and girl children up to the age of about thirteen, and well-brought-up boy children from about eight years on. . . ." He "liked Katharine Hepburn's face on the screen, no matter what was said about her pretentiousness . . . and old friends if I only saw them once a year and could remember their ghosts." But in general he liked very little.

> I saw that for a long time I had not liked people and things, but only followed the rickety old pretense of liking. . . . I couldn't stand the sight of Celts, English, Politicians, Strangers, Virginians, Negroes (light or dark), Hunting People, or retail clerks, and middlemen in general, all writers . . . and all the classes as classes and most of them as members of their class.[6]

On the movie screen which Fitzgerald watched, the successful author was replaced for a moment by an old depot master. "Better you don't talk to me,"[7] the old man muttered bitterly to someone. At last, there was an emotion that the broken author recognized. There was someone with whom he could feel kinship.

The movie about Fitzgerald had been written by one of the author's old friends, Edwin Knopf. The story was actually drawn from Knopf's own experience, not Fitzgerald's. But who had ever heard of Edwin-Knopf-the-famous-author? Who had ever associated his name with Dickens, Conrad, Hemingway? Who had ever seen him as the symbol of a generation? So he romanticized himself, took the cloak of Successful Author, and told his story as if dreams came true, as if he actually *were* Scott Fitzgerald. Knopf proudly sent his screenplay to Scott. In it, he called Scott and Zelda by their real names, but by the time the script had been transferred to the screen, the successful author had been renamed Tony Barnett.

Knopf had gotten his start in show business at about the same time Fitzgerald was getting started as a novelist. During those early years he had a theatre in Baltimore where he staged *The Czarina*. One day, during what was supposed to be a *closed* rehearsal, Knopf felt someone sitting in a seat directly behind him. He turned to see who it was.

"What are you doing ?" he asked indignantly.

"Watching you direct," answered a lanky, freckle-faced girl just out of Bryn Mawr.

She had been around the theatre before, looking for a part, so Knopf recognized her, but he could not remember her name.

"I gave her a long lecture," Knopf remembers. "I told her to go back to Connecticut and get married and have babies. I told her I didn't like amateurs."

But when the girl refused to leave, the young director began to reconsider.

—How would she like to be one of the ladies in waiting? The Czarina could always use one more.

—She would.

—She wouldn't have any lines.

—That was all right.

—But she would have plenty of curtsies.

—Fine.

It wasn't much, a curtsy, but it was something. Knopf remembers that she got up on the stage and, "By God! she curtsied." The director decided to ask the actress her name. She said that it was Katharine Hepburn. That was 1928.

After *The Czarina* Knopf wrote what was to be for him the fateful play. It was called *The Big Pond* and Miss Hepburn was cast in the leading role. But then came the breakdown. The strain of trying to do everything for his theatre—writing, directing, producing, publicizing, all at the same time—finally told. Knopf suffered a "crack-up" of his own and, ironically, the experience led him to Fitzgerald. On the advice of his doctor he turned over all his duties to someone else and went to France, where he found the author of *The Great Gatsby* at work on his next, his fourth, novel.

When Knopf returned to America after a summer of relaxation had pasted over the cracks, he sold *The Big Pond* to Warner Brothers, then followed his play to Hollywood, where he helped adapt it for the screen. During the years which Fitzgerald spent struggling to pull together *Tender Is the Night,* Knopf was working his way up in the Hollywood hierarchy, turning out picture after picture.

The script which had Fitzgerald as its hero was written with no particular studio in mind. Knopf was gambling that he could sell it—he was lucky. Samuel Goldwyn had recently dispatched George Oppenheimer to find a vehicle for Anna Sten, a beautiful Russian actress whom the producer hoped to make into another Garbo or Dietrich. After a year of searching, Oppenheimer recommended a script written by his cousin Mildred's husband, Edwin Knopf. The original title was *Broken Soil,* but this was soon changed to *The Wedding Night*—after all, the audience was coming to see a sex goddess, not the farmer's daughter—and they were in business. Miss Sten starred opposite Gary Cooper, who played Fitzgerald. The real Fitzgerald was impressed by his screen counterpart, but in a strange way. "Gary Cooper's appeal is just that he can't act," the author wrote. "But they think from his unwilling expression—I bet when he takes those silly clothes off he'd be twice as exciting as those silly actors."[8] *The Wedding Night* was directed by King Vidor, an old friend of Fitzgerald's who had been greatly acclaimed for his work on *The Big Parade, The Crowd,* and *Our Daily Bread. The Literary Digest* called the film a "fine, mature, and poignant motion picture."[9]

Knopf did not know that the same year his fictitious Scott Fitzgerald appeared on the screen as the very symbol of the romantic artist, the real Fitzgerald would be writing *The Crack-Up.* When these essays began to appear in *Esquire,* however, Knopf saw that being Scott Fitzgerald was a more difficult task than he had imagined. Then he began hearing of Fitzgerald's debts, all forty thousand worth. Writing *The Wedding Night* had given Knopf a special affection for the author—he knew that something had to be done.

It was sometime late in 1936 that Edwin Knopf took his idea up to the top floor of the Thalberg Building at MGM where the big boys were, sitting up there on top of everyone else. Knopf wanted to hire a writer, but to do that—to spend money—he had to get the approval of the College of Cardinals: L. B. Mayer, Sam Katz, Eddie Mannix. "I had a hell of a time," he remembers.

When Knopf suggested to Mayer, the dictator, that they hire a screenwriter named Scott Fitzgerald, the old man looked puzzled.

"Scott who?" he asked.

Sam Katz had never heard of Fitzgerald either.

Eddie Mannix was a little more accommodating. Sitting at his big desk in his big office with a sign above his chair which read DON'T LET MGM'S SUCCESS GO TO YOUR HEAD, he asked:

"What's he done lately?"

"Not much," Knopf confessed.

The story editor retreated, leaving the Cardinals to their steam bath, their masseur, and to each other. But he did not forget about his mission. It took a while, but he finally convinced the executives to take a chance on the man who had written *The Great Gatsby* and *Tender Is the Night.*

The next step was to contact H. N̶. Swanson. The chain worked
like this: Fitzgerald was represented in the East by his agent
Harold Ober, who in turn was represented in the West by his
associate "Swanie" Swanson. When Knopf and Swanson got
together, Knopf made his offer: he was authorized to pay Fitzgerald a thousand dollars a week if the author would come to
MGM as a screenwriter.

"I wouldn't insult him with it," Swanson said.

"It's a thousand a week more than he's making now," Knopf
said.

"No," said Swanson. "No deal."

"You're not the one who is going to make that decision," Knopf
told the agent. "Scott's going to make it."

Knopf, who never had an agent himself, was no particular
fan of Swanson's. He says, "Swanson is the kind of man who
would not be interested in Scott if he were making only a
thousand a week." When Knopf called Fitzgerald in Baltimore,
"He was so pleased," according to the story editor. The author
accepted a six-month contract. In an autobiographical sketch
called "Afternoon of an Author," which Fitzgerald wrote not long
before leaving for California, he described the "isolation" and the
"growing seclusion of his life" in Baltimore. He seemed to have
told all the stories he had to tell, and found himself "picking over
an already well-picked past." He wrote that he "needed reforest-
ation" and only "hoped the soil would stand one more growth."[10]
As a novelist Fitzgerald had little left to harvest, so he would
go to Hollywood now and sow his soil with exotic seed.

He would begin as a screenwriter, but it was to be only a
beginning. He had been thinking about Hollywood for some
time now, but what he really wanted was not only to write but
to direct—to be Jay Gatsby, stager of lavish entertainments, and
Dick Diver, the man whose charm gave shape and meaning to
the performance, with a dash of General Grant besides. He
wanted to run the show, to be both an artist and a leader of men.
To him the director was all of this, "a symbol of power."

2

The classic Roman columns stretched for almost half a mile along the front of the MGM studio, giving it the air of a great Coliseum. As Fitzgerald drove down Washington Boulevard that first day and passed along the colonnade, the studio must have looked like the capitol of an empire worth conquering. Of course the author had been to the studio before, back in 1931, and so he knew that the imperial front was really a false front just like the ones they used on the sets—the columns and the marble wall were really just plaster and wood. Once inside you saw that the vast building which appeared to be there was not there at all; the Roman façade which the public saw was just a fence to hide the jumble of shacks and sound stages which made up the studio. Still, the Coliseum effect made its impression, and Fitzgerald began to dream of "all the money and glory beyond the impregnable walls."[11]

Unfortunately, the world behind the fake columns was even more empty in July 1937 than during Fitzgerald's first visit to MGM. Thalberg was dead—in his place there now stood a new building which bore his name. Big and square and made of concrete, the structure looked a little too much like a mausoleum. Edwin Knopf's office was there and the novelist went up to report to him. He was ready to go to work.

"Here came this completely crushed and frightened man," Knopf remembers, "—the features were there, the drawing, but not the face. He had that almost blue paleness. Not big wrinkles but little wrinkles all over because he was sick."

Fitzgerald would later describe Stahr's face in *The Last Tycoon* in much the same way: "The face . . . was aging from within, so that there were no casual furrows of worry and vexation but a drawn asceticism as if from a silent self-set struggle—or a long illness."[12]

George Oppenheimer, who was now at Metro, was also surprised at the change in the author. In the 1920s it had been

Oppenheimer who sometimes felt unsure, out of place, while the Fitzgeralds, Scott and Zelda, seemed to be leading the parade. He even remembered an evening a long time before in New York when one member of the author's family had helped to kiss away his self-consciousness. It had happened at a party which Oppenheimer attended with Beatrice Kaufman.

> In the early part of the evening Bea and I became separated in the crowd [Oppenheimer recalls] and I found myself with famous faces all about me but no one whom I knew well enough to approach. Gradually the guests drifted into the dining room. I hung back, hoping that Bea would retrieve me. Just as I was about to give up hope, there appeared in the doorway F. Scott Fitzgerald and his wife Zelda. They were two of the most beautiful people I had ever seen and both were obviously in their cups. I had never met them but, to my amazement, Zelda came up to me as if I were an old friend, asked me to bring her a drink and some food and to join her on the fire escape since she craved air. Abruptly I was no longer a stranger, but one who had been singled out by the most beautiful woman in the room and, to boot, the wife of my literary idol.
>
> Deep into the night Zelda and I sat on that fire escape, talking, drinking, and necking (a tribal custom of the twenties). . . .
>
> As I walked home that night I was Amory, Anthony, Gatsby, and Anson lumped into one shimmering youth. Next morning I was still on a cloud, slightly edged with hangover, as I headed for the [Alfred] Knopf office. Just as I reached Fifth Avenue I saw Scott and Zelda about to board a bus.
>
> "Zelda! Scott!" I shouted and sprinted toward them.
>
> They turned and looked in my direction. I needed no lip reading to grasp what Zelda was saying. It was too clear in her bewildered expression. I could almost hear her dulcet voice inquiring of Scott, "Who the hell is that?" as the bus rolled away, leaving behind one more shattered illusion.[13]

But in Hollywood Fitzgerald and Oppenheimer seemed to have traded places. Now, incredibly, people were asking who the hell is Scott Fitzgerald. Now Scott was the one who felt like an outsider. So Oppenheimer invited the author and his daughter Scottie, who happened to be visiting from the East, for dinner one night. Fitzgerald came and seemed to have a good time, but he said almost nothing.

Shortly after arriving in Hollywood, Fitzgerald moved into a Beverly Hills hotel on Sunset Boulevard called the Garden of Allah, where many other screenwriters lived. The Garden had once been the estate of Alla Nazimova, the great silent-screen star; it was composed of small two-story stucco bungalows, each with two apartments, clustered about a main house which had a pool and patio. The effect was that of a small Moroccan village, except that the starlets lounging about the pool wore not veils but the 1930s one-piece. There were palm trees everywhere.

Fitzgerald shared his bungalow with Edwin Justus Mayer, the writer who twenty years earlier had said that Scott's success made him "feel dirty."[14] Other old friends out of Fitzgerald's past were also living at the Garden of Allah—people like John O'Hara, who had just written *Butterfield 8,* Marc Connelly, author of *The Green Pastures;* and Dorothy Parker and Alan Campbell.

Humorist Robert Benchley lived there too, and it was at a party in his bungalow that Fitzgerald and Sheilah Graham first saw one another. They did not speak, but each made an impression on the other. "Smiling faintly at him from not four feet away was the face of his dead wife, identical even to the expression," Fitzgerald would later write of Stahr in *The Last Tycoon;* of course the author's own wife was not really dead, only crazy. "Across the four feet of moonlight, the eyes he knew looked back at him, a curl blew a little on a familiar forehead; the smile lingered, changed a little according to pattern; the lips parted— the same. An awful fear went over him, and he wanted to cry aloud."[15] Fitzgerald stared at Miss Graham and then got up and rushed out of the room.

When he was gone, Miss Graham asked Benchley, "Who was that man sitting under the lamp? He was so quiet."

"That was F. Scott Fitzgerald—the writer," Benchley said. "I asked him to drop in. I guess he's left—he hates parties."

Miss Graham was sorry that she had not spoken to him. She had often used his name in her column "SHEILAH GRAHAM SAYS." When she wanted to suggest that someone was passé, she would say that they were "as old-fashioned as F. Scott Fitzgerald types." She had not, however, read anything that he had written.[16]

The author and the columnist met again at a Writers' Guild dinner dance at the Coconut Grove. Miss Graham noticed Fitzgerald sitting alone at Dorothy Parker's table; he was watching her. "Immediately things changed," Fitzgerald wrote in *Tycoon.* ". . . the people shrank back against the walls till they were only murals; the white table lengthened and became an altar where the priestess sat alone. Vitality swelled up in him, and he could have stood a long time across the table from her, looking and smiling."[17]

Miss Graham suggested that they dance. "I'm afraid I promised to dance the next one with Dorothy Parker," Fitzgerald said. "But after that—" But there was no after that; the speeches started and went on and on.[18]

The next Saturday, Eddie Mayer asked Miss Graham to dinner, sweetening the invitation with the information that Fitzgerald would be there, too. Actually Fitzgerald had asked Mayer to ask Sheilah. She remembers in detail what happened that night:

We met at the Garden of Allah and went to the Clover Club, a gambling place with dining and dancing upstairs. Scott said little on the way out—there was a reticence about him that made me feel he belonged to an earlier, quieter world. His clothes, too, spoke of another time: he wore a pepper-and-salt suit and a bow tie, and though this was July, a wrinkled charcoal raincoat with a scarf about his neck and a battered hat. It was hard to believe that this was the glamour boy of the twenties. At the bar we were introduced to Humphrey Bogart and his wife, Mayo Methot, "Won't you have a drink with us?" Bogart asked Scott.

He shook his head and said, pleasantly, no. Bogart seemed surprised. We sat with them for a few minutes and Scott made some light jokes about a picture he was writing for M-G-M. The Bogarts laughed and I caught respect and deference.[19]

After that, Fitzgerald and Miss Graham began seeing one another regularly. He bought a second-hand Ford coupé, which he would drive up her hill every evening about six o'clock. The car rattled and had a funny horn. Miss Graham says that Fitzgerald, "with his battered collegiate hat and raincoat, his pullover sweaters and jaunty bow ties . . . reminded me more and more of all I had read about American college boys of the twenties."[20] What she did not know was that Scott had written the jalopy and the costume and even a little of her into the picture on which he was working.

The movie, Fitzgerald's first assignment, was a comedy about an American Rhodes scholar and his adventures in England. The reputation the author had won for *This Side of Paradise* had stayed with him and so, twenty years after *Paradise*, he was put to work on a movie about the college scene. His producer was Michael Balcon, later the head of Britain's prestigious Ealing Studio and the dean of British film makers. With a genius like Balcon in command and an author like Fitzgerald writing his story for him, MGM might well have asked this production company to turn out a masterpiece—and received what it asked for. Instead, it asked them to turn out *A Yank at Oxford*—which was, after all, a funny film.

There was story conference after story conference, and then Fitzgerald got down to "the endless detail of script revision."[21] Knopf had assigned him an office in the Thalberg Building and there he sat day after day, a Coca-Cola bottle on his desk, scripts in cheery sky-blue covers beside the Coke. Above Fitzgerald sat the big boys. Below him in the basement were the archives, the "morgue," which contained many more unproduced scripts than the other kind. And all about him for miles around stretched the permanent sets—old castles and Western towns, and even the good ship *Bounty*. Here and there among the sets were great stacks of stock-piled icebergs, trees complete with stands, Greek columns with stands, Gothic towers (both miniature and life-size), and papier-mâché boulders as light as balloons—scraps left over from some of the biggest, most glutinous entertainment orgies ever staged.

3

The idea of doing a picture on Oxford had been hanging around Metro for years. The project was first entitled *Yale Versus Oxford*, but none of the writers could get hot on it. In 1937, when the studio decided to open up a new studio, and hopefully a new cinema frontier, in England, the Yale-Oxford story was revived. The tale was tinkered with; then Yale was expelled from the scenario so that the writers could concentrate on the English university alone. The title became *A Yank at Oxford* and Robert Taylor was picked to be the Yank. At a much publicized London lunch, L. B. Mayer, a powerfully built little fireplug of a man, explained the casting as follows: "If ever there was an American young man who could logically by culture and breeding be called a Britisher, it's Robert Taylor."[22]

The original "story idea" came from John Monk Saunders, the man whose chest had intoxicated the Fitzgeralds back in 1927. Alistair Cooke, writing in *The New Republic*, would later say:

> No Englishman could have written a story so contemptuous of Lakedale State College (founded 1903) or kneeled in such lyric fervor before the spectacle of dinner in hall or the ritual of a Bump Supper (what possibilities here for funny and sordid truth). A Rhodes scholar might have done it—and that in fact is the answer. A Rhodes scholar did, Mr. John Monk Saunders.[23]

Frank Wead, a veteran Metro screenwriter, was given first crack at turning Saunders' "idea" into a script. He had done a hundred and one pages when Fitzgerald arrived and was put on the story, writing behind him. This system for mass-producing scripts had been started by Thalberg; Fitzgerald described how it worked in *The Last Tycoon,* where Monroe Stahr tells Prince Agge:

> "We have all sorts of people—disappointed poets, one-hit playwrights—college girls—we put them on an idea in pairs, and if it slows down, we put two more writers working behind them. I've had as many as three pairs working independently on the same idea."
>
> "Do they like that?" [Prince Agge asks]
>
> "Not if they know about it. They're not geniuses—none of them could make as much any other way."[24]

Thalberg was dead, but his system wasn't. So Fitzgerald was given Wead's unfinished script and asked to touch up what was there and write an ending. For some reason he was not assigned a collaborator. They were giving him a chance to go it alone.

Scott got down to work, but before he had gotten far with his revisions, he was interrupted by an actress who said that she was in distress. Scott had long done his writing for a particular girl. At Princeton he had composed what amounted to whole books of letters to Ginevra King. Later he wrote Zelda miles of letters from New York. *This Side of Paradise* had been written, in part at least, to win The Girl, and it had succeeded. Now in Hollywood Scott was once again writing for a woman, Miss Maureen O'Sullivan, but scripting her lines was like paying homage to some Platonic conception of beauty: he had never seen his star in the flesh.

Then one day while he was writing, a messenger came to Fitzgerald's cubicle to deliver a note from the actress which said, "Miss Maureen O'Sullivan wishes you to have luncheon with her tomorrow. You may get in touch with her in her dressing room." (Scott kept the scrap of paper for the rest of his life.) When Fitzgerald reported to Miss O'Sullivan's dressing room, she asked him to come out to her house at Malibu at noon the next day. The writer accepted.

Scott drove his old Ford out along Route One past all the sea-food restaurants and seaside motels to where bright, expensive beach cottages were strung out single file on a shelf of land at the water's edge in much the same way that the Coke bottles were lined up in his office. Miss O'Sullivan had a motive for inviting Fitzgerald out to Malibu, where she had rented Jack Warner's house for the summer: she wanted to go over the script for *A Yank at Oxford* with him. She remembers complaining to Scott that the role of Molly read like "one of those very dull ingénue parts, just a love interest." She asked him "to liven it up, to make it more interesting, to come up with an angle."

Scott always fell in love with actresses. The first had been Ina Claire in *The Quaker Girl* and now the latest was Maureen O'Sullivan in *A Yank at Oxford*. Like Monroe Stahr's seaside home in *The Last Tycoon,* Jack Warner's beach house had an air of a sound stage about it—it was made for drama. Scott and Maureen were alone, playing what the movie people call a "Two-Shot Close-Up," and literature's retired leading man was doing all right. The writer who was quietly invisible about the studio was a changed man in the presence of his star. "He seemed flamboyant," Miss O'Sullivan remembers. "He seemed vital. He was great fun."

Fitzgerald's high spirits probably had two causes. First of all, he was warmed by the proximity of one of the most beautiful women in the world. But he was also warmed by what he was drinking. The author and the actress sat in a big room off the bar and toasted one another with mint juleps. Miss O'Sullivan was to Fitzgerald a strange constellation: she was Irish but she liked Southern juleps. She reminded him of his Old Country forefathers and of Zelda all at the same time. Fitzgerald reminded Miss O'Sullivan of her past, too. She was just over from Ireland and she found him "almost a European character."

Sobriety had held Fitzgerald down like some unforgiving hyper-gravity ever since he had arrived in Hollywood. Now the mint juleps seemed literally to give him wings. "He strode about the room," Miss O'Sullivan recalls, "with his arms waving in the air. It was a wonderful afternoon."

When Fitzgerald returned to the studio, he tried to find the angle which the actress, his fellow countryman, had requested. Evidently he succeeded. "I remember liking what he wrote for me," says Miss O'Sullivan. "He added the Fitzgerald touch."

Reading and rereading the script which he was to improve—Wead's script—Fitzgerald must have felt a little as if he held in his hands a dramatized version of his own autobiographical short story "The Freshest Boy." For Lee Sheridan (Robert Taylor) arrives at Oxford in much the same frame of mind as that which afflicts Fitzgerald's Basil Duke Lee when he arrives at St. Regis: he is arrogant, especially about his prowess at sports. Of course the similarity between Lee and Basil is a kind of family resemblance shared by almost all heroes of stories about brash New Boys who matriculate at Old Schools and must learn to conform to Old Traditions before they finally win everyone's respect. All the same, in Lee Sheridan, Fitzgerald met an old friend.

Still, he agreed with Miss O'Sullivan that something was missing in the Wead script, and he thought that he knew what it was. In Wead's story the conflict was sometimes between two individuals, sometimes between the individual and society, almost never between two cultures. The Yank could have been an Armenian at Oxford and it would not have changed the story; Molly was supposed to be English, but Wead made her sound like the kind of girl whom Lee might have found next door in Lakedale, U.S.A. Fitzgerald thought that that was wrong and so he set out to stress the Yank's Yankness and Molly's Britishness.

He began at the beginning, rewriting Wead's first scene completely. When he showed the scene to Balcon, the producer liked it. The upstart screenwriter had outwritten the veteran—it was that easy. When the cameras finally rolled in Denham with Jack Conway directing (he also did *The Redheaded Woman*), they photographed not the track-meet opening which Wead had written, but Fitzgerald's send-off at the train depot. Three college boys, costumed as fife and drummers of the American Revolution, march down the main street of Lakedale playing "Yankee Doodle." Lee Sheridan, who is surrounded by a crowd as he prepares to embark for England, laughs when he hears the musicians.

LEE: Hey, you nuts? Do you think I'm going to war?

OLD MAN (*in the crowd*): You never can tell.[25]

Lee climbs into the train, waving good-by and promising that he will take charge of matters once he gets to Oxford. Fitzgerald's hero was off for the mother country and Fitzgerald himself— clear the tracks, everyone—was on his way, too. Lee fully expected to become an important man on the other side of the ocean, and Fitzgerald surely expected to become the same in California: he wanted to be "Czar of the Industry right away." Lee was the great American athlete—if you didn't believe it, just give him an opening and he would tell you—and Fitzgerald was the great American author. There was no telling how far they might go.

The Spirit of Seventy-Six scene at the depot was a happy beginning for both the picture and the author's career, for it sets the stage for the drama of manners which Fitzgerald thought should carry his story. The old man in the crowd was right. Lee is going to war. He will be forced to fight the Revolution all over again on English soil, but instead of popping away with a musket, he will pop off with American slang. Rather than country against country, it will be the English culture versus the American, the Yankee Doodle dandy versus the Oxford "gentlemen."

Lee's problems begin almost as soon as he reaches Oxford and starts talking. The British students consider his constant bragging very un-Oxford and at one point remove his pants to cool off his self esteem. Nor does Lee like his fellow classmates any better than they like him. But there *is* one exception, the pretty English coed Molly Beaumont. In the Wead script the love story had been just another boy-girl romance—Miss O'Sullivan was bored just thinking about the role. Fitzgerald decided to enlarge the scope, to make the love story an America-England affair, and so wrote several new scenes.

In the most original of these, Molly and Lee go motoring through the English countryside—like a younger model of Scott and his own English girl, Sheilah, rattling through Beverly Hills. At one point they stop and Lee uses a bar of soap to decorate the car in what he calls American college fashion, scrawling all manner of slogans:

LEAP IN—LIMP OUT

HELLO, CHICKEN, HERE'S YOUR COOP

PAIR CONDITIONED—110° IN HERE

One of Lee's mottoes is LOVE AT WORK, but he might well have written NOVELIST AT WORK. Movies supposedly depend primarily on pictures, books on words, but in this scene Fitzgerald mixes his media and shows us pictures of words. Somehow these pictured words seem entirely appropriate for a novelist just embarking on a career in the movies. We seem to be atop the Great Divide which separates the publishing houses of the East from the picture studios out West.

Molly watches Lee for a while and then decides that she wants to play too.

MOLLY: Oh, I've got a good one. Why is our car like a baby? Because it has a rattle.

LEE (*touching Molly's head*): Rattle.

Molly grows more serious and asks Lee:

MOLLY: You're not really such a barbarian as you seem— you do eat the same food as we do . . . but do you speak the same language as we do?

Molly is right. She and Lee do not speak the same language, and that is their problem. Yet what separates them is more than any mere accent, for by language we are meant to understand more than words. We are meant to see language in a metaphorical sense as a kind of cornucopia containing all one's manners and mannerisms—one's culture, in short. If Lee does not speak Molly's language, she comes no closer to speaking his. As Fitzgerald pointed out in a note to his script, "Molly completely fails to catch the rhythm of Lee's American expressions. Hers are all stilted."

As the old Ford huffs and puffs back into Oxford looking like graffiti on wheels, Lee tells Molly, "It's good to see yourself as others see you." What he does not notice is that students, professors, policemen, and the general populace of Oxford are laughing themselves silly as the Ford rolls past. By this time Fitzgerald had learned that the moving-picture camera could do more than simply frame a story—it could help to shape it. Here it is an ideal tool for picturing irony. For centuries novelists —Fitzgerald included—had been achieving irony by showing us characters whose vision was more limited than our own. In reading about them we *seemed* to look over their shoulders smiling to ourselves. In *The Great Gatsby,* for instance, we *seem* to see the objects of Gatsby's love dream—the enormous house and Daisy—not only as he sees them, but in a larger context. But with the coming of pictures the audience could do more than *seem* to look over shoulders. We are actually there as Lee and Molly drive through Oxford, oblivious to the fact that they are the town joke. The larger context becomes the larger picture, the picture which the camera and the audience see, but Lee and Molly do not. When Molly finally does notice the hilarity, she abandons the car, flushed with embarrassment, but Lee never catches on at all.

Fitzgerald dutifully turned in this scene just as he had his "Yankee Doodle" opening, but someone—it could have been anyone from Balcon all the way up to Mayer himself—did not like it. In its stead, a roller rink full of lots of nice motion and very little meaning went before the cameras. Going around and around and around the rink, the hero and heroine encountered no noticeable cultural hurdles.

Most of the scenes which Fitzgerald wrote for *A Yank at Oxford* went the way of his rattle-trap Ford scene—they were junked. As the rewriting went on and on, the Yank had much of his Yankness bled out of him to the point where in the finished picture it is hard to see what Fitzgerald had been trying to do.

4

"Suffice to summarize," Fitzgerald wrote Mrs. Harold Ober of his first weeks as a full-time screenwriter. "I have seen Hollywood —talked with Taylor, dined with March, danced with Ginger Rogers (this will burn Scottie up but it's true), been in Rosalind Russell's dressing room, wisecracked with Montgomery, drunk (ginger ale) with Zukor and Lasky, lunched alone with Maureen O'Sullivan, watched Crawford act, and lost my heart to a beautiful half-caste Chinese girl whose name I've forgotten."[26]

Meanwhile his scenario was passed on to Malcolm Stewart Boylan and Walter Ferris, and they began working behind him just as he had worked behind Wead. Toward the end, George Oppenheimer was called in to nurse the script through its last revision. He had become what was known as a "screenplay doctor" and producers called him in, as one calls any doctor, when there was trouble.

At the endless story conferences where *A Yank at Oxford* was defended and debated and ridiculed, Oppenheimer, the doctor, managed to have some of Fitzgerald's lines restored. But most of the author's weeks of work on the motion picture were wasted, except as a lesson in Hollywood writing: Fitzgerald had learned something about how to put a scene together, but also how the scenes were likely to be treated.

As with most Hollywood productions, rewriting went on and on in accordance with Parkinson's Law: the reworking expanded to fill all the time allowed for it. So when Robert Taylor and the MGM production crew set off by rail for New York on their way to England, Oppenheimer was on the train. "I tried to write only one word a day," he says, "so that they would have to take me to England." But alas, Balcon decided in New York that Oppenheimer had done enough, and sent him home to Hollywood.

As for Robert Taylor, he set off for England like the character he was going to play, with bands blaring and girls cheering. But along the way he had some trouble and, by the time his ship docked on the other side of the Atlantic, he could not have been more out of character had he tried. If Lee Sheridan had come upon Oxford beating his own drum, Taylor wanted to slip ashore like contraband.

Things had started to go wrong in Phoenix, Arizona, where a girl threw herself onto Taylor's lap and then announced to the press that her boy friend's lap was more fun. The star began to feel insecure. Then in New York a reporter asked him if he had hair on his chest. He was so shaken that once at sea he informed Metro's publicity agents that he could not face the British press. The publicity men wired ahead to Howard Strickling, the studio's head of publicity who was then in London preparing a big welcome, to ask if they could sneak Taylor into England. Strickling wired back NOTHING DOING. When the ship bearing the star pulled up to the pier, Strickling told the reporters how frightened Taylor was, and asked them to lay off the hair on his chest and his widow's peak; then he went in to see Taylor and gave him to understand that this was a critical moment in his career. Both the actor and the press rose to the moment. The interview marked a turning point in Taylor's relations with newspapermen.[27]

L. B. Mayer, like any American going abroad, knew enough to take along plenty of American products like Taylor and Lionel Barrymore. But there came a point where native actors and actresses had to be hired, and this task was assigned to the Britisher, Balcon. All went well until Mayer noticed how much the producer had offered an unknown actress just out of the Royal Academy. He demanded that Balcon find someone cheaper, but the producer refused to back down and so Vivien Leigh was introduced to American movie audiences. Later, on the set of *Gone With the Wind,* Fitzgerald would write for Miss Leigh once again.

A Yank at Oxford was finished and ready for release in

February 1938. When the screen credits were finally passed around, Wead was left out and so was Fitzgerald. Instead, for one blink of the eye, the following appeared on the movie screens: Screenplay by Malcolm Stewart Boylan, Walter Ferris, and George Oppenheimer. By then Oppenheimer, the script doctor, was used to seeing his name at the end of such lists, although he was still a little sensitive about it. One day Bronislau Kaper, who had recently joined Metro's music department, told George, "I always thought your name was 'and George Oppenheimer.' "[28] The joke spread through the studio like gossip. Soon he was "and George Oppenheimer" to everyone. "He hated it," Edwin Knopf recalls.

A Yank at Oxford opened at the Capitol Theatre in New York on February 24, and not everyone liked it. Characteristically, *Time* magazine thought that *Yank* was un-American. "M-G-M made Robert Taylor what he is today," *Time* said, "but is far from satisfied. His saccharine cinema roles and cream-puff publicity have all too closely linked the word 'beauty' with the name 'Taylor.' Something had to be done to make him an unhissable he-man. . . . Last week cinemaddicts viewed the results: . . . with typical prodigality, M-G-M tries to save Robert Taylor's face at the expense of the U.S.'s."[29] Alistair Cooke told *New Republic* readers that the picture "was made by Metro in England and in awe." He called the film "a spellbound tribute to a conception of cultural leadership which probably survives nowhere but in the movies, but which thereby seeps through to two hundred million customers a week, grateful anyway to have their miasmic notions of Oxford jell into something."[30] Had such Fitzgerald scenes as the one where Lee decorates the old Ford not been cut, Cooke might have liked the picture better. At any rate, the Yank would have appeared brighter; he is obviously a better sloganeer than Molly.

The *New York Times,* however, liked the picture as it was, calling it "an uncommonly diverting show." But movie critic Frank S. Nugent could not resist a few digs at Taylor, commenting that "we still regard that widow's peak with a cynicism the feminine contingent rightly defines as envy." Nugent went on to say that *Yank* "evoked a wholly satisfying picture of Oxford life. . . . In fact, we even found ourselves rooting for Mr. Taylor in the Oxford-Cambridge crew race. But subconsciously that might have been because we were so glad to see him overseas."[31]

While *A Yank at Oxford* played at the Capitol, the Strand was advertising Edward G. Robinson in *A Slight Case of Murder* and Radio City Music Hall was showing David O. Selznick's acclaimed *The Adventures of Tom Sawyer. You Can't Take It with You* won the Academy Award that year; other outstanding pictures of 1938 included *Boys' Town* with Mickey Rooney and Spencer Tracy, *Test Pilot* with Clark Gable and Spencer Tracy, *Bringing Up Baby* with Cary Grant and Katharine Hepburn, and the nostalgic *Alexander's Ragtime Band,* with Don Ameche. Then toward the end of the year Fitzgerald's next picture appeared and it ranked with any of these.

The movie told the story of three Germans and their hardships after World War I. It won Fitzgerald his first screen credit and even a handshake from L. B. Mayer himself. By then Mayer knew the answer to "Scott who?" But he knew Scott Fitzgerald not as the author of *The Great Gatsby* or *Tender Is the Night.* He knew him as the man who wrote *Three Comrades,* one of the ten best movies of 1938.

☆ **7** ☆

Three Comrades:
Words, Words, Words

1

The huge barn of a building was dark except for one corner where two dozen people huddled near a bank of lights like campers warming themselves by a campfire. Some of them were drinking cardboard-tasting coffee from paper cups; when the job was done there would be a champagne party, but now they drank black brew.

"Let's have it quiet, please," someone said in a loud voice.

A bell rang and the talking changed to whispers and then to silence the way a theatre hushes when the lights go down. Beneath fifty artificial suns stood Robert Taylor and Margaret Sullavan. A make-up man was just running a comb through Miss Sullavan's hair—she was playing a downtrodden German girl, but that did not mean that her coiffure had to suffer, too.

"Roll 'em," said the director.

The camera began to make a very soft whirring sound almost as if it were breathing, nothing louder. The scene marker went in front of the lens for a moment, *whack*, and then the camera was looking directly at Taylor and Miss Sullavan. She was a frail lovely girl who, like one of the actresses in *The Last Tycoon,* had "starlight that actually photographed in her eyes."[1] She played a sophisticated rich girl who had lost all her money after the war; she said her lines, and the microphone suspended from the sound boom just above her head picked up her soft voice. Then the boom swung toward Taylor, who played a fumbling garage mechanic, as he answered Miss Sullavan's lines with his own.

"All right, cut."

The camera stopped its breathing; everyone relaxed, took another sip of coffee; then the bell rang and they did the whole thing over again. Miss Sullavan spoke and Taylor answered her. Cut. And again. Miss Sullavan and then Taylor. Cut. And again. . . .

"No," said the actress and this time the lines weren't from the script. She thought for a moment to be sure and then said, "I can't play this."

She meant that she could not play her lines, the ones F. Scott Fitzgerald had written for her. Suddenly everything stopped— the camera, the bobbing mike, the bells, the coffee drinking. If Miss Sullavan couldn't play her lines, then something had to be done to fix them. And Joseph L. Mankiewicz, the producer, thought that he was just the man to do it. He had rewritten other big names, so why shouldn't he rewrite Scott Fitzgerald? (Besides, even today Mankiewicz is a little skeptical of the whole Fitzgerald cult. "What would the Fitzgerald idolatry be like if he were ugly like Sinclair Lewis?") All Mankiewicz needed was a few nights without sleep, and then "Maggie" would be able to play her lines. It wasn't his idea. "Maggie was the one who blew the whistle."

That Mankiewicz rewrote Fitzgerald surprised few old-timers around the MGM plant—he had a reputation for reading scripts with a pencil in his hand to make "improvements." Edwin Knopf says of Mankiewicz, "It is both Joe's strength and his weakness that he thought that he could rewrite anyone." George Oppenheimer sums up the producer as follows: "Joe thinks he's Shakespeare." Ogden Nash was least surprised of all. He had recently done what he thought was "a respectable job" on a picture called *The Shining Hour*. He had worked on the script for months, only to have Mankiewicz rework it in twenty-four hours. The producer finished his rewrite job by applying his pencil to the credits: he crossed Nash's name off the picture.

But Fitzgerald had not yet learned to expect such help. The rewritten *Three Comrades* script led to a split between the producer and the writer which never healed. Fitzgerald got so angry that he wrote Mankiewicz a hate letter, but before he could send it off Sheilah Graham intervened. "You'll only antagonize him," she argued, "and he'll never restore your script."[2] So Scott tore up the letter and wrote a milder protest. Milder, but not mild. Ironically Fitzgerald, in pleading his case, said that he too was trying to help a distressed lady, he too was sorry for poor Maggie:

Dear Joe:

Well, I read the last part and I feel like a good many writers must have felt in the past. I gave you a drawing and you simply took a box of chalk and touched it up. Pat has now become a sentimental girl from Brooklyn, and I guess all these years I've been kidding myself about being a good writer. . . .

To say I'm disillusioned is putting it mildly. For nineteen years, with two years out for sickness, I've written best-selling entertainment, and my dialogue is supposedly right up at the top. But I learn from the script that you've suddenly decided that it isn't good dialogue and you can take a few hours off and do much better. . . .

. . . *but to say in detail what I think of these lines would take a book.* The last pages that everyone liked begin to creak from 116 on, and when I finished there were tears in my eyes, but not for Pat—for Margaret Sullavan.

My only hope is that you will *have a moment of clear thinking. That you'll ask some intelligent* and *disinterested* person to look at the two scripts. Some honest thinking would be much more valuable to the enterprise right now than an effort to convince people you've improved it. I am utterly miserable at seeing months of work and thought negated in one hasty week. I hope you're big enough to take this letter as it's meant —a desperate plea to restore the dialogue to its former quality . . . Oh, Joe, can't producers ever be wrong? I'm a good writer—honest. I thought you were going to play fair. Joan Crawford might as well play the part now, for the thing is as groggy with sentimentality as *The Bride Wore Red*, but the true emotion is gone.[3]

When this letter was published years later, people who had seen Joseph L. Mankiewicz' name on the screen many times but had never registered it, suddenly registered. Sure, Joe Mankiewicz, he was the one who wiped his feet on F. Scott Fitzgerald's script. The word even went around that Brady, the villain in *The Last Tycoon*, was modeled after Joe.

"I've often been asked to write my side of the story," Mankiewicz said, taking a break on the set of *There Was a Crooked Man* in June 1969. Leaning back in his canvas chair, he watched Henry Fonda shove a rifle butt into a prison guard's stomach. "When I rewrote Scott's dialogue," he went on, "people thought I was spitting on the flag."

But before Mankiewicz could continue the story of what happened between himself and Fitzgerald thirty years ago, a small black actor dressed as a servant came up. The producer did not like the black man's mustache.

"You're playing a Tom, you know," Mankiewicz said. "I don't think a Tom would have a mustache."

"Yes sir," said the Tom and hurried away to shave it off.

The mustache disposed of, Mankiewicz got back to Fitzgerald, explaining his side of what happened as follows:

"I hired Scott for *Three Comrades* because I admired his work. More than any other writer, I thought that he could capture the European flavor and the flavor of the twenties and early thirties that *Three Comrades* required. I also thought that he would know and understand the girl.

"I didn't count on Scott for dialogue. There could be no greater disservice done him than to have actors read his novels aloud as if they were plays. Mr. Hemingway, Mr. Steinbeck, Mr. Fitzgerald, Mr. Sinclair Lewis—all of them wanted to write plays and none of them could write one to save their soul. After all, there is a great difference between the dialogue in a novel and in a play. In a novel, the dialogue enters through the mind. The reader endows it with a certain quality. Dialogue spoken from the stage enters through the ear rather than the mind. It has an immediate emotional impact. Scott's dialogue lacked bite, color, rhythm."

Whom had Mankiewicz counted on for dialogue, if not Scott? At one point, he had assigned E. E. Paramore to collaborate with Fitzgerald, but the producer had not counted on him for good lines either. "Paramore was a Hollywood hack, a constructionist," according to Mankiewicz. He was there to help out with technical matters, that was all. In the final analysis Mankiewicz, as always, had depended upon himself. Or as he puts it: "I am a writer who was forced to become a producer. I'm still essentially a writer. I've done a great deal of writing on all the films I've produced, although I haven't taken any credit because the Screenwriters' Guild won't let me. Scott's dialogue was unspeakable. On the other hand, I *did* write *All About Eve* and I *had* been nominated for several Academy Awards as a writer. I was considered a damn good writer of dialogue."

Mankiewicz says of the Fitzgerald letter accusing him of not playing fair, "I never got it. Perhaps he was writing for posterity when he wrote that letter. He might have been boozing it." Mankiewicz says that the first time he saw the letter was when Edmund Wilson sent him a copy in 1944 and asked if he would object to its being reprinted in *The Crack-Up*. He wrote back:

> I regret to say I have many objections to the publication of the letter you sent me. . . .
> Aside from the extremely unpleasant characterization of me that emanates from the letter, I do not want it published for reasons that have to do also with Scott, his good taste and his sense of criticism.
> There were many other conferences with him . . . and he

was eventually happy with the final script. As a matter of fact, he offered me his support in a battle I had with the Hays Office about the anti-Nazi aspects of the picture—a quarrel which nearly resulted in my resigning from the studio. As for the points upon which Scott remained adamant, it is unfortunate—or fortunate, depending on the point of view—but he was proved wrong on everyone of them! . . .

In addition to my profound regard for Scott as a great American writer, I was extremely fond of him personally. To have our relationship characterized by a letter such as the one you have chosen, would not be fair either to Scott or to myself.[4]

The letter was not printed in *The Crack-Up,* but it was printed in Arthur Mizener's biography *The Far Side of Paradise,* which appeared in 1951. It caused the producer no little embarrassment. He might have changed some of Fitzgerald's words, but he was the producer. That was his job. He had to keep his people in line.

Fonda slammed the rifle into the guard's stomach once again and spat out his line, "Make you respect me?" Mankiewicz smiled at the words.

2

Three Comrades ended in a bitter feud in January 1938, but it had started out happily during the pleasant summer of 1937. Fitzgerald had come to town with a master plan for conquering Hollywood, and it looked for a while as if it were working out. "I must be very tactful but keep my hand on the wheel from the start," he had written his daughter, ". . . until, in fact or in effect, I'm alone on the picture[s]. That's the only way I can do my best work."[5] For a while he had *Three Comrades* his way— all to himself. And what a picture it was going to be! It was to be based on the novel *Three Comrades* by Erich Maria Remarque, and with Fitzgerald writing the screenplay there was no reason why it should not be another *All Quiet on the Western Front.*

Fitzgerald was enjoying his work and life in California. To his editor Maxwell Perkins back in New York he wrote: "Everyone is very nice to me, surprised and rather relieved that I don't drink. I am happier than I've been for several years."[6]

In late July, as Fitzgerald was just beginning work on the *Three Comrades,* the story of a tragic marriage, his fifteen-year-old daughter arrived from the East. Helen Hayes brought Scottie out to her father, the actress and the boarding-school girl making the long trip across the continent by train. In Hollywood there was no room for Scottie in Scott's Garden of Allah apartment, which he already shared with Eddie Mayer; she stayed with Miss Hayes and her husband Charles MacArthur, who had not only written *The Front Page* with Ben Hecht but also had scripted *Princess Alluria* with Scott during the summer of 1928 on the Riviera.

"We were holed up at the Beverly Hills Hotel in one of those bungalows," Helen Hayes remembers. "It was a lovely summer— Scott and Scottie and Charlie and I." A decade earlier, Miss Hayes and MacArthur, Scott and Zelda had roamed New York together. Now after the long bouts with insanity and alcoholism, the old symmetry of two couples had given way to a more baroque configuration: husband and wife, father and daughter. (In a screenplay called *Cosmopolitan,* Fitzgerald would later write scenes where a father pretends that a daughter can take the place of a lost wife.) The actress and her screenwriter-playwright husband seemed to represent all that Scott had failed to achieve in marriage and in his assaults on Hollywood, and yet MacArthur and Fitzgerald were absolutely alike in one painful respect: halfway through the 1930s, both authors had found that they could no longer write, and both were still struggling to make the writing go again. Years before, Scott had told Miss Hayes, "Don't worry about Charlie not realizing his talent. Other men have to *do,* Helen. Charlie only has to *be.*" Fitzgerald himself could not, however, take his own advice and so had cracked up trying to *do.*

"I remember so many evenings that we spent together," says Miss Hayes, "going to dinner at Stephen Vincent Benét's in Pasadena, or Zoë Akins', also in Pasadena, and the odd, strained evenings at Norma Shearer's in Santa Monica." Fitzgerald could never forget that crazy Sunday at the Thalbergs in 1931, according to Miss Hayes, and so he "never felt comfortable there—he was apt to kick over the party."

But Scott's daughter, now Scottie Smith, remembers enjoying those dinners at Miss Shearer's more than anything else in Hollywood. Too young to feel the tension, she responded to what she calls the "glamour" of sitting down at the same table with the actress who had played Juliet in the movies and who seemed to embody the great romance of the play itself. "So far Scottie is having the time of her young life," her father wrote Maxwell Perkins, "dining with Crawford, Shearer, etc., talking to Fred Astaire and her other heroes."

"Scott relaxed most and was most bedazzled at Marion Davies'," Miss Hayes says of the star who lived in the Hearst castle as William Randolph Hearst's protégée. "He might have invented the whole way of life in that Mount Vernon by the sea, like his marvelous 'The Diamond as Big as the Ritz.' I remember one evening that Scott reveled in at Marion's when Charlie Chaplin and Bea Lillie got into a hot competition singing cockney songs and doing comical dances together on that white marble bridge over the swimming pool.

"There were many things that delighted him," Miss Hayes remembers, "but all in all, I think Scott was unhappy there from the start. Hollywood was so much more bizarre than even he could be. He hated the awful discipline of the studios. Pictures took writers right back to the working climate of high school. And he was not in the best shape spiritually; he was afraid that his writing gift was going through a tunnel. His few high spots were our evenings together, especially when we went to the Benéts'. At the Benéts' he always felt like a first-class passenger again."

One afternoon, riding through the streets of Hollywood in a taxicab, Fitzgerald leaned close to Miss Hayes and explained in his low, dry way a view of life which sounded like the Biblical story of Joseph. "One changes one's whole life, not just incidents but one's spiritual life, every seven years," he said. "A snake changes its skin every year, our own skin changes every seven years, and so do our lives."

"He was looking for a new start," the actress says. "A new cycle. He was three years into famine, but his hope was that after four more bad years he would reach the seven years of plenty."

When Rosemary left Dick Diver in *Tender Is the Night,* he missed her and so sought her in the only place where he could still find her, on film at the movies. On the day Helen Hayes left California to return to the New York stage, the Fitzgeralds, father and daughter, reserved a projection room in the basement of the Thalberg Building where "as a sort of 'wake' for you" (Scott wrote) "Scottie and I ran off *Madeleine Claudet.*" Fitzgerald went on to say: "Charlie dropped in, and the Fitzgeralds contributed appropriate tears to the occasion—an upshot which, as you will remember, Garbo failed to evoke from this hardened cynic, so I think you have a future. Remember to speak slowly and clearly and don't be frightened—the audience is just as scared as you are." The motion picture *The Sin of Madeleine Claudet* had been produced by Thalberg and largely scripted by MacArthur. It told the story of a mother who is separated from her son. Shortly after Miss Hayes' departure, Fitzgerald was separated from his daughter. "I must say," he wrote to friends back east of Scottie's trip, "that it was an *Alice in Wonderland* experience for her," but added, "reports about the talent scouts following her around are somewhat exaggerated."[7] The daughter went back to school at Ethel Walkers and the father went back to Sheilah Graham.

The letters which Fitzgerald wrote Scottie that fall showed a new joy in his daughter ("I was very proud of you all summer") and in his work. He seemed to like juggling the shiny names of the stars who would act out his story when he wrote:

News about the picture: The cast is tentatively settled. Joan Crawford had her teeth in the lead for a while but was convinced that it was a man's picture; and Loretta Young not being available, the decision rests at present on Margaret Sullavan. Certainly she will be much better than Joan Crawford in the role. Tracy and Taylor will be reinforced by Franchot Tone at present writing, and the cameras will presumably roll sometime in December.[8]

Later Robert Young took Spencer Tracy's place as the third comrade, but that was the only change.

Of the three comrades, Robert Taylor was to have the most important role, that of Bobby Lohkamp. Taylor, of course, had also had the lead in *A Yank at Oxford.* But *Three Comrades,* the new Fitzgerald-Taylor vehicle, would differ from *Yank* in one significant way: it was an important story. The picture was to chronicle the rise of Nazism in Germany—and this on the eve of World War II.

Sheilah Graham remembers how Fitzgerald felt about Hitler:

On Sunday mornings we sit before the Cases' enormous console radio, listening to Hitler's speeches. They infuriate Scott. He jumps up and pads restlessly about the room. "They're going to do it again. They're going to have another war—and we'll be in it, too." He sits down, lights a cigarette, listens again to the ranting, hysterical voice, the thunderous "*Sieg Heil! Sieg Heil! Sieg Heil!*" It echoes through our little beach house. He turns to me. "I'd like to fly over there and assassinate Hitler before he starts another war. I'd do it, too, by God!" He tells me, with a sudden disarming smile, "You know, Sheilo, I wanted to fight in the last war. They pulled the rug from under me. The Armistice came and I never got across."[9]

When Mankiewicz's fight with L. B. Mayer over the anti-Nazi material in the movie erupted, there was no doubt on whose side Fitzgerald would enlist.

After spending August, September, and most of October alone on the picture, Fitzgerald made one of his regularly scheduled trips back east to see Zelda in her sanitarium. These visits were always difficult, even more so this time because Scott was pre-occupied with California worries. He was afraid that when he returned to Hollywood he would find a collaborator waiting for him there. Scott wired Mankiewicz about his fears, and the producer wired back:

DEAR SCOTT YOU MUST STOP READING ALL THOSE NASTY STORIES ABOUT MOTION PICTURE PRODUCERS. THEY'RE NOT TRUE . . . I WOULDN'T TRY TO HIRE SHAKESPEARE BECAUSE BRITISHGAUMONT HAS HIM TIED UP STOP . . . WHERE DID YOU GET THAT BUSHWAH ABOUT ANOTHER WRITER BEST WISHES JOE.[10]

The news was especially welcome under the circumstances. Now that Fitzgerald was sure that he wouldn't have a new partner in Hollywood, he could concentrate on helping his old partner—what was left of her. When Scott returned to Holly-wood, he forgot about the rumors he had heard and got down to work finishing his screenplay. Everything went very well for two weeks, and then Mankiewicz introduced Fitzgerald to the collaborator he had been promised he would not have.

The producer had decided that Scott needed some help and had assigned E. E. (Ted) Paramore to write with him. Fitzgerald must have welcomed his new co-worker with the embarrassment of a man who suddenly encounters someone he thought he had killed long ago. For Paramore, whom Fitzgerald had known years before in New York, had appeared in *The Beautiful and Damned* as a simpering but "well-intentioned" male Florence Nightingale who labored among the poor trying to teach them to be more like rich folks. Of course the author had changed Ted E. Paramore to Fred E. Paramore, but that fooled no one. At one point in the story, Paramore gets drunk, crawls about the Patches' living-room on hands and knees whimpering, "I'm not a guest here—I work here."[11] Now at MGM twenty years later Fitz-gerald had to face the real Paramore and try to *work here* with him.

As might be expected, the two were not an ideal team. They

spent much of their time not writing but quarreling about who was in command. At one point, after they had all but stopped speaking, Scott wrote Paramore:

> I totally disagree with you as to the terms of our collaboration. We got off to a bad start and I think you are under certain misapprehensions founded more on my state of mind and body last Friday than upon the real situation. . . . When you blandly informed me yesterday that you were going to write the whole thing over yourself, kindly including my best scenes, I knew we'd have to have this out.[12]

Paramore was not allowed to completely rewrite Fitzgerald's script, but on the other hand Fitzgerald never had the picture to himself again.

Relations between the two collaborators never improved. Fitzgerald accused Paramore of writing "Owen Wister dialogue" for a story about Germans. It infuriated Scott, for example, when he would pick up Paramore's stuff and find a German sergeant popping off with expressions like "Consarn it!"[13]

After the picture was finished, Fitzgerald put his exasperation with his collaborator into a short, if somewhat self-righteous, fable:

A FABLE FOR TED PARAMORE

A great city set in a valley desired a cathedral. They sent for an eminent architect who designed one distinguished by a great central tower. No sooner was it begun, however, than critics arose who objected to the tower, calling it useless, ornamental, illogical, and what not—destroyed his plan and commissioned another architect to build a cathedral of great blocks and masses. It was very beautiful and Grecian in its purity, but no one ever loved the cathedral of that city as they did those of Rome and Vienna and the great Duomo of Florence.

After thirty years wondering why, the citizens dug up the plans of the first architect (since grown famous) and built from it. From the first Mass the cathedral seized the imagination of the multitude and fools said it was because the tower pointed heavenward, etc., but one young realist decided to dig up the artist, now an old man, and ask him why.

The artist was too old to remember, he said—and he added, "I doubt if I ever knew. But I knew I was right."

"How did you know if you don't know your reasons?"

"Because I felt good that day," answered the architect, "and if I feel good I have reason for what I do even if I don't know the reason." So the realist went away unanswered.

On that same day a young boy going to Mass with his mother quickened his step as he crossed the cathedral square.

"Oh I like our new cathedral so much better than the old," he said.

"But the academy thinks it's not nearly so beautiful."

"But it's because of the mountains," said the little boy. "Before we had the tower I could see the mountains and they made everything seem little when you went inside the Church. Now you can't see the mountains so God inside is more important."

That was what the architect had envisioned without thinking when he accidentally raised his forefinger against the sky fifty years before.[14]

While the job had gone well, Fitzgerald had not needed gin, but with the coming of Paramore his needs changed. When the letter to his collaborator referred to his "state of mind and body last Friday," he meant that he had been drunk. Since his letter to Perkins about everyone being "relieved that I don't drink," he had done some backsliding.

Once Fitzgerald had gone A.W.O.L. from the studio to accompany Miss Graham to Chicago, where she was to broadcast her gossip column over the CBS radio network. He brought along a bottle of gin on the plane. The trip was planned as a kind of honeymoon for the couple, who had met in Hollywood almost exactly six months before. When in Chicago Sheilah was introduced to Arnold Gingrich, the young editor of *Esquire* magazine, she shocked him by explaining that she and Scott had come to his city "to consummate our affair." Girls didn't talk that way—not in 1937—but Gingrich thought, "Maybe English girls are different."

The editor remembers Scott's and Sheilah's Chicago "honey-moon," a honeymoon he was trapped into sharing, as follows:

"Sheilah had to go to her broadcast and she left Scott sitting in the Drake Hotel. Naturally he picked up the phone and called me, since I was just across the street, and said, 'Come over here.' The son of a bitch had to pick the one day when I couldn't. We were firing a guy, Jay Allen. Dave Smart would do the impulsive hiring, but he would turn to me to do the firing.

"I told Scott, 'I'll call you back just as soon as I can.'

"This was a very bad reversal of our relationship—one of high priest to altar boy. I was a Fitzgerald fan who just happened to have a magazine, but I was a prisoner in my own shop. Scott began calling more and more frequently. He had nothing to do so he was drinking, ordering gin. By the time I pried myself loose from the Jay Allen discussion in the afternoon and ran across to see Scott, he was up in his room absolutely polluted.

"Scott had tumblers lined up as if he were going to play musical glasses. They looked like glasses of water, but they were glasses of gin. He was a real Dr. Jekyll and Mr. Hyde character when he had taken on board large amounts of liquor—a vicious drunk, one of the worst I have ever known. He could hardly talk, slur-ring all his words, trying to tell me about Sheilah, this great new English girl.

"Scott was rather puritanical. He was the obverse of Ernest in this way. Very, very rarely would he embellish his speech with a lot of he-man obscenities. But when he was drunk, he was differ-ent, and he kept saying, 'I just got to have this cunt.' At this point he hadn't yet.

"I thought, My God! let's see if we can't get this son of a bitch sobered up a little. I ordered a steak sandwich and a big pot of coffee.

"I told Scott, 'Jesus, you're a mess. You're not fit company for a dog.'

"Unless he sobered up, it was going to be no honeymoon. He wasn't up to consommé, much less consummate. I held his nose and poured the coffee down, but he wouldn't eat.

"I said, 'Just pretend it's medicine.'

"He said, 'No.'

"I said, 'I'll feed you.'

"I literally tried forcing the sandwich into his mouth. Scott thought that it would be a cute idea to eat my finger. The son of a bitch bit my hand as hard as he could. I screamed, *yeoooowww!* At this point Sheilah, whom I had never seen before, walked in.

"I yelled, 'The son of a bitch bit my finger!' That was my opening line to her. I was on the floor for some reason, hands and knees.

"Sheilah looked at Scott and practically said, 'Who's that?' She just didn't recognize this mess. He was pissy-ass, falling-down drunk. Scott was in no shape to travel, and she was very upset because they had a plane to catch.

"Sheilah said, 'Scott has to be in Hollywood tomorrow. His option comes up for renewal tomorrow.'

"I got him to drink some more coffee, and then he wanted me to run across the street and get those sketches he'd written, and read them to Sheilah. Sheilah was perfectly willing to read them herself, but no, *I* had to read them. He lay down on the couch and pretended to be napping, but he was listening to every word, watching Sheilah's reaction. She was watching him and I was doing a bad job reading because I had one eye on him, too. It was an odd way to meet *The Crack-Up.*

"When we left the hotel room, I had to pick Scott up and carry him like a sack of potatoes. I had carried him halfway across the lobby of the Drake Hotel when he said, 'I'm all right now.' I felt like a fool. He walked across the lobby, down the stairs, and got into the airport limousine. He seemed fine.

"Later, Sheilah told me what happened on the ride to the airport.

"Scott asked Sheilah, 'Did I do a good job?'

" 'What?' she wanted to know.

" 'Pretending to be drunk,' he said. 'That little snot was putting me off all day long. He was too busy to see me and I wanted to make him sweat a little.'

"Sheilah relaxed.

"There was a girl sitting just ahead of them and Scott said, 'Hasn't she got the nicest face?' He was going on and on, as if he were writing a character in a book, practically making verbal love to the girl. She turned and smiled, and he said, 'Silly bitch!'

"There was another bad moment when they opened the door of the limousine. Scott got out and fell flat on his face."

When Miss Graham got Fitzgerald inside the airport, he was so drunk they refused to allow him on board, so she loaded him into a taxi and drove him around until the next plane was scheduled to take off for the West. That was not until five in the morning. They were in that cab for five hours.

Fitzgerald was afraid that when he returned to the studio after his desertion, he would get fired. But somehow he managed to soothe the angry and to live with the "I-told-you-so" stares. Before long he was back to serious work on *Three Comrades*.

But relations with his collaborator and producer were growing more and more exasperating, and they never improved. "All the brains come in," Scott told Sheilah. "They sit around a table. They talk about everything except the subject at hand—and when they do talk about that, they don't know what they want, they don't know where we're going, they repeatedly change their minds—it's disgraceful."[15]

3

Toward the end, Fitzgerald and Mankiewicz could no more appreciate one another's point of view than Tom Buchanan could sympathize with Jay Gatsby or Gatsby forgive Buchanan. Fitzgerald was a romantic when it came to motion pictures: the script on which he labored became his compelling dream. The producer's only contribution seemed to be getting between Scott and the green light across the bay. Mankiewicz, on the other hand, had not gotten to be a practical Hollywood success by being a dreamer. *Three Comrades* was one of many pictures that he would do and he had no romantic illusions about it. It was *his* picture and he planned to exercise the same authority over it which Tom Buchanan exercised over *his* wife. On Fitzgerald's side, it can be said that Mankiewicz was often too heavy-handed; he ruined lines which he probably did not even understand. On Mankiewicz' side, however, it should be pointed out that he was sometimes right in the changes he made, especially when it came to cutting some of his writer's longer, wordier speeches. Mankiewicz at least was accustomed to telling stories with pictures rather than words.

It was appropriate that Fitzgerald be given a novel to adapt for the screen, but occasionally the assignment encouraged bad habits such as thinking like a novelist rather than a screenwriter. He sometimes could not resist backsliding into a world where stories are told in words and the only pictures are on the dust jackets. Fitzgerald wanted to begin his screenplay, for example, by literally spelling out what had happened to Germany in the years since the war. He wanted to put titles on the screen which would tell the movie audience that in the 1920s, while the rest of the world grew rich, Germany had grown more and more wretched. He even suggested a graph to show that the national wealth of Germany had fallen dramatically while the cost of living had risen sharply.

Mankiewicz was not happy with all those words and charts on the screen. He called one of his weekly story conferences ("That's the only way you can work with writers"), and they went over the beginning again and again. All these meetings were much the same. "A four-hour wrangle in a conference room crowded with planets and nebulae of cigarette smoke," Fitzgerald had once written. "Three men . . . suggesting or condemning, speaking sharply or persuasively, confidently or despairingly."[16] In such a room, Mankiewicz scrapped Fitzgerald's graphs and titles. What the producer wanted was action, motion, and conflict right from the start.

"There should always be a fight between Lenz and Koster," Mankiewicz told Fitzgerald. "Have them get excited about this. Lenz says: 'I can't just dismiss everything I've dreamed about the last four years.' Koster defends his own point of view: 'To hell with all that. Theories! That's what we've been fighting for. *Now,* we've got to fight for *bread.*' Bobby adores both of them. He agrees with Koster and with Lenz."[17]

Mankiewicz soon got conflict, all right, but between his writers rather than the comrades in the screenplay. Fitzgerald had come up with what he thought was a good idea for a dramatic opening: a grenade tossed into a plane as it sat on the runway. Paramore took the idea and embroidered it with speeches about the hardships of both war and peace; by the time he was finished, he was as guilty as Fitzgerald had been of wordiness.

"I think the opening is terribly unwise," Fitzgerald wrote Mankiewicz of the Paramore rewrite job. "My idea of blowing up the airplane is now completely talk. I wanted to have a glimpse of the Comrades, with possibly a dozen short speeches to show the difference between Lenz and Koster, and then go with a bang into Germany as it is today. The material as it is has been said in *They Gave Him a Gun, The Road Back,* and in a thousand editorials until the mere mention of it strikes the brain cells dead."[18]

Fitzgerald was learning that too many words were as bad as fog when it came to pictures. In his best scenes, the author overcame his instincts as a novelist and managed to tell his story visually. In one such scene, for example, the comrades, driving a strange-looking car which they built themselves out of automobile scraps, get into a race with an expensive, fashionable Buick. Nor is the race all motion and no meaning, for in a way it symbolizes what the story is about: the comrades, who are garage mechanics, will be racing all their lives against the kind of people who can afford Buicks. After the comrades win the race, they meet the Buick's owner. His name is Breuer and he insolently asks Gottfried the make of the comrades' mongrel speedster.

GOTTFRIED: Well, the grandpa was a sewing machine, the grandma was an old radio, and the papa was a machine gun—[19]

Here we have a good example of what Mankiewicz (or someone) accomplished in rewriting Fitzgerald, for in the movie theatres the comrade was made to say:

> GOTTFRIED: Well, the grandpa was a sewing machine, the grandma was an old radio, and the papa was an alarm clock—[20]

The difference between the two lines is the difference between an alarm clock and a machine gun. Mankiewicz' line is a joke, Fitzgerald's a subdued threat.

The Fitzgerald scene which caused the most consternation portrayed a telephone call from Bobby to a girl named Pat. The contents of any script in progress is usually a well-guarded secret even within the walls of a studio itself: there is that persistent fear that people will steal anything that isn't copyrighted. But somehow, despite the attempted secrecy, the story of what Fitzgerald had done got out and it spread like scandal. "It upset everyone at the studio," Edwin Knopf remembers. The scene began with Bobby at a telephone. CUT TO: Saint Peter in heaven sitting at a switchboard. This saintly operator rings Pat's number for Bobby. CUT TO: Pat answering her phone. This humor went over like a fly in L. B. Mayer's chicken soup. It was not long before all the MGM lions up there on the top floor were roaring. The one who roared the loudest was Eddie Mannix. From beneath his MGM's SUCCESS sign he bellowed, "What the hell does he think he's writing about?" And anyway, "How do you photograph *that?*" Saint Peter was hastily cut from the script.

Once Bobby meets Pat, we begin to see that Remarque's novel *Three Comrades* was, strangely, the kind of book which Fitzgerald himself might have written. It was about his kind of people. Pat had once been one of the very rich and, although the war had stripped her of her fortune, she still possessed the tastes of the rich: music, the dance, the opera. Bobby, on the other hand, was nothing but a garage mechanic. In better days he might have risen higher, but in postwar Germany he was trapped in his caste, and his feelings of despair as he courts Pat remind one of Fitzgerald's own as he kept trying somehow to put together enough money to persuade Zelda to marry him. "She's a rich man's girl," Fitzgerald had Gottfried say of Pat. "What can Bobby do?"[21]

Much of what Bobby does do in his attempts to win the rich man's girl is embarrassing, and it is out of this embarrassment that Fitzgerald creates some of his most affecting scenes. One of these depicts Bobby's first call on Pat at her apartment. When the front door is opened to him, he finds his way barred by a baby grand piano which stands athwart the entrance. Pat asks him to go around to the bedroom door, explaining that with so little space she was forced to choose between having a door and a piano. Bobby shyly refuses the bedroom door, making his entrance by crawling under the piano. In Remarque's novel there is no piano in the way. We are told only that Bobby "began to feel rather awkward."[22] But here Fitzgerald managed to think in terms of moving pictures rather than words. The piano becomes a visible metaphor for all that stands between Bobby and Pat. And yet Bobby, for all his awkwardness, penetrates this cultural barrier. Mankiewicz seems to have liked the scene, for it was filmed and used in the movie.

In another scene, however, Bobby crosses cultural boundary lines and literally falls apart. Dressed in makeshift evening clothes—borrowed tails which are threadbare, tie held down in back with string, top hat which won't open—Bobby takes Pat to the opera and then dancing. All goes well so long as Bobby remains perfectly still, but when he rises to dance trouble dogs his steps. As he begins to try to waltz, pins fly, strings come undone, and the suit splits under the arms, the rips forming great gaping smiles which seem to participate in the general laughter. In the novel Bobby feels out of place at the night club, but all his discomfort is trapped inside his head—there is nothing to see. Fitzgerald rethought this discomfort in terms of what a camera could record, and came up with a way to actually picture Bobby's composure coming apart. Mankiewicz filmed the scene just as Fitzgerald had written it.

When Bobby rejoins his friends after his dance-floor disaster, Koster comforts him with advice which echoes *The Crack-Up,* where Fitzgerald wrote, "At three o'clock in the morning, a forgotten package has the same tragic importance as a death sentence . . . and in the real dark night of the soul it is always three o'clock in the morning, day after day." What Koster tells Bobby is:

> KOSTER: Forget it. Very few things will stand inspection at three o'clock in the morning.[23]

Mankiewicz rewrote Fitzgerald's scene so that most of the three-A.M. bitterness was emptied out of it. The grimness of the original lines became the Brothers Grimm in the producer's version:

> KOSTER: Hello, Cinderella—got both your slippers on?[24]

In the margin of his copy of the final shooting script, Fitzgerald wrote, "This is 'authors talking' about a script. This isn't writing. This is Joe Mankiewicz. So slick—so cheap."

Fitzgerald and Mankiewicz often disagreed over characterization. Mankiewicz did not like the way Bobby was turning out and he was worried about Pat. One day he called Fitzgerald in and told him, "Be very careful with Bobby. Give him some smart answers now and then. Don't make him too much of a dolt. When Lenz kids Bobby, let Bobby kid Lenz. Don't let Pat fall in love with a ninny."[25]

Mankiewicz's objection to Fitzgerald's treatment of Pat was more specific. Scott thought that Pat should use whatever she had left in the way of money and influence to help the comrades, but Mankiewicz blocked that idea. He called his writers into the conference room and told them how he saw Pat.

> I don't agree . . . that Pat has to make some physical contribution to the well-being of those three guys, particularly since the entire motive of Pat's taking her own life at the end of the picture is the realization that she can be of no help to these three men. . . . Pat is a spirit—the spirit of the silver dress. These men fight to keep this for Bobby. But the dress

must tarnish and fade. All she can ever do for Bobby, she has already done. She can now only grow weaker—older and uglier. All she can ever be is a memory, and maybe being a living memory is what brings such hardships to the three. . . . At the beginning of the story, she gave up fighting for her own life—how can she go on and fight for them?[26]

Fitzgerald accepted this eloquently phrased view of Pat but was furious about other Mankiewicz changes. In one scene Scott had placed Pat at her prized piano where all through the dialogue she plays snatches from the classics. Mankiewicz moved the scene into the comrades' garage and replaced the music with the regular thud of Koster's hammer as he repairs a car. Fitzgerald felt that he had written a highly civilized scene only to have someone with mechanic's grease on his hands come along and smudge it up. In that letter which Mankiewicz says he never received, Fitzgerald wrote that "Example number 3000" of what the producer had done wrong was "taking out the piano scene between Pat and Koster and substituting garage hammering. Pat the girl who hangs around the garage! . . . I feel *somewhat outraged.*"[27]

In another scene Fitzgerald had Pat tickle Bobby's nose with an anemone. Bobby guesses that the flower is a rose, then a violet, then a lily. "I've always got by on those three,"[28] he tells his new bride. Mankiewicz rewrote the scene so that Bobby's limited horizon—something else to blame on the war—is pointed up more bluntly. Bobby asks the cliché question: what will they talk about for the rest of their lives? Pat says that she will teach him books and music, and they will talk about those since they're always safe. Fitzgerald saw his heroine being made over into a kind of schoolmarm and exploded:

> ". . . books and music—she's going to teach him." My God, Joe, you must see what you've done. This isn't Pat—it's a graduate of Pomona College. . . . Books and music! Think, man! Pat is a lady—a cultured European—a charming woman. . . . I thought we'd decided long ago what we wanted Pat to be![29]

The author's protest was ignored.

Producer Mankiewicz had hired Fitzgerald because he would know and understand a girl like Pat. Once she falls ill, her lungs hemorrhaging, and is forced to retreat to a Swiss sanitarium, Fitzgerald found himself writing out of his own despair. Know the girl indeed!

In Paris one day back in 1930, Zelda had been so afraid that she would be late for her ballet lessons that she had started changing into her tights in the taxicab. When the cab got held up in traffic, she bolted and ran the rest of the way. Fitzgerald took her from the dance studio to a hospital at Malmaison where she stayed ten days repeating over and over:

> "It's frightful, it's horrible, what's going to become of me, I must work and I no longer can, I must die and yet I have to work. I'll never be cured, let me go, I have to see 'Madame' [her dancing teacher], she has given me the greatest joy in the world, it's comparable to sunlight falling on a block of crystal, to a symphony of perfumes, to the most perfect strains of the greatest masters of music."[30]

From Malmaison, Fitzgerald took his wife to sanitariums in Switzerland and then to others in this country, including the Phipps Clinic of the Johns Hopkins University hospital.

Yes, Fitzgerald knew about the late twenties and early thirties and what they could do to a man's girl. Pat was not only no stranger, she was practically a member of the family. No wonder there was misery to pay when Mankiewicz "took a box of chalk" and touched up her portrait.

Fitzgerald had written *Tender Is the Night* out of his and Zelda's tragedy, and now in *Three Comrades* he was telling the story all over again. From the point of her hemorrhage on, Pat— like Dick Diver's Nicole—will be not only Bobby's wife but his charge. She will be his to love but also to nurse and care for. Nor is the illness of either wife, Nicole or Pat, merely a personal catastrophe: it is also a social catastrophe. Their infirmities mirror the world's own.

The war has cost Pat more than her fortune.

PAT: Everyone said that I was a fool—that I ought to save my money and go to work. I wanted to be very gay and irresponsible. (*Pause.*) I was frightened enough sometimes—as if I was in the wrong seat at the theatre.[31]

Of course what Pat says is true: her family was once rich and it did lose its money. But what we later come to see is that Pat is really talking about the loss of her health, not her riches. Weakened by the war, she is heading for a crash, but she has decided to go on living to the full, living on margin "even if only for a little while." This scene went into the movie untouched.

This idea—that one could go bankrupt physically, even emotionally and morally, as well as financially—had been embedded in Fitzgerald's imagination for years. In 1931 he had published a story entitled "Emotional Bankruptcy." Later on he had carried the theme over into *Tender Is the Night,* where Dick Diver gives so much to so many undeserving people that he wears himself away from inside. And Fitzgerald thought the same thing had happened to him. At about the same time that he was working on *Three Comrades,* he was writing letters to his daughter which warned:

> Our danger is imagining that we have resources—material and moral—which we haven't got. One of the reasons I find myself so consistently in valleys of depression is that every few years I seem to be climbing uphill to recover from some bankruptcy. Do you know what bankruptcy exactly means? It means drawing on resources which one does not possess. I thought I was so strong that I never would be ill and suddenly I was ill for three years, and faced a long, slow uphill climb. Wiser people seem to manage to pile up a reserve.[32]

And now, in his movie script, the author tried to infuse his own heritage of bankruptcy into Pat's lines. "Everyone said that I was a fool—that I ought to save my money and go to work"—how many people had said the same of Scott. And now he and Zelda, like Pat, were bankrupts in their own way, but they had lived as they liked "even if only for a little while."

The script's closing moments take place in a cemetery where the surviving comrades have come to visit Pat. Koster says the only words, "There's fighting in the city."[33] Along with these last pages, Fitzgerald handed in a request:

> About the ending. I beg you not to fool with it too much. The effect was obtained in a happy moment and shifting about may completely ruin it. . . . The tp-tp-tp of the gun, the walk down the hill like the descent from Calvary, and Koster's single understated remark—have greater emotional rhythm than any static picture of a grave that can be devised. It's like the wreaths floating in the water in *Captains Courageous*. If you stand still in the presence of death your emotions grow dead, too.[34]

Fitzgerald's plea failed to convince Mankiewicz that the ending could not be improved. He did not have the comrades stand still, as Scott had feared, but rather run away—at least, flight is implied. There in the cemetery, just before the fade-out, Mankiewicz had Bobby say that he wished Pat were going to South America with them.

When Fitzgerald saw that Mankiewicz had the comrades fleeing the fatherland, he not only complained to Joe, but also wrote a letter to Joe's bosses, Eddie Mannix and Sam Katz. The letter, which Scott decided not to mail, read as follows:

Dear Sirs:

I have long finished my part in the making of *Three Comrades* but Mank——— has told me what the exhibitors are saying about the ending and I can't resist a last word. If they had pronounced on *Captains Courageous* at this stage, I feel they would have had Manuel the Portuguese live and go out west with the little boy, and *Captains Courageous* could have stood that much better than *Three Comrades* can stand an essential change in its story. In writing over a hundred and fifty stories for George Lorimer, the great editor of *The Saturday Evening Post*, I found he made a sharp distinction between a sordid tragedy and a heroic tragedy—hating the former but accepting the latter as an essential and interesting part of life.

Certainly this step of putting in the "new life" thought will not please or fool anyone—it simply loses us the press and takes out of the picture the real rhythm of the ending, which is:

The march of four people, living and dead, heroic and inconquerable, side by side back into the fight.[35]

Fitzgerald thought that by going to South America the surviving comrades turned the story from tragedy into escapism. All right, so their dreams were—in the words of *The Great Gatsby*—"already behind them, somewhere back in the vast obscurity beyond the city, where the dark fields . . . rolled on under the night." But that was no reason to stop fighting. The only brave step was to "beat on, boats against the current," even though they could not win, even though they would always be "borne back ceaselessly into the past."[36] Of course, when Gatsby was killed, Nick Carroway retreated to the Midwest just as Bobby and Koster were retreating, but Fitzgerald had gone beyond that now. He had cracked up and then come back to fight again, and he expected no less of others.

Could Mankiewicz have foreseen the ironic tricks which history would later play, perhaps he would have been more anxious to listen to Fitzgerald's objections to sending Bobby and Koster to South America. But how could he know that after World War II thousands of Nazis would themselves flee Germany for South America, almost as if following the comrades?

The picture went before the cameras in January. All through the winter and into spring the shooting continued, and Mankiewicz went on making improvements.

4

L. B. Mayer, Mankiewicz, and a Nazi sat together in a projection room in the basement of the Thalberg Building. As the unruly German crowds poured onto the screen, the little room itself seemed crowded, too. The Nazi was obviously uncomfortable and Mayer, who watched the German the way a honeymooning wife watches her husband, was uncomfortable, too. When Gottfried was killed they both seemed pained, but perhaps for the wrong reasons. Mayer had invited the Nazi, a representative of the German consulate in Los Angeles, to this secret screening, to see if he had any objections to the film. He had, but Mankiewicz said that he would not make any cuts.

Joe Breen, the censor, was brought into the fight, and he applied pressure, too. After his office reviewed the film, he had a suggestion to make which he thought would resolve all the problems and save the picture. Why not schedule some retakes, he said. With a little rewriting these scenes could be made to indicate that this was not the rise of Nazism in Germany, but the rise of communism. Mankiewicz said that if they turned his Nazis into communists, he would resign from the studio.

"The next day I went into the commissary," the producer remembers, "and Scott was there. He ran up, threw his arms around me, and kissed me."

By the time the picture opened in June 1938, Fitzgerald's affection for Mankiewicz had vanished. Scott took Sheilah Graham to the première and as they drove toward Hollywood he told her, "At least they've kept my beginning." In the theatre, however, as the lights went out, the gloom descended. Miss Graham remembers:

> As the picture unfolded, Scott slumped deeper and deeper in his seat. At the end he said, "They changed even that." He took it badly. "That s.o.b.," he growled when he came home, and furiously, helplessly, as though he had to lash out at something, he punched the wall, hard. "My God, doesn't he know what he's done?"[37]

Fitzgerald and Miss Graham, Ted Paramore and Mankiewicz —they all waited for the notices. Some of the reviewers agreed with the disappointed Scott, holding that the story was too sentimental. "If you have tears prepare to shed them, for *Three Comrades* is a tear jerker," Philip T. Hartung said in *Commonweal*. But he added that even though "the whole affair is too sentimental . . . conditions in Germany after the war warrant emotion and tears."[38] *Time* magazine called the picture "a story, beautifully

told and consummately acted, but so drenched in hopelessness
and heavy with the aroma of death . . . that its beauty and
strength are often clouded and betrayed."[39] Otis Ferguson wrote
in *The New Republic* that the film seemed a little wordy. He
went on to say that the story

> wrings the heart rather than warms it. . . . It is a queer picture
> to talk about: there is no doubt it is a good one, and strange;
> but the goodness is mostly in its eloquent statement of the
> fringes of a national tragedy, things so sobering and deep that
> I scarcely know whether it is your duty to go to see it and be
> torn, or to keep clear and just see *Vivacious Lady* over again.[40]

When the *New York Times* reported its verdict, however,
Mankiewicz felt that his picture had been vindicated. Frank S.
Nugent wrote: "Let us come to the point at once: The Metro-
Goldwyn-Mayer version of Erich Maria Remarque's *Three Comrades* . . . is a superlatively fine picture, obviously one of 1938's
best ten, and one not to be missed." He praised the director Frank
Borzage for achieving "once more the affecting simplicity that
marked his *Seventh Heaven* . . . and *A Farewell to Arms.*"
Nugent also lauded the actors: Franchot Tone, who "turned in a
beautifully shaded portrait of Otto Koster," and Robert Young,
"almost equally effective as . . . Gottfried." Margaret Sullavan
overwhelmed him. He spoke of "a shimmering, almost unendur-
ably lovely performance. . . . Invite us now and you'll have us
nominating her for Scarlett. . . ." Nugent chided only the widow-
peaked actor Robert Taylor, whom he had not much liked in
A Yank at Oxford either. The critic said, "As the third of the comrades, Mr. Taylor has his moments of sincerity, but shares them
with those suggesting again the charming, well-fed, carefully
hair-groomed leading man of the glamour school of cinema."[41]
    Mankiewicz could not resist gloating a little. He pointed
out that the tears in Fitzgerald's eyes for Margaret Sullavan "were
quite the most unnecessary he ever shed."[42] Besides the plaudits
of the *Times,* she won the New York Critics Award and the
British National Award for her performance.

The picture did well, but Fitzgerald never forgave Mankiewicz for retouching his script. In one of his Pat Hobby stories he had a writer much like himself threaten a producer much like Joe: "When I *do* write a book . . . I'll make you the laughingstock of the nation."[43] And the author did have cause to complain. "37 pages mine," he scrawled on the producer's shooting script, "about ⅓, but all shadows and rhythm removed." And it is certainly true that Mankiewicz cut many good Fitzgerald scenes while building up the sentimental ones which remained. On the other hand, for all the tears which should have been wrung out of the last reel, the picture was nothing to be ashamed of—it was a good movie. Moreover, irony of ironies, the producer whom Fitzgerald hated the most was also the one who used more of what the author wrote than any other Hollywood producer before or since. Scott even got a raise—up to twelve hundred fifty a week from one thousand—as a result of his work for Mankiewicz. And his contract was extended for another twelve months.

Most important of all, it was at the bitter première of *Comrades* that Fitzgerald saw his name on the screen for the first and last time. Thanks to this screen credit, which he shared with Paramore, the author received a letter from Quigley Publications which said that *Three Comrades* had earned the rating "Box Office Champion," and that his name would therefore "find a prominent place in the 1939 edition of *FAME*"—*FAME* was written in red letters. Fitzgerald was no longer Scott Who?—he was making a name for himself as a script writer. But if Hollywood was beginning to discover who he was, the author himself was not so sure: he began to wonder about his own identity. One day he sent himself a postcard: "Dear Scott,—How are you? Have been meaning to come in and see you. I have been living at the Garden of Allah. Yours, Scott Fitzgerald."[44]

In his next script Fitzgerald turned his imagination from the foreign soil of Germany to more familiar ground. The new story, an original, was to star Joan Crawford, and it read like *The Great Gatsby* revisited. He cared about this film, to be called

Infidelity, even more than he had about *Three Comrades,* but the obstacles inevitably arose and Fitzgerald found that there was nothing to do but break his heart against the stone wall of the Hays Office.

Infidelity:
A Picture Worth a Book of Words

1

Hunt Stromberg was jittery. He tried to sink back in the projection room's big red overstuffed chair and just enjoy the movie, but of course he couldn't. Albert Hackett could not relax either. His wife Frances was even worse; she sat nervously thumbing the papers which she held in her hand. They were watching Joe Breen, the industry censor who had come over from the Hays Office. He in turn was watching the screen suspiciously, his eyes like moral spectroscopes straining to pick up anything off-color. Putting something over on Breen was not going to be easy. After all, any man who would order Walt Disney to erase an udder from one of his animated cows was definitely a moral force to contend with.

Only a few days before, Stromberg, the Hacketts, and Breen had been in the same chairs in the same projection room. Now they were having to go through the whole thing again. Reason: Breen had objected to some scenes in Stromberg's new film *Wife Versus Secretary.* Today he had returned to see what whitewash the producer proposed so as to cover his moral lapses. Every time they came to one of the "objectionable" scenes, Stromberg would have the projector stopped and signal Mrs. Hackett to read the changes they had concocted. But the trio still hoped to pull the celluloid over Breen's eyes where one scene was concerned. Stromberg had briefed the Hacketts carefully. When they came to this particular scene, the projector would not stop—perhaps he wouldn't remember, perhaps they could slip it right past the watchdog's nose. Of course, if he did remember, if he said something, then they would stop and have Frances read the new version.

On the screen Jean Harlow could be seen leaving a fashionable apartment complex on New York's East River. She walked quickly —it was a business-like stride—down to the water, where she boarded a huge motor launch. She stood proudly on the prow of the launch as it bore her down-river to a wharf where she was met by a long, black, chauffeur-driven limousine. The limousine in turn ferried her to a tall office building which seemed to be designed to show just how big Big Business could be. Jean stepped from the limousine and entered the building. Deferentially, the elevator boy said, "Good morning, Miss Whitey." At the top of the building she got out and moved down the hall; everyone whom she met smiled when she smiled; everyone kowtowed with, "Good morning, Miss Whitey." She went on into her office, closing the door behind her, and then it happened: she sat down at her desk and started typing. She was a secretary!

Breen coughed. He said that no good secretary could earn that kind of money. She had to be selling something besides her shorthand. But the projector did not stop. Stromberg and Breen had wrangled about this opening sequence the last time they met, and Joe had agreed to let it stand if the rest of the picture was cleaned up.

Shortly, however, the film was stopping every few minutes to give Frances Hackett a chance to read the changes which were to bind up the film's moral abrasions.

Then Stromberg's jitters grew worse, Albert Hackett leaned forward a little in his seat, and Frances unconsciously pawed her pages. Clark Gable was on his way up to Jean's apartment. Would

Breen remember? Gable walked down the hall into a fantastic penthouse which could have been borrowed from the set of *Marie Antoinette.*

"Hold it!" said Breen. He remembered. Stromberg turned to signal Frances and she began to read. Yes, the apartment would be cut down to size so that it looked like it belonged to a secretary and not some other kind of woman. After all, they wouldn't want to suggest that adultery paid. And yes, they remembered the Breen rule that if a man and a woman were on a bed together, at least two feet had to be on the floor at all times. (It was a standing joke that this rule only encouraged perversion.)

Before they went on, Breen told a story just so that they would know where he stood. The story was about a certain Mae West picture: Miss West, Breen explained, had invited a prize fighter up to her room. "Make yourself comfortable," she told him. "Take off your coat." As the evening wore on, Miss West grew more and more ebullient until the camera, for modesty's sake, had to look away. While the audience's imagination overflowed, so did the river. A flood washed across the screen, with people being helped out of windows, and horses and cows and houses floating away. "It was one of the funniest scenes I ever saw," Breen said, "but of course I had to cut it."[1]

That was the cast of mind which Fitzgerald was up against when he began work in January 1938 on a script provocatively entitled *Infidelity.* Coming a year after *Wife Versus Secretary* played the nation's movie houses, it too was about a wife pitted against a secretary, and a Stromberg production also. Breen was doubly suspicious, for, as the producer had already proved, the censor had a good memory.

"We felt so desperately for Scott," the Hacketts recall, "because we knew it couldn't be done. They wouldn't allow it just because it was about infidelity. About the only infidelity you could have in pictures in those days was a man taking another man's wife to lunch. We didn't tell Scott that it was impossible because we couldn't bear to break his heart. He was enthusiastic about his script; he wanted very much to do it. It was the first thing he really came to life on. But *Wife Versus Secretary* probably put the nail in his picture's coffin."

Ironically, seven years earlier Fitzgerald had helped drive a nail into that coffin himself. The nail was *The Redheaded Woman.* Fitzgerald's script for the picture had not been used, of course, and the project had been passed on to Anita Loos, who had written a very funny script. But not everyone had laughed: some had left the theatres shaking their fists rather than their sides. What bothered them most was not that the Redhead (Harlow) slept around through most of the movie. They were angry because after sleeping around she had not paid the price. Instead, she ended up as the happy mistress of a French noble-man (Charles Boyer, before stardom). Such happiness they could not forgive. The outcry was so great that the Hays Office was frightened into getting tough about censorship, and soon it was busy promulgating new rules. To begin with, the censors decided to whitewash the talkies' talk, prohibiting the use of such ex-pressions as: cripes, fanny, the finger, Gawd, goose, hell, damn (except in *Gone With the Wind*), hold your hat, in your hat, madame (if she had girls), nance, nerts, nuts (except meaning crazy), pansy, raspberry (the sound), SOB, son of a, tart, tom-cat, and whore, along with all the traveling-salesman and farmer's-daughter jokes.

Moreover, as a direct result of *The Redheaded Woman,* the Hays Office issued the following edict concerning infidelity: "Adultery, sometimes necessary plot material, must not be ex-plicitly treated, or justified, or presented attractively."[2] Fitz-gerald's poignant story flew in the outraged face of this industry law.

It also flew in the face of L. B. Mayer and his highly touted respect for motherhood and the family. Like the Hays Office ruling which allowed all the adultery you wanted so long as it was not justified, so long as the adulterer paid for his or her crime, Mayer's own code had that same smell of Hollywood hypocrisy.

Hedy Lamarr was one of many who had a chance to study

Mayer's code in a private face-to-face meeting, or rather it would have been face to face if Mayer had been a little taller. The two met in Europe, where Miss Lamarr had just finished *Ecstasy*, in which she went swimming nude. Mayer had seen the film, and it offended his good taste.

"Ah yes, my dear," the studio head told the star, patting her ass casually, "I know you would not make a vulgar picture intentionally. But in Hollywood, such accidents don't just happen." (The irony of this, Miss Lamarr says, was lost to her at the time.) "We have an obligation to the audience—millions of families. We make clean pictures . . . of course . . . if you like to make love . . . fornicate . . . screw your leading man in the dressing room, that's your business. But in front of the camera, gentility. You hear, gentility."

Miss Lamarr threatened to go.

"You have spirit. I like that," Mayer said, looking down the actress's dress with eyes which stood just cleavage-high. "And you have a bigger chest than I thought! You'd be surprised how tits figure in a girl's career."[3]

Caught between Hollywood's defenders of the faith—Breen on one side and Mayer on the other—Scott never had a chance.

2

One April day Scott and Sheilah drove out along the ocean following Route One, where they hoped to find a home among the "gaudy shacks and fishing barges" of Malibu. They decided on a "cottage" with green shutters, a sunroom, a dining room, a captain's walk, four bedrooms, and a garden, which rented for two hundred a month—half of what Fitzgerald had been paying at the Garden of Allah.

Scott would leave the cottage every morning and drive for miles along the ocean and then across the city to the studio. In *The Last Tycoon* he remembered that long drive to work with "the cars stacked and piled along the road, the beaches like ant-hills without a pattern, save for the dark drowned heads that sprinkled the sea." On the way to work he would see the sun bathers with their "blankets, matting, umbrellas, cookstoves, reticules full of clothing—the prisoners had laid out their shackles beside them on the sand."[4] In the evenings Fitzgerald would drive the same road home and the beach people would still be there. Scott lived by the sea but he never sun-bathed, never swam, nor could he imagine what these people did there on the sand all day.

In a sense the cottage became Scott's hermit's cave. "By early 1938 we were virtual recluses in Hollywood,"[5] Sheilah Graham remembers. Scott himself wrote, "I'm through. From now on I go nowhere and see no one because the work is hard as hell, at least for me, and I've lost ten pounds. So farewell, Miriam Hopkins, who leans *so* close when she talks, so long, Claudette Colbert, as yet unencountered, mysterious Garbo, glamorous Dietrich, exotic Shirley Temple—you will never know me. . . . There is nothing left, girls, but to believe in reincarnation and carry on."[6] When the screenwriter and the young gossip columnist did come out of seclusion to attend a rare social function, the couple still seemed like recluses even in a roomful of guests. They would usually withdraw to a corner or a divan of their own. At a party which Alan Campbell gave for the visiting Somerset Maugham, Maugham told his host, "I'm told F. Scott Fitzgerald is in Hollywood. I should like to meet him." Campbell replied, "You did, tonight—here."[7] The Fitzgerald who in 1927 had made himself "conspicuous" on his first trip to Hollywood now seemed to be transparent.

And his hypochondria was acting up again. There were all kinds of pills in the Malibu medicine cabinet—depressants to ease the insomnia, "bennies" to accompany the morning coffee, other pills to cure the imagination of its many ills. Scott worried about his tuberculosis flaring up again. He even worried about Miss Graham's driving. When she went over twenty he would say, "My God, slow down, you're killing me."[8] When they went to the movies, Fitzgerald would move two or three times during the evening because he felt the people behind him kicking his chair. For some reason, Miss Graham's chair was never kicked.

But if the author handled himself and his health with an old maid's care, he was developing new vigor and dash in at least one area of his life: his writing. It was almost as though he consciously conserved his energy so that he would have it to run the writing machine. He took his job of creating for the movies seriously and went about it systematically.

In his younger days, Fitzgerald had methodically analyzed the plots of one hundred *Saturday Evening Post* stories. He was teaching himself the genre. Now in Hollywood he wanted to teach himself another story form, moving pictures, and he took up the task in much the same way: he had countless movies run off for him in a classroom-sized projection room where he carefully studied each one.

Since he was supposed to write Joan Crawford's next film, he gave himself a special course in her pictures. Back in the twenties Scott had been captivated by the star. "Joan Crawford is doubtless the best example of the flapper," he had noted then, "the girl you see at smart night clubs, gowned to the apex of sophistication, toying iced glasses with a remote, faintly bitter expression, dancing deliciously, laughing a great deal, with wide, hurt eyes. Young things with a talent for living."[9] But now that admiration was as far away as the author's own youth. When Miss Crawford had wanted to play Pat in *Three Comrades*, Fitzgerald had been worried. When she was persuaded to pass up the role, he was greatly relieved. But now he had been assigned to write a movie specifically for her. There was nothing to do—Miss Crawford was going to be his star. All through February Fitzgerald studied her films the way a man who has fallen out of love studies his wife, watching her critically, every familiar gesture an aggravation, and yet making the best he could of the situation.

On the screen: *Chained*, starring Joan Crawford. Fitzgerald watched intently. The camera zoomed in for a close-up and the screenwriter took a blunt-pointed stub of a pencil down from behind his ear and wrote, "Why do her lips have to be glistening wet?" The actress seemed to be amused at a kind of private joke and the author put down, "Don't like her smiling to herself—or such hammy gestures that most actresses get away with." Joan's smile turned a little sour and Scott noted, "Cynical accepting smile has now gotten a little tired." Moments later he wrote, "Bad acting to following the stage direction 'as an afterthought.'" The drama heated up. To break her chains, Joan had to prove that her will was stronger than Clark Gable's. Fitzgerald was unimpressed. "She cannot fake her bluff," he scrawled, bearing down hard, "or pretend to."

But the hour and a half which Fitzgerald spent alone with Joan's image in the small theatre was not all agony. He found that she actually did some things rather well. In one scene she was at the wheel of a motorboat and Scott decided, "Her smile brighter in outdoor situation than in drawing rooms. . . . Outdoor girl better." The smile changed into laughter and the star's critic liked that better still. "Hearty laughter rather good," he put down.

As the movie unwound, however, growing sadder with each reel, Fitzgerald saw that he liked the star better when the smiles and laughter were wiped away. "A sad smile not bad," he observed, "but the serious expression best." As he renewed his acquaintance with Miss Crawford, her image told him a lot about what his own opening would have to be like. "Absolutely necessary that she feel her lines," he wrote. "Must be serious from first. So much better when she is serious. Must have direct, consuming purpose in mind at all points of the story—never anything vague or blurred. Must be driven." Up on the screen, Crawford saw Gable in a gun shop, and Fitzgerald noticed that there was "a touch of Louise Perkins . . . Has that groan." But at the end of the film, the star, the shopgirl's idol, burst into tears and the effect was spoiled. "Don't like her voice crying—tremulous."[10]

Another day Fitzgerald had *The Woman* run off for him. Later he saw Miss Crawford in a movie called *World's Fair*, and his mind must have gone back to the late 1920s when he himself had planned a novel with that title.

In March the author wrote Gerald Murphy:

I am writing a picture called *Infidelity* for Joan Crawford. Writing for her is difficult. She can't change her emotions in the middle of a scene without going through a sort of Jekyll and Hyde contortion of the face, so that when one wants to indicate that she is going from joy to sorrow, one must cut away and then cut back. Also, you can never give her such a stage direction as "telling a lie," because if you did, she would practically give a representation of Benedict Arnold selling West Point to the British.[11]

When Fitzgerald, now well acquainted with the star on the screen, finally encountered her in person, he told her, "I'm going to write your next picture."

"Good," she said, drawing her face into that serious, driven expression the author had admired in her movies. "Write hard, Mr. Fitzgerald, write hard!"[12]

As the script progressed there was much searching about for a co-star. When the studio finally made up its mind, it chose as Fitzgerald's hero an actor who had once portrayed Scott himself in a movie. In a sense, he would be playing the same character over again. The leading man, star of *The Wedding Night*, was Gary Cooper.

Hunt Stromberg was Fitzgerald's new boss. The producer towered over Scott and had a luxurious crop of hair which waved at the top of his flag-pole height. His round-lensed glasses and the formal three-piece suits which he sometimes affected gave him the air of a junior faculty member at a university. Since a screenwriter's prestige in Hollywood was umbilically tied to the prestige of his producer, the move from Mankiewicz to Stromberg was something of a step up for Fitzgerald. In the Stromberg unit he joined a writing staff which included such old friends as Dorothy Parker, Alan Campbell, and of course the Hacketts.

Stromberg had helped the Hacketts when they needed him most, back when they were working for John Considine ("Oh, that dreadful man"). He rescued them and they remained forever grateful; they remember the producer as "creative and understanding." "With Stromberg," they explain, "you had a real participation in casting. If someone objected to your script, he would be on the writer's side, fighting." And most important of all, he was not under the impression that he was Shakespeare: when he was given a script, he did not immediately sit down to rewrite it.

Fitzgerald liked Stromberg much better than Mankiewicz. He called him "a sort of one-finger Thalberg, without Thalberg's scope, but with his intense power of work and his absorption in his job." Still, he confided in a letter to Maxwell Perkins, "Relations have always been so pleasant, not only with you but with Harold [Ober] and with [George] Lorimer's *Saturday Evening Post*, that even working with the pleasantest people in the industry, Eddie Knopf and Hunt Stromberg, I feel this lack of confidence."[13]

Like most movies, this one began with a long wait. Fitzgerald stayed in his office so that he would be there in case the telephone rang—of course, it never did. He tried to catch up on his letter writing, tried to plot out a few stories, but that silent phone could be more distracting than someone who chattered incessantly. So for the most part the author looked out his office window, listened to voices in the hall, cleaned out his desk, sharpened his pencils, waited.

One afternoon when Fitzgerald was sitting in his office, the phone finally rang. It was Stromberg's secretary: the producer wanted to see the screenwriter right away. Fitzgerald would be right over. When he entered the producer's office, he found that Stromberg had a title ready for him. What would Scott think of a movie called *Infidelity*? Fitzgerald said that it sounded interesting. "Kick it around for a while," the producer instructed. That was how Stromberg often worked. He would call a writer in, drop a title in his head, and then the waiting would start all over again. Now the gestation could begin in earnest. The screenwriter at least had a seed to work with: a name.

The waiting went on and on as the writer "kicked around" Stromberg's idea. Days passed. The weekend came and Fitzgerald retreated to Palm Beach, where he had an idea. When he returned to the studio, he decided to fill some of his waiting time by writing out plots which had occurred to him. As he attacked his tablet, he grew excited:

> I have been playing with [an] idea [which is] utterly fantastic. . . . What would one think of Othello in modern dress on the screen? It would be [a] fascinating job for a writer and, I should think, for a director. Of course the great parts of the Moor, Iago, and Desdemona belong to the ages. There is infidelity for you on a grand scale. The more I think of it, the more I like it. . . .

Then in the middle of his excitement, Fitzgerald cooled: "However, I guess this is too fantastic an idea for Joan Crawford, and . . . the Moor would have to be changed for the Southern trade. . . ."[14]

From Shakespeare, Fitzgerald turned next for inspiration to another classic showman: Benny Goodman. The author outlined his story idea as follows:

> Put Shakespeare aside for a moment. My other brain wave last night concerns a story I thought of in Palm Beach last week. The name of it is *Trap Drummer*. I have noticed that the drummer in Benny Goodman's orchestra, to the younger generation, is such a hero that any night at the Palomar last summer one could see hundreds of kids standing around, staring at him. I wondered if he had a wife and what she thought.
>
> Now, supposing there was a trap drummer and Joan Crawford met him and helped him up to a position where he was practically a society pet, an Eddie Duchin; and supposing at this point he met a society girl and Joan Crawford sacrificed him and told him to go off with the society girl and she herself, after the divorce, married a man whom she admired and respected as she never had the trap drummer.
>
> Business of accidental encounters of the two couples.
>
> The trap drummer's romance with the society girl goes to pot, however, and he needs Joan Crawford; and, seeing that he is drinking himself to death and that his career is going to

pieces, she leaves the comfort and security that she has found, goes back to the trap drummer, and there she is again the trap drummer's wife, sitting in a corner in the night club, watching as he plays sometimes—and people pointing to her with a sort of pity, saying: "Yes, that's his wife. Isn't it a pity he's married to her." But she knows in her heart that she has done the right thing and knows that he, in the midst of his drumming, looks through the stares of adulation of the young . . . to her and he knows she is the rock and love of his life.

It is, of course, the woman following her maternal instinct rather than her instinct to be protected. As such it is a true and essential human story. Also it is, as far as I know, absolutely original in that nobody has yet written about orchestra people except in musical terms in the Ben Bernie pictures. . . .

Fitzgerald ended his story with a question: "Do the story and the title have to be the same, or can a story featuring John Crawford be called *Trap Drummer*? Or would it have to be called *The Trap Drummer's Wife*?"[14]

Stromberg was interested, but neither idea bowled him over, so Fitzgerald went away to think again. This time he forgot Shakespeare and put the big-band sound out of mind, too, in order to return to his imagination's favorite prompt book: his own experience. Infidelity was no stranger to Fitzgerald. He outlined a somewhat autobiographical story to Stromberg and the producer liked it very much. He asked how fast the writing would go. No longer a self-employed novelist but a worker in a movie factory, Fitzgerald was happy to submit a timetable:

SCHEDULE

Sequence I		Feb.	23rd	The Waldorf
			24th	Home and morning
			25th	Office
Sequence II			28th	Seeing her off
		Mar.	1st	" " "
Sequence III			2nd	Old Secretary
			3rd	" "

Sequence IV {
    4th Abroad
    7th   "

    8th Revise
    9th   "   FIRST ACT
    10th "   45 pages.

Sequence V {
    11th Montage & auto
    14th Apartment
    15th   "
    16th Discovery

Sequence VI {
    17th Church & Office with phone
            number
            Door closes.
            TIME LAPSE

Sequence VII {
    18th Breakfast room, phone & bound
            for party
    21st Party

Sequence VIII {
    22nd CUT TO husband and back to
            old beau
    23rd With beau
    24th Crisis with beau and switch
            CUT TO husband.
    25th Revise
    28th   "   SECOND ACT
    29th   "   50 pages.

Sequence VIII {
(Cont'd)
    30th New Man
    31st Crisis with New Man

Apr. 1st Husband
        4th   "
        5th Reunion
        6th Revise   THIRD ACT
        7th Revise   25 pages.

    8th DELIVERY OF SCRIPT

    Total 120 pages.[15]

Fitzgerald pointed out:

> That is less time than I took on *Three Comrades,* and the fact that I understand the medium a little better now is offset by the fact that this is really an original with no great scenes to get out of a book. . . . My plan is to work about half the time at the studio but the more tense and difficult stuff I do better at home away from interruptions.[16]

Stromberg agreed to let Fitzgerald work at home some of the time, which was a rarer privilege than one might imagine. Being cleared for home work was something like a prisoner's being made a trusty. Sheilah Graham recalls what Scott was like when he worked at their beach house:

> Scott, at Malibu. He is in an ancient gray-flannel bathrobe, torn at the elbows so that it shows the gray slipover sweater he wears underneath. He has the stub of a pencil over each ear, the stubs of half a dozen others—like so many cigars—peeping from the breast pocket of his robe. . . . In his room, off the captain's walk, the floor is littered with sheets of yellow paper covered with a large flowing hand. He uses his stubby pencils—he sharpens them carefully with a penknife, but never to a fine point because he bears down heavily—and writes at furious speed. As soon as one page is finished he shoves it off the desk to the floor and starts the next.[17]

3

The movie script which was piling up almost like waste paper at the author's feet was to be an experiment, something so new that it was also very old, as old as silent film. One could almost imagine that Fitzgerald in undertaking this experiment had been taking lessons from Monroe Stahr. In *The Last Tycoon* Stahr develops a scene in which a girl enters an office, lights a fire in the stove, and then burns a pair of black gloves. When the telephone rings, she answers and says, "I've never owned a pair of black gloves in my life." All the while a strange man is "watching every move the girl makes." A British writer named Boxley complains that the story is "just melodrama." But Stahr says, "Not necessarily. . . . In any case, nobody moved violently or talked cheap dialogue or had any facial expressions at all. There was only one bad line, and a writer like you could improve it. But you were interested."[18] Fitzgerald in *Infidelity* tells a story which is very different from Stahr's, but in some respects he tells it the same way. There are very few lines of dialogue, and he hoped that there would be no strained facial expressions, but we are interested. Fitzgerald explained what he was trying to do in a memo to Stromberg: "Note how we . . . engrave our characters and our situations with practically no dialogue—a completely new technique and one that is not without its air of intrigue and appealing mystery."[19]

Actually, the technique was not as new as Fitzgerald thought. When the movies had first learned to talk, they had seemed to jabber incessantly, but soon, like a boy with a changing voice, the industry grew unsure of its new vocal cords, and movies became noticeably quieter for a time. Alfred Hitchcock promptly labeled this new reticent breed of films "silent talkies."[20] This reaction to talk reached its peak in the late thirties just as Fitzgerald was beginning as a screenwriter. Not surprisingly, he suffered much the same sort of growing pains. His *Three Comrades* was a little like the early talkies, heavy on dialogue; then in *Infidelity* he decided to shut up and let the pictures do the talking for him. His "silent" talking picture was not so much completely new as very up-to-date. And effective.

On the first page of Fitzgerald's script we are introduced to two characters known simply as Gray Hair and Rumpled Hair. Descended from Nick Carroway in *The Great Gatsby*, they are the outside observers through whose eyes we see the story. The two men are at a night club on the roof of the Waldorf, where they entertain themselves by watching several couples at faraway tables through opera glasses. The motion-picture audience was to have been allowed to look through the glasses along with Gray and Rumpled, for the scenes were to have been photographed "through a frame shaped like this ∞."[21] The couples, as viewed through the glasses, were to have been seen moving their lips, but no dialogue was to be recorded on the soundtrack: Fitzgerald by now had decided that the old adage about being seen and not heard should be applied to motion pictures—an art which was, after all, not yet grown up.

Rumpled and Gray look from table to table trying to decide which couples are engaged (ecstatic), married (bored), or cheating (nervous). Like Nick Carroway, the two men with the opera glasses help us to see what matters in the action of others: they help us get the right moral labels stuck on the right people. Fitzgerald was using Rumpled and Gray to educate his audience on how to *see* his story. Of course, no one ever did see it. Joe Breen took care of that.

At first, Gray and Rumpled's game seems easy. It grows more difficult when they turn their glasses on a man and woman who are obviously not strangers, but who treat one another with the caution and politeness usually reserved for new acquaintances. Fitzgerald called the couple "silent and inscrutable"—they are bound to one another and yet there is a barrier between them. The man and woman are the hero and heroine of the story, Nicolas and Althea Gilbert. Puzzled, Gray Hair and Rumpled Hair decide that this spying is a silly game anyway; they give up and leave the roof. It is left to us to judge where Nicolas and Althea, more complicated than the other couples, fit in along that spectrum which runs from engagement through marriage to infidelity.

As Fitzgerald fashioned the story of Nicolas and Althea Gilbert, his thoughts went back to southern France and the fall of 1924, when he and Zelda had met a French flier named Édouard Josanne. Josanne was hard and handsome and brave like Tommy Barban in *Tender Is the Night*. Zelda wrote that he had a head of gold like "a Christmas coin . . . broad bronze hands . . . convex shoulders . . . slim and strong and rigid." When Fitzgerald discovered that the flier, who came evening after evening to sit in the garden and talk about smoking opium in Peking, was also Zelda's lover, the bitter fights began. Josanne departed, leaving Zelda a letter in French and his photograph. "It was the most

beautiful thing she'd ever owned in her life, that photograph,"
Zelda wrote of herself. "What was the use of keeping it? . . .
There wasn't a way to hold on to the summer, no French phrase
to preserve its rising broken harmonies, no hopes to be salvaged
from a cheap French photograph. What ever it was that she
wanted from [him], [he] took with him. . . ."[22] At first, things
seemed to get better. A month after the affair ended, Fitzgerald
wrote in his ledger that he and Zelda were "close together" again.
But years later he admitted: "That September 1924 I knew something had happened that could never be repaired."[23]

That was the emotion behind *Infidelity,* but he told the story
with the roles reversed. Althea accompanies her mother on a
vacation to Italy. A former secretary who once loved Nicolas
drops by his office one afternoon, stays for dinner, then goes home
with him at night to see the house she might have lived in if his
father had not intervened. The butler is clearing away the breakfast dishes the next morning when Althea returns unexpectedly.
Indicating her plate, the butler asks the secretary if she is
through. She is, of course, and so is Nicolas and Althea's marriage
as they have known it.

Throughout his screenplay Fitzgerald continued to emphasize
sight over sound, pictures over words. *Picture:* Althea, "with a not
too emphasized gesture, turns her wedding ring with her thumb."
Picture: Althea, passing the fireplace, catches her fur coat on the
spike of an ornate andiron; she frees herself quickly and goes on,
but Nicolas remains behind to quickly bend off the offending
point. *Picture:* At breakfast, Althea waits to see if Nicolas will
notice that she has ordered a new kind of ham for the cook to
prepare. Nicolas brightens when he notices his wife's attention.

ALTHEA: Well—?

NICOLAS (*puzzled*): Well?

ALTHEA: Nicer?

NICOLAS: What, nicer?

ALTHEA: The ham. It's sent up from the South.

Nicolas' eagerness fades. One cannot help wondering if Zelda, reared near Montgomery, Alabama, ever had ham sent up from the South.[24]

To forget the night which ruined his marriage and to stop thinking for a while, Nicolas decides to give a party on his Long Island estate. Once the backdrop for weekends of consuming love, it has now lain idle for two years. To this party Nicolas invites not the senators, bankers, and heiresses of his social set, but the entire cast of a Broadway show in which he has invested. This is to be an evening where Jay Gatsby himself could walk the bright lawns and feel at home.

As the show people gather and the great house is lit once again, Nicolas talks with an actress named Alice:

> ALICE: I never understood what you'd do with a big house unless you had a thousand children.
>
> NICOLAS: Nothing but vanity. Or else sometimes you think you're so much in love that your love could fill the biggest palace conceivable.[25]

By this time, Nicolas and Althea's love no longer fills the palace, nor have they filled it with children. In *The Last Tycoon* Stahr's tragedy is the barren "Waste Land of the house [begun] too late."[26] In *Infidelity*, the Gilberts' tragedy is the Waste Land of a house abandoned too soon. The kingdom is to have no heir. We were to witness the fall of the Gilberts just as the author himself, in a different way, had witnessed the fall of the Fitzgeralds.

Rather than a thousand children, Nicolas filled his mansion with actors and actresses, dancers and musicians. There are rows of limousines hired to ferry the guests to and from the party: there is a big swing orchestra: there is a huge canvas sprawled across the lawn and covered with dancers. But Nicolas is still lonely even in this crowd. The irony of infidelity is that rather than joining Nicolas to more of humanity, it has cut him off from even those to whom he once belonged. While the party roars downstairs, the master of this mansion makes a solitary tour of empty bedrooms. Once again the story was to have been told in pictures without words. The deserted rooms were to have provided a visual metaphor for the fall of the House of Gilbert. Nicolas sees a live mouse, the unlikely inheritor of this abandoned place. He passes among billiard tables, all of them covered with canvas sheets. He enters the master bedroom, where the chairs, the bureau, and the lady's vanity are all shrouded in canvas. The last scene in the unfinished script ends with Nicolas staring at a large bed which, like everything else, has been covered to keep off the dust.

4

Fitzgerald believed in his script the way one believes in an old friend: it was like a visit paid to the world of *The Great Gatsby* thirteen years after the book's publication. Like the 1925 novel, it told the story of the infidelity of a husband set against the backdrop of expensive New York homes and lavish country estates on Long Island's fashionable northern shore. What separated *Infidelity* from *Gatsby*, however, was the author's feelings toward the adulterer. As Fitzgerald had grown older, he had come to better understand Tom Buchanan's sin. First there had been Zelda and Josanne, and now Scott and Sheilah.

In a memo to Stromberg, Fitzgerald says of the secretary who destroys Nicolas' marriage:

> A turn of the wheel . . . a flip of the coin . . . and this girl [Myrna Loy] might have been Gary's [Gary Cooper's] wife. How often this happens in life! And this is one of the big broadsides we are firing dramatically. . . . For every man—and every woman—has more than one woman in their lives. . . . How strange it seems sometimes that a certain relationship was not consummated—and yet it is simple to explain—everyone knows the thread of incidents affecting each life.[27]

Years before, Fitzgerald had written of Gatsby's loss of Daisy: "He must have felt that he had lost the old warm world, paid a high price for living too long with a single dream."[28] By 1938 the author himself had lost Zelda—not to another man but to insanity. Now he too knew what it was to pay the high price of the single dream, so he tried to believe that there could be more than one dream. He tried to believe that by living with Sheilah Graham he could recoup some of his losses. In *Gatsby*, when Nick Carroway discovered that Tom was unfaithful to Daisy, he felt like calling the police. In *Infidelity*, when the same crime is discovered, the author calls for understanding. By now he knew what it was like to be in the adulterer's place.

In fact, that was to have been the key to the last few minutes of his movie. Fitzgerald outlined what he had in mind in a treatment where Althea actually sees herself—and the audience sees her on the screen—in the place of the secretary who falls in love with Nicolas. The experience teaches her compassion. Fitzgerald used to say that a writer never wasted anything. His inspiration about characters in a movie seeing themselves in someone else's place never made it onto the screen, but it did make it into a book. In *The Last Tycoon* Boxley is brought in to doctor a script that a team of veteran writers have bogged down on. He has an idea. "Let each character see himself in the other's place," Boxley suggests. "The policeman is about to arrest the thief when he sees that the thief has *his* face. I mean, show it that way. You could almost call the thing *Put Yourself in My Place*."[29]

Stromberg was uncertain about this idea. He knew the old rule: fantasies don't make money. (That was before *Mary Poppins*.) One problem was that photography was such a realistic art that it often undercut any make-believe one attempted to film.[30] Still, Fitzgerald's idea might have worked. It played, after all, on the movie's magic for making audiences see themselves as anything from Tarzan swinging through the jungle to Little Caesar mowing down everyone who got in his way. By carrying this one step further, Fitzgerald hoped to convert the audience's imagination into a moral force. If people could see themselves as Iris (or Nicolas or Althea), then perhaps they could understand and forgive the infidelity. Perhaps such understanding was the function of art. The screenwriter never got a chance to find out. Before he could finish his script, something happened.

At the bottom of page 104 of the script, Fitzgerald wrote: "There will be about 15 or 20 pages to the end." Then he turned in his nearly completed scenario to Stromberg and headed east. Like Nicolas Gilbert, Fitzgerald did not have much of a family anymore, but he was determined to spend Easter with what he had left of one. Since he was anxious to prove to that family that he was still a writer and a good one, he took along a copy of *Infidelity*. The father met his daughter Scottie in Baltimore and they set off by rail for Norfolk, Virginia, to collect Zelda from her hospital. In a compartment in the Baltimore-Norfolk train, Scottie, who was then just sixteen years old, read her father's story about the tragedy of adultery. It was a dismal Easter for these people who now only followed the rickety old pretense of being related to one another. Scott and Zelda fought, and Scott drank. But at least one good thing had come out of the visit: the father had proven something to his daughter.

When he returned to Hollywood, however, he discovered that the script which his daughter had admired was not going to be produced. With only twenty pages to go, Joe Breen had blackballed it. This was an era when everyone was making movies for the family, and America's First Family was not the Roosevelts but the Hardys. Almost everyone in the country knew Andy Hardy (Mickey Rooney), Judge Hardy (Lewis Stone), Mother (Fay Holden), Aunt Millie (Sara Haden), Andy's girl friend Polly Benedict (Ann Rutherford) and the little girl next door who sang (Judy Garland). *Infidelity* had no place in this world.

Fitzgerald wrote his daughter:

We have reached a censorship barrier in *Infidelity*, to our infinite disappointment. It *won't* be Joan's next picture and we are setting it aside awhile till we can think of a way of half-witting halfwit Hays and his Legion of Decency. Pictures needed cleaning up in 1932–33 (remember I didn't like you to see them?), but because they were suggestive and salacious. Of course the moralists now want to apply that to *all* strong themes—so the crop of the last two years is feeble and false, unless it deals with children.[31]

In *The Last Tycoon* the disappointed screenwriter would state flatly that Hollywood's "golden age [came] before the censorship."[32]

After a scheme to change the picture's name from *Infidelity* to *Fidelity* miscarried, there were other attempts to outwit the halfwit censors. Breen thought that Scott's projected ending—the reconciliation between Althea and Nicolas—was tantamount to advertising that crime paid. So the author worked out what he hoped would be a compromise. He outlined his idea to Stromberg this way:

> First let me state it in terms of a parallel, highly justified in this case because adultery is a form of thievery. . . .
>
> A certain man [Nicolas], in co-operation with an unknown accomplice [Iris], has stolen from his partner [Althea]. The partnership is dissolved.
>
> After ten years the partners meet. The thieving partner has been forgiven in a certain way but has not been reinstated in partnership nor does he expect it. He finds, though, that his unknown accomplice has returned and is engaged in once again trying to steal from his former partner [having an affair with Althea's new husband].
>
> . . . He steps in to right the wrong. In the process of so doing, it is necessary that the old accomplice be ruined—and also that he shall be received back into partnership.

Fitzgerald went on to explain: "A Catholic like Breen would, I think, accept the morals of this situation completely. The thieving partner is redeemed. The unreformed accomplice is punished."[33] But Breen did not accept it. The idea got nowhere. Finally Stromberg's patience wore out. He was through fighting the Hays Office. He gave up and assigned Fitzgerald to another story. Like Nicolas Gilbert's unborn children, Scott Fitzgerald's unborn screenplay—one of the best he would ever write—went into permanent storage.

After working for three months on the picture, Fitzgerald came home one evening and told Sheilah, "I've been taken off the story."

She knew how much *Infidelity* meant to him, so she tried to cheer him up. "Let's have some people over," she suggested. "Why don't you invite a lot of your friends."

"That's it," said the author. "We'll have a party."

And they had one: to celebrate the disaster. When the guests began to arrive, they included Eddie Mayer, Nunnally Johnson and his wife Marion, Cameron and Buff Rogers, Bill Warren (who helped with the adaptation of *Tender Is the Night*), and with him the lovely actress Alice Hyde. For most of the evening Fitzgerald was an excellent host, organizing Ping-Pong matches, boxing with Eddie Mayer's seven-year-old son Paul, serving drinks, being his old expansive Dick-Diver self. Best of all, the only thing that he would drink was water.

Some neighborhood children came over and the author brought out a deck of cards. "Would you boys like to see a wonderful card trick?" he asked. "Only one other man in the world can do this. And he's a lifer at San Quentin, who spent ten years in solitary where he thought up this trick." He rolled up his sleeves. "Watch! Abracadabra." He closed his eyes and whirled three times. Then out of the deck on demand came an ace, a king, a ten, a four.

The prized script seemed to have been forgotten. Fitzgerald seemed happier than he had in some time. Suddenly Sheilah realized why. The water that Scott had been drinking was gin. The drink soon began to take its toll. The author took Alice Hyde aside and told her confidentially that Bill Warren had syphilis. After the news had had time to do its mischief, he took Bill aside and asked, "What's the matter, old man? Seems she can't stand you. You haven't said anything offensive, have you?"[34]

As the guests began to leave, Fitzgerald escorted them to their cars. As he was escorting Nunnally and Marion Johnson, he suddenly changed his mind about seeing them out and asked Johnson to step into the den.

"He seemed a little frantic, a little wild," Johnson remembers. "He locked the door and dramatically dropped the key in his pocket. Then he began ordering me to leave town."

With the door locked, Johnson was not sure how that was possible.

Scott told him, "Listen, Nunnally, get out of Hollywood. It will ruin you. You have a talent—you'll kill it here."

Johnson recalls the rest of what happened that evening as follows:

"This was a crusade for about twenty-five minutes. He wanted to deliver me from this hell I was in. I told him that since I was doing better than I had ever done in my life, I didn't want to be saved. I finally asked Scott, 'Have I got to fight to get out of this room?' My wife and Sheilah started knocking on the door. When he let me out, we went outside to the car and started to drive away, but he followed us down the road. I stopped to see what he wanted and he said, 'I don't suppose you'll ever come back!'

"I asked him, 'Why not, Scott?'

"He shouted, 'Because I'm living here with my paramour!'

"I had seen that word written down before but I had never heard it spoken. I turned to my wife and said, 'Good God, I didn't know Scott was a Methodist.'

"My wife said that he wasn't, that he was a Catholic, but I said that no one but a Methodist would use a word like that."

Johnson had escaped from Fitzgerald's house, but neither he nor Scott escaped from Hollywood. Johnson went on to write the fine script for *The Grapes of Wrath;* Fitzgerald's next writing job was on a movie which was to star Irving Thalberg's widow. But even while he was writing dialogue for the new screenplay, he kept submitting plans for the revival of the story which the censors had stopped. A year later, when he began *The Last Tycoon,* the author wrote his daughter that the novel was his "first labor of love . . . since the first part of *Infidelity*."[35]

The Women:
Epitaph for the Spoiled Heroine

1

Hunt Stromberg looked at his watch nervously. Fitzgerald had reported to his office to discuss what they were going to do about repairing the first few pages of his script for *The Women*. Stromberg didn't like them. But as the writer tried to talk his story—never his strength—the producer's nervousness made him nervous, too. He could not help noticing the perspiration which gleamed across his boss's forehead and gathered in bright pools about his eyes. The producer looked at the time once again. Stromberg was obviously paying more attention to his watch than to his writer. But he was not clocking Fitzgerald to see how long he had been talking—it had been only a few minutes. Nor was he expecting an important director or star. He wasn't even looking to see how long until lunch. What Stromberg *was* doing was checking to see how much longer the pain inside of him would last.

Suddenly the producer stopped Fitzgerald. He wanted to know if Scott could come back later, say in two hours, when they would take up the conference again. Of course Fitzgerald would come back—that was his job. The writer left and Stromberg waited alone. The doctor was coming with the drugs; he would be there soon. The man in pain shifted in his chair and looked at his watch once again.

When Fitzgerald reported back two hours later, Stromberg seemed more relaxed at first. But soon he was after his watch again. Again he was waiting for the doctor to come. Again he put the writer off. Could he come back in the morning?

That night Stromberg decided that he could not wait until morning to solve the opening. He called Fitzgerald at home in Malibu. Could Scott come right over? The writer drove his old Ford—the one which just missed being immortalized in *A Yank at Oxford*—along ocean-hugging Route One, then cut inland to Beverly Hills. When he parked his runt of a jalopy in front of Stromberg's mansion, it seemed to make the huge house look even bigger. Fitzgerald was shown in and then taken not to the living room or the study but to Stromberg's bedroom. Scott found the producer waiting for him in bed, sick. It was a shock, but Fitzgerald understood about being ill and working anyway—many of his short stories had been written while he was confined to bed. The sickroom became their conference room. The author sat beside the bed and, as his superior fought back the pain, they plunged into their comedy, trying to make it funnier and funnier.

Fitzgerald would later write in one of his notebooks that he was tired of his own "rhythm and the rhythms of the people in Hollywood. He wanted to see people with more secrets than the necessity of concealing a proclivity for morphine."[1] But Stromberg had a good reason for his proclivity. Not long after Fitzgerald transferred to his unit, he had developed a slipped disc which kept him in constant pain, and Stromberg was terrified of pain. He began wearing a corset which was supposed to do the work of his damaged backbone, holding the weight of his head and shoulders. That helped, but the pain continued, and along with the pain, the drugs.

Even loyal old-timers like the Hacketts, people with years of good will behind them, found it hard to face this new, diminished

Stromberg. "It was impossible to work with him anymore," they remember.

The fatal day, so far as the Hacketts' screenwriting careers were concerned, came when Stromberg called them into his office and told them that from now on they would be writing one *The Thin Man* picture and one Jeanette MacDonald-Nelson Eddy picture a year. "The first *Thin Man* was a refreshing comedy," the Hacketts recall, "but after that each one kept getting thinner and thinner." The couple were equally tired of writing sweet little stories for Jeanette and Nelson. "When I heard what they wanted us to do," says Albert Hackett, "I went back to my desk and cried and puked into my typewriter." That day the fabulously successful couple quit the movies and began packing. They were going home to Broadway. MGM lost two of its best screenwriters, Fitzgerald two of his best friends.

As the Hacketts were leaving Hollywood, giving up once they were convinced that the best had already been, Bill Warren was just getting settled in California, hoping to break in. Columbia Pictures brought him out from New York because they were impressed with the detective stories he had been writing at pennies a word for the pulps. He moved into an eight-dollar-a-week room in a Los Angeles boarding hotel and thought that he was living in comparative affluence. When Fitzgerald saw the room, he said, "What are you doing in a dump like that? Come down and live in Malibu."

Warren moved in with Scott and Sheilah for the summer. "I was nothing but a lackey," he remembers. "It was always, 'Boy, bring the drinks.'" It was usually late by the time Scott got back to the beach house after a day's writing at the office. There would be little conversation at dinner. If Scott said anything, it was likely to be something like, "I had an awful fight with so-and-so today."

Wednesdays Fitzgerald would stay home from the studio. When Warren asked him why, Scott would say, "Well, I'm sick." On those days when he was "sick," the older author would take the younger one to the Pickwick Bookstore, where, Warren says, "He would buy me books he thought I should read." Scott would take Bill to lunch at Musso Frank's, where other writers ate, where he would be known.

Fitzgerald normally shunned the beach, but one night at about ten P.M. he led Sheilah and Bill down to the edge of the ocean. He was taking them to see what Stahr showed Kathleen in *The Last Tycoon:* little silver fishes which came rolling in "twos and threes and platoons and companies, relentless and exalted and scornful, round the great bare feet of the intruders, as they had come before Sir Francis Drake had nailed his plaque to the boulder on the shore."[2]

One summer day a new boarder arrived at the beach house. He was a big, powerful man and, when he shook Warren's hand, he gripped him by the fingers and squeezed until Bill sank to his knees. Ernest Hemingway, who, Fitzgerald had written, "talked with the authority of success," had come to Scott, who "talked with the authority of failure," for a place to stay and some spending money. Fitzgerald had written that he and Ernest could "never sit across the same table again"; he said that they had "walked over one another with cleats." In "The Snows of Kilimanjaro" Hemingway had written that the very rich had ruined Scott Fitzgerald, and since then he had more than once hinted that movie money had taken up the job where the Eastern rich had left off. But now Ernest, who said that he was waiting for a check from one of the national magazines, needed some of that Hollywood wealth. Scott gave him twenty-five dollars a week allowance. Ernest insisted on cash so that there would be no record.[3]

Hemingway would set up a card table out on the beach at night, station a kerosene lantern on it, and, with the waves rolling and the wind tugging at his pages, write *For Whom the Bell Tolls* in longhand. Warren told Fitzgerald, "He's just waiting for a columnist to come along and discover him writing that way." One night Bill went out to watch and Ernest called out, "Boy,

take a look at this." ("Hemingway always resolutely refused to
remember my name," Warren says.) The novelist handed Bill a
page on which the handwriting formed an inverted pyramid.
Warren says that it was one of the sleeping-bag scenes. At the
bottom of the pyramid was the orgasm. The earth moved. Hemingway asked Bill what he thought of it. "I don't understand it,"
said the young man, whose life had been at least more sheltered
than Ernest's. "What does it mean?" After Ernest explained, Bill
liked the scene better.

One morning Scott woke Bill and said, "We're going to Metro."
Fitzgerald wanted to introduce Hemingway to the powers at the
studio, proud to show off the famous author to his bosses, proud
to dangle impresarios like Louis B. Mayer before Ernest. They
rattled up to the Thalberg Building in Scott's old Ford for what
was to be Hemingway's grand entrance. Deferentially, Fitzgerald
guided his friend into the office of Bernard Hyman, a small, retiring man who was one of the most powerful producers at MGM.
Ernest looked the little fellow over.

"You're doing pretty well for a 'Heeb,' " he said.

Mayer was the next to be honored with an introduction. The
two bullies were bound to resent one another. Hemingway's
power was in his body, in the guns he shot game with, in the
courage he thought he had. Mayer's power was in his empire and,
as it turned out, his police force. The great American individualist
shook hands with the head of the great American corporation.
The oak tree looked down at the fireplug. In Mayer's office,
Hemingway was so rude that Metro's dictator called one of his
house cops and said, "If this man isn't out of my office in five
minutes, it's your job."

After Hemingway had been thrown out, all Fitzgerald said
was, "He doesn't have a car. How's he going to get back to
Malibu?"

At the end of the workday, Scott and Bill went to look for
Ernest. They found him across the street in a bar called the
Retake Room. Ernest was inside telling everyone how he had

put L. B. Mayer in his place. Scott had a few drinks and soon he too was making Ernest the hero of the incident. As the third member of that party recalls, "Little Billy Warren, who was waiting outside the bar and who didn't even have a license, had to drive the two drunks home."

One night Fitzgerald came home to Sheilah as happy as if he had been drinking, but he hadn't. He had seen an advertisement in the *Los Angeles Times*: The Pasadena Playhouse was going to première a new play based on F. Scott Fitzgerald's "A Diamond as Big as the Ritz." He called the Playhouse and asked them to reserve two seats "somewhere near the back." Then he ordered a limousine and chauffeur; this event was too showy for his bouncy Ford. Sheilah wore a gray and crimson evening gown; Scott had on his tuxedo. They could have been on their way to one of the debutante parties which the younger Fitzgerald immortalized.

When they reached the Playhouse, there were no crowds in front of the theatre. Fitzgerald wondered if it could be the wrong night and went off to find out. When he returned, he said, "It's the students—they're giving the play in the upstairs hall." The two first-nighters, dressed for box seats and velvet chairs, sat on wooden benches at the back of the hall, once again alone. Just before curtain time about a dozen students wandered in, the girls in skirts and slacks, the boys without ties.

Scott laughed all through the play and at the end decided, "I'm going backstage. It might encourage them to know the author came to see them." The young actors could not hide the fact that they were surprised to see Fitzgerald—they had assumed that he was dead.[4]

Fitzgerald helped Miss Graham into her silver-fox jacket and they returned to the rented elegance of their limousine. The fur was the first that Sheilah had ever owned. Scott had given it to her for her birthday. He always laughed at her when she wore it because of the way she sat forward in her seat so as not to crush the fur. Like the old Ford which the author had written into his script for *Yank,* the fur coat was written into the script on which he was now working. It became a prostitute's badge.

2

"Scott would rather have written a movie than the Bible, than a best seller," says Warren, but once again Fitzgerald had run into trouble on a picture, so that his goal now seemed further away than ever. Warren remembers that one evening "Scott showed me a scene that he had written that day. I was aghast. It was night. The heroine was in her room. The wind was blowing and Scott had her recite 'Invictus': 'I am the captain of my soul . . .'"

Bill told Scott, "My God, that would take a whole reel."

Scott answered, "What do you know? That's what I get for asking a peasant."

It is not easy to understand why Fitzgerald was given this particular writing job in the first place. To begin with, the play which he was supposed to adapt had been a smash Broadway comedy; Fitzgerald had written only one comedy since he left Princeton, *The Vegetable,* and it had flopped in Atlantic City long before it got anywhere near Broadway. Furthermore, the play which he was to make into a movie was by a woman, Clare Booth, and was very much the kind of play a woman would write. There were not even any men in the play, none, the all-female cast being a gimmick which Miss Booth had exploited quite successfully. And yet they wanted Scott to write a woman's comedy about women to be called *The Women.* Hollywood was like that.

Being assigned to *The Women* was a double disappointment for Fitzgerald. Not only had *Infidelity* been stopped, but he had been transferred onto, then off of, a story which promised to become a classic film memorial to Irving Thalberg. In a sense the picture *Marie Antoinette* was Thalberg's own *The Last Tycoon*— it was to have been his masterpiece, but his death left it unfinished. Fitzgerald had been drawn to Thalberg as the last of the great producers: he was drawn to the producer's hero,

Louis XVI, as the last of another line, the last of the Sun Kings. In his 1921 novel *This Side of Paradise,* Scott had described "a new generation . . . grown up to find all Gods dead, all wars fought, all faiths in men shaken," but the author himself had never stopped believing in the Gods, wars, kings, and heroes. He wrote only five pages of script for *Marie Antoinette,* but in these he found space to resist the Age of Steinbeck and to recall a different age which thrived on different beliefs.

"You see, we believe in kings, you and I," he had Ferson tell the queen; the courtier is trying to explain to Marie why he will not run away with her, why she must stay with Louis. "Oh, I know it's not the fashion at present. There's another spirit in the air. But it was a great human idea—the king. You and I were brought up to believe it. We shall die believing it."[5]

After a few days, however, Fitzgerald learned that he was not to be allowed to continue telling this story of monarchs shaken off the world's chessboard by the masses. Instead of kings and queens and battlefields, he was given a bridge table and asked to tell the stories of the women gathered around it. Fitzgerald had little enthusiasm for the new project, but he was at least no stranger to the kind of woman he was supposed to write about. In a way, they were like the girls he had described in *This Side of Paradise,* but now, like the author, they were twenty years older. In *Paradise* Rosalind had thrown over Amory because he showed no signs of growing rich enough to spoil her. All the girls in *The Women* have solved that problem: they have found men rich enough. Fitzgerald's Gloria Gilbert, heroine of *The Beautiful and Damned,* had been cut from the same lace; Nicole in *Tender Is the Night* and Pat in *Three Comrades* had needed spoiling, too, but they had an excuse: they were sick.

The pampered heroine had served Fitzgerald well for many years, but an estrangement was coming. Mary Haines, the protagonist of *The Women,* would be the last heroine in this tradition about whom the author would ever write. In a note to Stromberg, Fitzgerald imagined "what sort of woman" Mary is when we first see her at the beginning of the story. His descriptions reads like an epitaph for all his old heroines, the ones who were beautiful and damned.

She is a member of a group, a clan who are brought up with a curious dualism. They are given the best education, tutoring, instruction and chaperonage, but at the same time they are told in a subtle way that they have no special obligations to fulfill, no price to pay for these advantages. Their brothers are at least expected to attain the minimum requirements at Yale, Harvard, Princeton, to fit them to become part of New York's ruling caste—but not the women. Merely satisfying high school requirements is enough to saturate them with expensive cars, mink coats, fabulous jewelry, so at the age of eighteen they have anything they want, no sense of reward or punishment. They own the earth. We are not going to preach a sermon, but we start with the supposition that this is true. If we make Mary a middle-class woman we have falsified the intention of the play. She belongs to this class and when she sees its general shiftlessness and viciousness she has a hard time getting out of it. That too has a definite part in this story.

This class is pretty new—it grew up in the twenties—her mother was a rich woman but raised in a religious atmosphere —a moral atmosphere. In Mary's world a woman acts almost entirely according to her temptations. But she must have inherited some taste from her mother and her own home, for she is plainly several cuts above her friends in her standards of conduct.

She had an English nanny, then a French mademoiselle and at twelve was sent to the Spence School in New York, where among her classmates were the plain, clever Nancy, the witty and amusing Sylvia, and Edith, who was perhaps her cousin or a friend of early childhood.

About 1928, when they were nineteen, the four girls made their debut at dances at the Ritz. Nancy wasn't popular with men—she loved someone who didn't love her—but the other three were very quickly engaged to three eligible young bachelors. Mary, the prettiest and sweetest, was the first to marry.

She had had little time or occasion to think before marriage and the first few years afterwards were much the same. She was mad about her husband and her two babies. She played occasionally at all the sports she had learned in girlhood—their summer house had a pool and though she quit tennis after the babies came, she still played golf in the nineties and always meant to play more if only to keep her still girlish figure from departing.

What was it that singled her out for a very special blow of fate? She had conformed in every way to the traditions of her class, she had not even availed herself of its privileges of occasionally straying. Why did she lose her husband to a rather low predatory-type female?

It was above all because she was a giver and not a taker, everything had to come to her, not for the asking, but without asking, because she was beautiful. A beautiful girl does not have to fight for men—she has no such training as a girl whose weapons must be guile and charm.

Her beauty has even formed her position among women. Even there life has been easy—she has such a sweet nature that her friends cannot even be jealous of her beauty, so she does not quarrel and cat with them. They show their better sides and she does not suspect their baser motives.

Nevertheless, her best friend has grown to be Nancy—she feels that Nancy is alive. As her twenties pass she has a better time with Nancy, who has ideas and talents, than she has with Edith and Sylvia. These two she takes for granted—part of her life—part of her past.[6]

This note to Stromberg, this history prepared to fill in the past of a Clare Booth character, must have been for Fitzgerald the cause which would prepare for the effects of the drama. Always one with a keen sense of history, he had to know Mary's background before he could write about her present. But no sooner did he have it down, Mary's then and now, than he began to think of changing it. He had already done the old Mary, had already written countless stories about girls who had been ruined by their own wealth. Now he wanted to do something different.

So Fitzgerald wrote another note to Stromberg:

Let us change Mary from a passive, simple, easily influenced character, to the exact opposite—an active, intelligent, and courageous character, and see what effect this would have upon the plot of *The Women.*

For the present, I shall keep to the general line we have, but what she does in the play on good advice she will do now from good sense of her own, and whatever she does on bad advice, she won't do in quite such a dumb way. Let her actions speak for themselves. . . . Immediately you see we have a new Mary.[7]

To echo the author, immediately you see we have a new kind of heroine, one in some ways more like Sheilah Graham, who took care of Scott, than the Zelda who required so much care herself.

But this new Mary did not intrigue Stromberg or the front office. Fitzgerald was back to the old, familiar heroine he began with. He decided to introduce her to the movie audience much as he had originally described her to Stromberg, by going back and filling in her past, by beginning at the beginning and showing her growing up spoiled. The first shot was to have shown Mary and her friends as babies wheeled through Central Park by German and French nurses. As Fitzgerald pointed out, "Plain American nursemaids or colored girls would be a step down socially."[8]

Stromberg said no. He did not like Fitzgerald's little baby-carriage prologue and besides he had an idea of his own. Scott described how that idea came to the producer in one of his Pat Hobby stories:

"Wait a minute! Wait a minute!" the producer said . . . "I seem to see a dog." They would wait, tense and breathless, while he saw a dog.

"Two dogs."

A second dog took its place beside the first in their obedient visions.

"We open on a dog on a leash—pull the camera back to show another dog—now they're snapping at each other. We pull back further—the leashes are attached to tables—the tables tip over. See it?"9

Fitzgerald saw it. He returned to his desk and wrote the opening scene just as the producer had dictated. Nor did he particularly mind losing his prologue. Later, in *The Last Tycoon,* he would have Stahr tell his writers, "When you extend a play with a prelude you're asking for it."10

The Women is a very talkative play. After all, its subject is gossip. Consequently, Fitzgerald's adaptation of *The Women* is more a step backwards in the direction of the talkative *Three Comrades* than a step forward into the quiet world of *Infidelity.* But most of all, Fitzgerald's screenplay was a step into the classic Metro-Goldwyn-Mayer mold. To be sure that Fitzgerald understood what type of script was expected of him, Stromberg sent him off to one of the studio projection rooms to see Metro's *Grand Hotel.* Ever since the early thirties when Thalberg produced the movie, an all-star extravaganza which paraded many of the company's most dazzling beauties, including Greta Garbo and Joan Crawford, Metro had been known as "the Grand Hotel of the studios."11 Besides the mystical Garbo and the voracious Crawford, this distinctly feminine studio also boarded Jean Harlow, the goddess-whore; Myrna Loy, the unlikely wife; Joan Fontaine, the governess who married well; coy Paulette Goddard; musical Jeanette MacDonald; tragic Luise Rainer; and Rosalind Russell, the heavyweight bust. The studio's favorite subjects were polished, sophisticated, stagy dramas like *Hotel. The Women,* a polished comedy which would make work for several of the studio's most important girls, was an ideal MGM property.

The play was not, however, an ideal project for Fitzgerald—it allowed too few moments for screenwriting greatness. Too much of the work had already been done, too much of the dialogue already written. Often the screenwriter followed Miss Booth's play almost word for word. He could not sharpen her sharp tongue, but he could—in fact, he often had to—censor it. Once again Joe Breen had to be placated. Fitzgerald's writing on the screenplay soon wore itself into a kind of rut, one familiar to veteran Hollywood writers: Copy a few lines, put in something original now and then just to convince yourself that you are still something more than carbon paper.

Miss Booth's play, and therefore Fitzgerald's movie script, was a modern-day, Park Avenue *School for Scandal*. As Fitzgerald wrote his daughter, "I am doing the screenplay of *The Women* for Norma Shearer. My God, what characters! What gossip! Let me remind you never to discuss my affairs with a living soul."[12] Miss Shearer was to play Mary Haines, the victim of the gossip. The cast also embraced Rosalind Russell as Sylvia, described by Fitzgerald as a "Park Avenue b——"; Joan Fontaine as Peggy, who wants children but cannot afford both them and rich friends, too; Phyllis Povah as Edith, who has seen so much of money and maternity that she is bored with both; and Joan Crawford as Crystal, the girl all the others are talking about.

At the beginning of the play Sylvia tells her bridge partners of a fascinating morning she has just spent at the hairdresser's. While having her nails manicured, some gossip was dropped into the still pool of her mind and she cannot wait to start it making ever wider circles. Miss Booth had Sylvia say of her informant, a young manicurist named Olga, "You know how those creatures are, babble, babble, babble, babble, never let up for a minute! When suddenly she said: 'I know the girl who's being *kept* by Mr. Haines!' "[13] Fitzgerald knew Breen well enough to change the line to, "I know the girl that Mr. Haines is crazy about."[14] By the time the movie was finally made, they had cut the line completely.

In the play Sylvia goes on to philosophize about men, swearing, "I wouldn't be sure of the Apostle Paul."[15] Fitzgerald knew that Breen, a Catholic, along with many movie-goers, *would* be sure, so the saint was spared, i.e., cut from the script. The movie as filmed followed Scott's lead and also spared Paul.

Not content to do nothing but copy words out of someone else's play, Fitzgerald would occasionally add a joke of his own, usually a serious one, since he had grown into a grim joker. At one

point he had his women get into an argument about which building it was that one of their friends threw herself off of. "It was
the one with the ledge," Edith says, "—because the papers said
she bounced."[16] The talk here is reminiscent of that scene in
Tender Is the Night where Hannan and McKibben argue about
whether it was the Racquet Club or the Harvard Club to which
Abe North, beaten nearly lifeless in a speak-easy, crawled home
to die.

Paired with this macabre cynicism in Fitzgerald's screenplay,
one finds a sentimentality about hearth and home. All through
Miss Booth's tough little play, he wrote in lines praising home
wherever he could. In one speech he had Mary tell her friends
that home means "everything in the world"[17] to her. Now that
his own home had come crashing down about him like so many
dropped trays, Fitzgerald seems to have developed an orphan's
respect for the institution.

Mary Haines' home is threatened by Crystal Allen. Crystal be-
stows her favors on Mary's husband and he in turn opens his
charge accounts to her. Armed with her new visa to the world of
the upper classes, credit, this shopgirl boldly invades an exclusive
couturier's in a determined quest for the lingerie equivalent of a
Diamond as Big as the Ritz. "I'd like to see," Crystal announces
proudly, "the best underwear in the world."[18] To go with her fine
underthings, Mr. Haines buys his paramour a gift which becomes
her most prized possession: a silver-fox jacket.

Why did Scott write Sheilah's silver-fox fur into his script? Was
it the bitch in him? Or was he simply being the good artist, never
wasting anything? Helen Hayes remembers that "Sheilah Graham
was good to Scott, but he wasn't nice enough to her—ever." The
actress believes that the gossip columnist "represented to Scott's
fevered mind the second-rate he had fallen into." Zelda had been
first-rate, like the twenties, but with the twenties' fatal flaw,
burning with the bright, short-lived flame of paper when set
afire; she had been greatly admired, but in a moral sense never
quite admirable. Sheilah embodied a diminished decade, the
thirties; she was not dazzling the way Zelda had been, but as a

worker, an achiever, a caring nurse, she *was* admirable. Zelda and Sheilah were opposites which the author held unreconciled in his mind: the beautiful girl who was damned, and the not-so-beautiful girl who was his personal savior. In his writing Fitzgerald was turning away from young "flappers" in favor of heroines who could better cope with the new, harder times, but still he felt the loss, and sometimes made Sheilah feel it, too.

Although Fitzgerald did not invent the story or the characters, *The Women* turned out to be a good vehicle for the author's continuing ambivalence toward the very rich and the very spoiled. The opposing emotions in the author's mind were matched by opposing characters in the play. That is, some of the rich women in the story are sympathetic, but others are what Scott called rich "b——s." Fitzgerald sorted out the one from the other, of course, according to whether they were spoiled by their fortunes or did something worth while with them. This concept of *"richesse oblige"* reveals less about the way Fitzgerald's mind was working than do his examples of what he thought of as worth-while uses of wealth. Once again he chose to recommend the home: the good rich use their money to strengthen the home, the bad rich neglect their families.

Mary's greatest problem is that she has spent too much time with the do-nothings of the social world, the Sylvias, Peggys, and Ediths, so when her home is threatened she too does nothing. Her daughter, Little Mary, pleads, "Oh, mother, why don't you *do* something!"[19] But instead of fighting, Mary retreats to Reno.

The Beautiful and Damned had been a kind of vindication of a leisure class who never did much of anything, but now Fitzgerald was sick of that type. In July, while he was hard at work on *The Women,* he wrote a shrill letter to his daughter which made his opinion of idlers very plain:

> . . . [Zelda] wanted me to work too much for *her* and not enough for my dream. She realized too late that work was dignity, and tried to atone for it by working herself, but it was too late and she broke and is broken forever. . . .
>
> For a long time I hated *her* mother for giving her nothing in

the line of good habit—nothing but "getting by" and conceit. I never wanted to see again in this world women who were brought up as idlers. . . . I think that idlers seem to be a special class for whom nothing can be planned, plead as one will with them—their only contribution to the human family is to warm a seat at the common table. . . .

You don't realize that what I am doing here is the last tired effort of a man who once did something finer and better. There is not enough energy, or call it money, to carry anyone who is dead weight, and I am angry and resentful in my soul when I feel that I am doing this. . . . *You* have spent two years doing no useful work at all, improving neither your body nor your mind, but only writing reams and reams of dreary letters to dreary people. . . . It is like an old gossip who cannot still her tongue.[20]

It is almost as though Fitzgerald had gotten his daughter confused with one of the characters in the screenplay which he was writing.

One of the advantages of authorship over parenthood is that fictional characters have to do what the man with the pencil wants them to. So at the end of his screenplay Fitzgerald reformed Mary as he often despaired of reforming his daughter (who after all was not nearly so wild as he had been). Through most of the script Mary serves simply as another spoiled heroine, but in the end she becomes something more: a defender of the home. As a girl, Mary's head, like that of Rosalind and Gloria before her, might have been turned by the glitter of society, but as a middle-aged mother her heart is moved by her family. To make this point, Fitzgerald thought nothing of changing Clare Booth's ending.

In a note to Stromberg he argued that "the biggest triumph is not of Mary over Crystal but of the home over the more predatory and destructive habits of the female." He went on to suggest that this point could be best made by changing the setting of the play's last scenes. On Broadway these scenes had taken place in the powder room of a fashionable night club: word is sent into the powder room that Stephen Haines wants to see his wife, and the original Mrs. Haines (Mary), rather than the new Mrs. Haines (Crystal), goes out to meet him. "But I think in the picture," Fitzgerald wrote, "it would be best to take the action back to Mary's house. . . . The last scenes should show Mary coming into her house, waking her daughter, having a momentary scare whether or not Stephen is coming—then the door slowly opening from outside."[21]

The movie, when filmed, chose neither the suspense of Clare Booth's ending nor the return home of Fitzgerald's. One of Mary's friends simply comes into the powder room and says, "Stephen's out there—he's waiting for you."[22] Mary starts out to meet him, spreads her arms, The End.

Throughout Fitzgerald's screenplay one has the sense of a visit paid to the world of *This Side of Paradise* twenty years later. A real sadness lies half-hidden in that last scene, for The Home emerges as the place where paradise is supposed to be when a man or woman reaches middle age, as Fitzgerald had; but twenty years after the publication of *This Side of Paradise* a real home was exactly what Fitzgerald did not have.

3

Fitzgerald's script ended happily for Mary, but once again the author was not so lucky. As with *Three Comrades,* he had no sooner finished his solo script than a collaborator was put on the story with him. First, he was teamed with Sidney Franklin, who was not so much a writer as a brilliant director. Since their talents were so different, the two men did not really track up one another's snow.

But then Franklin was moved out and Donald Ogden Stewart moved in. Fitzgerald and Stewart had grown up in St. Paul together, and evidently the two boyhood rivals wasted no time in becoming studio rivals, for Fitzgerald later wrote in his notebooks:

> Don Stewart, unlike Elsa Maxwell, yearned after higher
> things. This yearning he indulged in a series of modest paro-

dies which he declared were "better than *Candide.*" However the attempt to convince himself brought on a short paranoia during which he made efforts to pull down the pillars on all our heads and hide in the ruins.[23]

The Fitzgerald-Stewart collaboration came to nothing. "Hunt was difficult to please," Fitzgerald later recalled, ". . . and toward the end Don and I lost interest."[24]

One day Stromberg had an idea. Get a woman! He called in Jane Murfin to adapt *The Women* for the screen. This time Fitzgerald was spared the pain of seeing someone else rewrite his words. Miss Murfin simply threw out his scripts entirely and started over from the beginning. Fearing the wrath of the censor, she was even more of a schoolmarm than Fitzgerald had been. Like him, she cleaned up Miss Booth's language so that ladies would not be afraid to come and see *The Women.* But she went even further. She cut one of the funniest scenes in the play, one which Fitzgerald had had the temerity to retain. It took place in the maternity ward where Peggy visits Edith and her newborn baby only to discover that, over the protests of nurses, the new mother has elected to suck on a cigarette while the baby performs a similar action on her. Peggy says, "Oh, Edith, isn't he divine!" Then stepping closer she cries, "What's that on his nose?" Edith: "What nose? Oh, that's an ash."[25] Inasmuch as Hollywood was anxious not to offend motherhood—it being widely held that Mother chose the movies the family would see —Miss Murfin allowed no ash to tarnish the madonna image.

By April 1, 1939, almost a year after Fitzgerald had begun the job, Miss Murfin finished it. Or so she thought. The blue cover came off her neatly mimeographed script and the pages were slipped into the new gold binding which signified final shooting script. The cameras were ready to roll. Then Stromberg reread the script one more time just to be sure, and discovered that he was not sure at all. Something was wrong. He had another idea. Get another woman!

Anita Loos was in her office working on dialogue for Gable or

Tracy or Garland or someone when her phone rang. Stromberg wanted to see her. When she reported to his office, he told her what the problem was. "We had to take out all of Clare Booth's dirty jokes," he said, "and now the script isn't funny any more." He wanted her to put laughs back into the story—clean laughs. They didn't hold up the picture. Miss Loos rewrote the script on the set, staying sometimes days, sometimes hours ahead of the camera.

The director to whom Miss Loos fed her dialogue was George Cukor. Known as a woman's director, he had just been replaced by Victor Fleming on *Gone with the Wind* because Clark Gable and David Selznick thought that he was giving all the best scenes to Scarlett O'Hara. Cukor in turn replaced Ernst Lubitsch on *The Women*, Lubitsch switching over to direct *Ninotchka*, and the movie-factory wheels kept turning. In fact, the assembly line turned out to be so impersonal that Cukor never realized that his old friend Fitzgerald had ever worked on the movie which he was given to direct.

Besides a woman screenwriter, Cukor had a cast of one hundred thirty-five women to direct, among them the studio's top stars. In a manly effort to keep the same cat fights from erupting off-camera as were being photographed on, the director developed a new method for calling his ladies to the sound stage when shooting was about to begin. Tradition dictated that the star be called first, but when a picture boasts Shearer, Crawford, Goddard, Fontaine, and Russell, all at the same time, who is *the* star? Cukor solved his dilemma by dispatching five boys to knock on all five doors simultaneously.

At a party one night Ernst Lubitsch saw Rosalind Russell dancing with Cukor and cracked, "Trying to get a close-up in the picture, I see!" He thought a while and then, referring to Irving Thalberg's widow, added, "But if you want to *stay* in the picture, you'd better dance with Miss Shearer."[26] Miss Russell took his advice: she and Miss Shearer danced the next number together.

Even before filming began, there was concern that especially Miss Shearer and Miss Crawford would try to live rather than act their clawing roles: long-time rival top cats at the studio, they had never before worked the same picture. When Thalberg had been alive, Joan had complained, "How can I compete with Norma when she sleeps with the boss?"[27] Now that Thalberg was dead, she was damned if she was going to treat her rival as Queen of Metro. The worst moment came during rehearsals for the only scene which Norma and Joan would ever play together in this picture or any other. It was, appropriately, the scene where the wife (Norma) confronts her husband's mistress (Joan). Miss Crawford, as actors' courtesy demands, was "feeding" Miss Shearer lines while Cukor rehearsed shots which would be made of Norma alone. But Joan's full attention was not on aiding her rival; she was also knitting, her needles clicking loudly. Norma asked Joan to stop, but Joan wouldn't. Then Norma turned to the director and demanded, "Mr. Cukor, I think Miss Crawford can go home now and you can give me her lines."[28] Cukor ordered Crawford off the set. That night Miss Shearer, who had once sent Scott Fitzgerald a telegram to try to patch over an embarrassing moment, received a wire from Miss Crawford which resulted in their never speaking to one another again—except to finish their cat-fight scene in the movie.

The picture premièred in September 1939 and soon had everyone gossiping. *Time* magazine liked the film but noted that "Prima Donna Shearer, for purely professional reasons, saw to it that she was billed above rival Prima Donna Crawford, stipulated that her name should be advertised in type half as large as the title and twice as large as that Lesser Luminary Russell."[29] Philip T. Hartung, writing in *Commonweal*, took an old-fashioned high moral line. "Men will find *The Women* unbelievable (if they have any gallantry)," he said. "Women will find *The Women* beautifully costumed, exaggerated and vulgarly frank . . . Children will find *The Women*—children better stay home."[30] Otis Ferguson observed in *The New Republic*, "It is a holiday from Hays all right: there is more wicked wit than Hollywood has been allowed since *The Front Page*."[31] Frank Nugent in the *New York Times* declared:

. . . the most heartening part of all . . . is the way Norma Shearer, Joan Crawford, Rosalind Russell, Paulette Goddard, and the others leaped at the chance to be vixens. Miss Shearer . . . is virtually the only member of the all-female cast who behaves as one of Hollywood's leading ladies is supposed to. And even Miss Shearer's Mary sharpens her talons finally and joins the birds of prey. . . . We don't know when we've ever seen such a terrible collection of women. They're really appallingly good, and so is their picture.[32]

Once again one of Fitzgerald's pictures had gotten good notices, but he failed to share in the glory. By the time the movie was released, he was looking for another job. While *The Women* was making money all across the country, Fitzgerald wrote his agent Leland Hayward that it would be futile to ask Stromberg for employment. "Hunt and I reached a dead end on *The Women*," he said. "We wore each other out. He liked the first part of a picture called *Infidelity* that I wrote so intensely that when the whole thing flopped I think he held it against me that I had aroused his hope so much and then had not been able to finish it."[33]

At the beginning of his work on *Infidelity* Fitzgerald had written to a friend, "this time I have the best producer in Hollywood."[34] Half a year and two unproduced scripts later, he scrawled in an uneven hand on a scrap of paper:

> Stromberg's assorted pickles gather near
> The wedding of the sickle and the dove
> All bridle-stiff with waiting we are here
> To make a song of petty-bourgeois love
> And flog dead horses through the afternoon
> Specifically the Metro-Goldwyn mare
> We who were meant to sing a newer tune
> Lie fallow in the Metro lion's care
> Stromberg, the name is like a solemn drum
> Beaten upon an ice floe in the north
> Grant that we shall not always rest here dumb
> Give us a date, let us for god pour forth

The woes of pretty faces
The mistakes[35]

In the fall of 1938, as Fitzgerald began work on his fifth script for Metro, he was growing panicky. "I am intensely busy," he wrote his daughter. "On the next two weeks, during which I finish the first part of *Madame Curie,* depends whether or not my contract will be renewed."[36]

☆ 10 ☆

Madame Curie:
Brave New Heroine

1

Aldous Huxley spread a batch of French newspapers on his desk for Fitzgerald's inspection. Scott's French was not very good despite those years on the Riviera, but it was good enough to catch the scent of scandal.

"If we could tell *that* story," Huxley told Fitzgerald, "we might really have something."

It had already occurred to Fitzgerald that working with Aldous might be more fun than trying to get on with the Hollywood hacks he had so often been teamed with. Now he was sure. Not that he really wanted to team with anyone. After all, he had not needed any help to write his novels nor had Huxley needed any help to write his, so why should they have to lean on one another like two cripples to put together a movie about Mme. Curie? But Hollywood was like that. At least he and Huxley spoke the same language.

Still, Huxley's success at MGM must have been a little hard for Fitzgerald to take—all the more so because of the way he had gotten into the business in the first place. Scott had come three thousand miles from the East to try to break into pictures; Aldous had come to Beverly Hills for his health, not looking for a job at all, but Anita Loos was a good friend of his and before long she convinced him to help with the movie adaptation of Jane Austen's *Pride and Prejudice.* With Greer Garson as Elizabeth and Laurence Olivier as Darcy, the picture turned out to be a Hollywood classic. Huxley had made a brilliant beginning and was highly regarded at Metro.

After *Pride and Prejudice,* Huxley was assigned to *Madame Curie* along with Fitzgerald; the movie was to be based on Eve Curie's biography of her mother. It was Hollywood typecasting: the author who had described the brave new world of the future was a natural choice to tell the story of the discovery of the brave new element, radium.

Huxley read Eve Curie's book, but in the true scientific tradition he wanted to know more. He sent to Paris for all the back issues of French newspapers which had anything in them about his heroine. When the papers arrived, he found headlines about Mme. Curie's new element and her Nobel Prize. But there were other headlines too, and it was among these that Huxley made his own discovery: a new element in the great Mme. Curie herself. She had had a love affair and reporters had turned it into a grand scandal. Huxley could almost see the little hunchbacks with their loads of papers moving through the cafés of Paris, crying the news to the patrons. This café society might not understand radium, but it would understand an *affaire d'amour.*

This was the story which Huxley told Fitzgerald. Marie Curie's lover had been the young assistant in Pierre Curie's own laboratory. He showed Scott a picture of a cheap hotel on the Left Bank of the Seine. There was another picture, one of a room inside the hotel—*the* room. It was a big box with no decorations, barren as the Curies' laboratory itself, but with a bed pushed into one corner and above the bed a single picture, a photograph of Professor Pierre Curie. The young wife and the young assistant had hung the aging husband above the bed where (as Huxley later wrote) he "was . . . always looking at you, like Big Brother in Orwell's *Nineteen Eighty-Four.*"[1]

If they could only tell *that* story. But of course as long as Joe Breen had anything to say about it, great lady scientists would act like ladies and not like tarts. In the movies you had to give the kids something to look up to.

For the time being, the two writers put aside these clippings and went to work on the story they *could* tell. Aldous was selected by producer Sidney Franklin to write the treatment. In short order he turned out a hundred-page outline which gave the movie people the Mme. Curie they wanted to see. His best scene showed Marie as a miserable young girl working as a governess to earn enough money to go to the university. Since she is so unhappy, she tells one of her charges, a little boy, the story of the Spartan boy who hid a young fox under his coat while at school and then let the fox bite him to death rather than cry out. Taking the story to heart, the little boy tells his governess, "I wouldn't want to be a Spartan. Would you, Miss Marie?" Marie answers, "*I* wouldn't want to be a crybaby."[2]

Huxley soon tired of the regimentation of studio work and quit MGM to return to "literature." Years later, however, he decided to put in writing the story which he could not tell in a moving-picture house: the story of a young wife and the young assistant who made love while a gloomy old scientist looked on from his place on the wall as if this were nothing more than another experiment. "Maybe the total reality is always too undignified to be recorded," Huxley wrote in his novella *The Genius and the Goddess*, "too senseless or too horrible to be left unfictionalized. All the same it's exasperating, if one happens to know the facts, it's even rather insulting, to be fobbed off with Soap Opera."[3]

With Huxley gone, MGM decided to allow Fitzgerald to go it alone with *Madame Curie*—they were giving him one last chance. On this picture Fitzgerald got a break: a producer whom he continued to get on with very well. Sidney Franklin, whom Scott first met while working on *The Women,* had been one of Irving Thalberg's most trusted lieutenants. Thalberg had picked Franklin to direct Norma Shearer in her second talkie, *The Last of Mrs. Cheney.* He also directed Miss Shearer, Fredric March, and

Charles Laughton in *The Barretts of Wimpole Street,* and Paul
Muni and Luise Rainer in *The Good Earth.* He was even entrusted with handling the famed stage performers Alfred Lunt
and Lynn Fontanne in their first film, *The Guardsman,* a picture
whose discarded rushes are said to have been more prized than
the movie itself. It seems that Miss Fontanne was bathing while
a camera trained on her nude back. When a phone rang the
actress turned to see what it was—turned directly toward the
camera as Franklin screamed, "Cut! Cut!"[4] But Franklin was not
only good with actors—he was good with writers, too. Even after
Fitzgerald left Metro, he included Franklin on a list of movie
executives "who *do* like me."[5] (He had a longer list of people
who didn't.)

One newspaper reported that "F. Scott Fitzgerald . . . has
drawn the scenario writing assignment for which most Hollywood writers would have given a right arm. . . . He is adapting
The Life of Madame Curie for Greta Garbo."[6] It was a dream
assignment, but if dreams are the stuff that movies are made of,
they have little to do with the actual manufacture of pictures.
To begin with, Eve Curie thought that Garbo, star of *The
Temptress* and *Flesh and the Devil,* was too exotic to play *her*
mother, so Greer Garson was cast in the role. Miss Garson, who
described herself as "Metro's Glorified Mama,"[7] had played the
wholesome bride in *Goodbye Mr. Chips,* as well as Elizabeth in
Pride and Prejudice; later she would play the title role in *Mrs.
Miniver.* She seemed safe enough. But the trouble in finding a
star forecast more trouble to come for this star-crossed picture.

2

Fitzgerald began work on the new script in a new house. Sheilah
Graham had been afraid that the Malibu beach house would be
too cold for Scott in the winter, so she rented a place in Encino
in the warm San Fernando Valley. Their new home was located
on actor Edward Everett Horton's estate, which—to Fitzgerald's
dismay—was called "Belly Acres." For years there had been
people from Ernest Hemingway right through to Joe Mankiewicz

who thought of Fitzgerald as a whiner. Now Scott could almost
hear them laughing until their stomach muscles hurt. The Old
Belly Acher had found his true home at last! "How can I tell
anyone I live in 'Belly Acres'?" he asked Sheilah, outraged.

There was a huge lawn and a garden full of roses all hemmed
in by a picket fence; there was a swimming pool and tennis
court and magnolia trees with deck chairs under them; a little
way off stood a fir and birch wood. But Fitzgerald remained cold
toward the place.

When Buff Cobb came for a visit, he asked her, "Don't you
think this is a rather uninspired house?"

"I don't know," she said. "The garden is lovely. . . . And all
those little pickets look like little gravestones in a Confederate
graveyard."

"Sheilah," Scott called, running into the house. "She's made
the place livable! We've got romance in the house."[8]

It was about this time that Miss Graham decided to read
Fitzgerald's books. "Scott," she said one evening, "I feel badly.
Here you are, a famous writer, and I've not read a thing you've
written. I want to read every one of your books."

"Do you really?" he asked, a little like a girl who has been kept
waiting too long for a proposal. "All right, Sheilo," he said. "I'll
get you my books. Let's get them tonight."

After dinner the couple paid a visit to Hollywood's largest
bookstore. "Have you books by F. Scott Fitzgerald?" the author
asked.

"Sorry—none in stock," the young clerk told him, and turned
to a customer whose tastes were more up to date.

"Do you have any calls for them?" Fitzgerald insisted.

"Oh—once in a while," the boy said. "But not for some time,
now."

Sheilah suggested, "Let's try another place," but the second
store was like the first.

At the third store they found a gray-haired man up on a ladder.
He had no Fitzgerald in stock either but was good enough to

suggest, "I believe I can get hold of a title or two. Which ones are you interested in?"

"I'd appreciate that," Scott said and ordered *This Side of Paradise, The Great Gatsby,* and *Tender Is the Night*.[9]

Shaken by this experience, Scott wrote to Maxwell Perkins at Scribner's, begging for a new life for his works:

Dear Max:

Since the going-out-of-print of *Paradise* and the success (or is it one?) of [Hemingway's] *The Fifth Column* I have come to feel somewhat neglected. Isn't my reputation being allowed to let slip away? I mean what's left of it. I am still a figure to many people and the number of times I still see my name in *Time* and *The New Yorker,* etc., makes me wonder if it should be allowed to casually disappear—when there are memorial double deckers to such fellows as Farrell and Steinbeck.

I think something ought to be published this spring. You had a plan for the three novels . . . the recession is over for awhile and I have the most natural ambition to see my stuff accessible to another generation. . . . A whole generation now has never read *This Side of Paradise*. . . .

You can imagine how distasteful it is to blow my own horn like this but it comes from a deep feeling that something could be done, if it is done at once, about my literary standing— always admitting that I have any at all.[10]

The weeks passed and the Los Angeles bookstore finally located the Fitzgerald titles Scott had ordered. Sheilah took them and started her reading where the author had started his writing, with *This Side of Paradise*. When she had finished, he asked, "What do you think?"

"Well," she said, "it's not as good as Dickens."

Scott was irritated. "Of course it's not as good as Dickens,"[11] he growled.

Sheilah liked the short stories, *The Great Gatsby,* and *Tender Is the Night* much better, and that pleased Scott. But it must have seemed to him that this girl with whom he now shared his life was the only one still reading his books. He desperately wanted to get his name back before the public, and if Scribner's was not going to put him in the bookstores, then perhaps Metro would give the author who had been famous for twenty years that half second of fame which a screen credit represented. Fitzgerald knew what he had to do. As Joan Crawford might have put it, he had to write hard on *Madame Curie*.

3

To jog his imagination he would play Pierre Curie and Sheilah would play Marie, and they would act out the scenes together as if *they* themselves were on the trail of something new. They were. They were helping one another and that kind of in-harness cooperation was to be an important part of what the picture was about. In fact, the real subject of Fitzgerald's screenplay was not so much the discovery of a new element as the discovery of a new kind of marriage, something unlike anything he had ever known with Zelda. The great experiment which absorbed the writer and his girl, like the Curies in his script, had to do with sharing work and love at the same time. To Fitzgerald that kind of partnership was like radium: very rare.

Sometimes when Scott played Pierre and Sheilah, Marie, they wouldn't have much to say to one another—they could almost have been acting out their parts in different rooms. Perhaps Scott would say that he hoped that Sheilah didn't whistle the way his last laboratory assistant had, and Sheilah would assure him that she did not; then silence again. That was the kind of picture the author wanted it to be—one with many quiet scenes which recalled the quiet of *Infidelity*. At the same time, however, he was learning more about how to use a sound track, so sound was to be as important in some scenes as silence was in others. He was moving in the direction of a balanced script, one not too loquacious but not too quiet either. He was also moving in the direction of a new heroine.

Within the spectrum of Fitzgerald's women, Marie Curie is

much closer to, say, Kathleen in *Tycoon* than she is to Fitzgerald's
earlier heroines, those in the tradition of Gloria Gilbert, who had
to be cared for. Just as in his own life Fitzgerald had moved
from Zelda, whom he took care of, to Sheilah Graham, who often
had to take care of him, so in his writing he moved from
Gloria Gilbert to Kathleen and Mme. Curie. In *Tender Is the
Night* the hero had been a doctor to the heroine, but in "An
Alcoholic Case," a story which Fitzgerald wrote during his
first year in Hollywood, the hero has fallen: now it is he who is
nursed by the heroine. In this story Fitzgerald's heroine had
just been to see the movie *Pasteur,* and it brings back memories
of her student nursing days when she and the other young nurses
would "swing across the streets in the cold weather at Phila-
delphia General, as proud of their new capes as debutantes in
their furs going to balls at the hotels."[12] It is this tradition to
which Mme. Curie belongs: she is an anti-debutante.

Like his fictional nurse, Fitzgerald too had seen the movie
about Pasteur, had been moved by it. That was the kind of film
he wanted *Madame Curie* to be. At the beginning of the project,
he addressed a note to his bosses: "As one who believes that such
a production as Suez set pictures back by three years—insulting
the public it gained in Zola and Pasteur by distorting history
into grotesque musical comedy—I approach this book [the
biography of Mme. Curie] with honest reverence." He wrote that
Mme. Curie represented "work and the creation of the modern
woman," adding that "from the Victorian lady who specialized
in China painting and refined music we travel, in the course of
one lifetime, to the achieved perfection of Madame Curie."

"The picture will be doing a great wrong," he said, "if [we]
do not present Madame Curie as an image of everything the
woman of the future should aspire to. We must frighten no one
away by a moral tale, but we must send them off at the end of two
hours feeling that they spent that time with someone so fine that
they will remember it for months and years."[13]

Some of Fitzgerald's earlier heroines had had much in common
with that "Victorian lady" who painted dishes, but his new

heroine, "the woman of the future," would "aspire to" much more, would pour out her art and energy on a stage much greater than a china dinner plate.

Fitzgerald worked on *Madame Curie* because he had been assigned to it, not because she was the one person in the world whom he most wanted to write about. And yet a real empathy comes through in his descriptions of her, for the problems which she faced were in some ways the problems which he faced, too. "It is not a story for cheap sentimentality," he wrote.

> We must be true to Mme. Curie, who did not like fools— in high places or low. We must dramatize the fact that much of the great work of the world is done in loneliness and neglect—and to do that we must concentrate, as she did, upon the work itself, and its glory. We must see her as a gorgeous instrument of human achievement. We must not ape the public that she ran away from by making a goddess of her—a great impossible close-up of a monster, what the public calls a genius. No, we must pull aside a curtain and let others see as individuals what they would like to have seen in Marie's lifetime—what it was that made her so great and fine and good, so that those who came to adore remain to love.

Once courted, once called "genius," Fitzgerald too knew what it was like to labor in loneliness and neglect. He too was trying to "concentrate" upon the "glory" of work, to be a serious writer.

Fitzgerald's new heroine led the writer naturally to a new kind of love scene, one where the prom or country club or villa is replaced by a scientist's laboratory. Pierre Curie and the then Marie Sklodowska are strangers to one another when, by chance, they are assigned to share the same lab. Their first interest in one another depends not upon one human being's need for another, but upon their common need for a particular scientific scale. There is only one such scale in their laboratory and Marie and Pierre soon learn that they must share it.

Fitzgerald wanted to begin his courtship scene by showing a close-up of Marie at the balance. She is carefully removing a mineral specimen from one pan, a weight from the other when Pierre appears in the frame.

PIERRE: May I?[14]

He picks up the scales and weights and carries them to his own workbench. A few moments later Marie, working in a wrinkled white smock, misses something she needs and begins to look for it. Remembering, she crosses the laboratory to Pierre's side.

MARIE: May I?

She picks up the balance and carries it back to her own table. Not long after, Pierre reappears at Marie's bench to retrieve it, but she is busy weighing a grain of uranium.

PIERRE: Don't hurry.

While he waits, he tries to tell the girl about something Professor Becquerel discovered that day. Marie waves him silent as she notes something down, then looks up. A little snubbed, Pierre takes up his story of the uranium which Becquerel wrapped in sensitized paper, placed in a dark drawer, and promptly forgot.

PIERRE: When he opened it, there was an impression of its shape on the paper.

His story finished, Curie indicates the scales and asks:

PIERRE: Through?

Marie is, and Pierre disappears with the balance. A few moments later, however, he returns, carrying the instrument. Marie looks up, surprised, as he replaces the scales on her table.

MARIE: Thank you.

This scene is in the right setting, the laboratory, with the right unhurried pace, characteristic of scientific investigation, and Fitzgerald gives us the right visual metaphor, the scientific balance. Marie and Pierre's love for one another will soon grow to be as delicately "balanced" as the piece of scientific machinery

which brought them together. We see in this one scene Fitzgerald's matured definition of marriage. The Curies are a sharing
couple: they share a balance, a laboratory, and later their life
work. There will be no room in the Curie's laboratory or in their
lives for someone like Gloria Gilbert, someone who would tip
the scales in her own direction. Appropriately, the scene also
reveals another kind of balance, a technical one: the poignant
use of silence is married to a few lines of simple dialogue.

Near the end of Fitzgerald's unfinished screenplay, Marie's
extravagant love for her father and her Polish fatherland force
her to abandon a brilliant scientific career and the genius who
could have helped her forge it. She plans to return to Poland to
become a tutor, and Pierre believes that he will never see her
again. On the way to the train which will carry Marie into self-
exile, the two lovers pause in a courtyard. In a well-worn room
above them, a tired man at a piano plays Chopin's Waltz in C
Minor. The pianist is Ignace Paderewski, a Polish refugee living
in poverty who will later become prime minister of a liberated
Poland. The music strengthens what Fitzgerald called the "emotional backbone" of his story and yet it is introduced without
relying on the contrived device of background music. The piano
is a part of the story, a voice, and its lines are as important as
any others.

Marie boards her train and begins the trip which carries her
farther and farther from Pierre and physics, but halfway home,
she writes a letter to the man left behind in Paris. "I realized
that half of me was missing," she tells him. "I could never be a
complete person alone. So I am coming back in the fall—and
we will solve the equation together."[15] To Fitzgerald, who was
aged beyond his years, the proper metaphor for life was no
longer "paradise." It was an equation, a problem, which could
not even be attempted alone.

4

"I am intensely busy. On the next two weeks, during which I
finish the first part of *Madame Curie*, depends whether my con-

tract will be renewed. So naturally I am working like hell—"
Fitzgerald had written his daughter around Christmas, then
added, "—though I wouldn't expect you to understand that—
and getting rather bored with explaining the obvious over and
over to a wrong-headed daughter."[16] In other words, Scottie
was behaving more like an early Fitzgerald heroine than like a
Marie Curie, and Scott was displeased.

Perhaps he sensed that he was failing at MGM just as he had
failed at Princeton twenty years before, and so he naturally
assumed that Scottie, so much like him, would be failing out of
Vassar too. In his panicky frame of mind he felt it his duty to
warn her. *"The whole damn thing about going to the college is
to keep it in proportion,"* he wrote. "Did you ever hear of a college
boy, unless he were an idiot, racing from Smith to Vassar to
Wellesley? There are certain small sacrifices for a college education or there wouldn't be any honor in having gone to college."[17]

In his next letter the father gave a kind of play-by-play of the
fall he foresaw for his daughter:

> Knowing your character, here's about the way things will
> go in the next month. You have four weeks before Christmas
> and probably you intend to try hard, but at the moment you
> have gotten into some entanglement in Baltimore that you
> either want to go deeper into or get out of, or put on ice—
> in any case, that will require two or three days of letter
> writing absorption. Then you will do well for three days—
> until the reply to your letter sets you off again. By now your
> impetus will be exhausted and you will have a good three-day
> low—the movies and New York, forget to hand in a theme, or
> something like that. Two weeks gone. Then, alas, one of those
> things will happen against which only the wisest will guard—
> a two-day cold, an unexpected change of Christmas plans, some
> personal trouble or upset. Then there's only a week left and
> despite frantic hours you will have another failure on your
> hands. Don't you see that this is just how it happens? Where's
> that "common sense" that you boast about?[18]

And then a little later:

> Your letter came. Touched that you wish I wouldn't worry
> about the marks and enlightened to know why freshmen are
> marked hard. "I don't see why you're so furious because I'm
> not brilliant" is a sentence that touches my heart. I don't know
> whether it's the thought or the style that impresses me most.

The father went on to make fun of a play Scottie had written.
"Which was your philosophical poem?" he asked. "'Be my little
little little, little wife?'"[19] A year later—after Fitzgerald had
calmed down—he liked his daughter's poem better, so much
better in fact that he used it in his best screenplay, *Cosmopolitan*.

Scottie, of course, managed to stay at Vassar much longer than
Scott stayed at Metro. No one still alive seems to remember just
why Fitzgerald was fired halfway through *Madame Curie*. He
had known that the renewal of his contract depended on how well
the Curie script went, but it seemed to be going brilliantly. On
the other hand, Scott was not a brilliant diplomat. He never had
been. At Newman, when he was in his teens, he had been "the
freshest boy," the one who knew it all and told you so. He had
also been the loneliest boy there. Now he was the freshest screenwriter. Not that he really said that much to anyone, but he was
always writing an endless succession of bitter letters and memos,
indelible angry words which remained on his bosses' desks long
after verbal outbursts would have faded into silence. The angry
boss who finally bounced Fitzgerald was probably Bernie Hyman,
or at least Scott thought so. Hyman, one of Metro's College of
Cardinals, hardly fit the central casting stereotype of a Hollywood
impresario: he was modest, soft-spoken, and even a little shy.
But Fitzgerald was sure that "Bernie Hyman quite definitely
doesn't like me. I don't know why because I've scarcely exchanged
two words with him."[20]

Fitzgerald explained his removal from *Madame Curie* to his
agent as follows: "We [Scott and producer Franklin] were buck-
ing Bernie Hyman's preconception of the thing as a love story.

Hyman glanced at what we had done and shelved the whole project. Franklin had been very interested up to that time."[21] When *Madame Curie* was taken out of Scott's hands, he wired Hyman:

> RESPECTFULLY SUGGEST THE BEST WAY TO GET $5000 WORTH OF USE OUT OF MY CONTRACT IS TO ORDER A 1200 WORD ORIGINAL FOR SOME SPECIAL ACTORS STOP I HAVE AN IDEA FOR BEERY AND GARLAND AND COULD CERTAINLY PRODUCE A COMEDY OF MANNERS IDEA FOR SOME YOUNG ACTRESS STOP AM AT YOUR SERVICE OF COURSE BUT ORIGINAL IDEAS ARE PART OF MY STOCK IN TRADE THAT YOU HAVEN'T YET TAPPED STOP[22]

No original was ordered. Fitzgerald was through at MGM. In his notebook, he wrote, "Mayer started as a junk dealer—now he is again."

The love-science equation which Hyman thought Fitzgerald had failed to solve went on to become a legendary writer-breaker. No one seemed to be able to get it right—*right* being defined as the way Hyman wanted it. As an unnamed Metro executive told a *New York Times* reporter, "One [writer] would get carried away with the romantic elements of the Curies' life and would stress that to the detriment of the scientific features. Another, scientifically minded, would be too intent on the physicist angles, and the romance would suffer."[23] As the years went by, writer after writer worked on the script, only to be fired or transferred to another picture.

The war began and still the work on *Madame Curie* dragged on. Sometime toward the beginning of 1942, a CalTech physicist named Dr. Rudolph M. Langer was called in as a consultant. He set up a laboratory at Metro where he and Franklin re-enacted the major experiments which had led the Curies to radium.

The problem of making desperately static laboratory experiments dramatic on the screen at first led the movie makers to help on some visual melodrama. Stealing from all those mad-scientist movies, they planned to fan the drama by showing sparks sizzling about the lab as the Curies searched for the new element. Fortunately Dr. Langer was on hand to complain that "it would be false to science."[24]

Soon everyone at MGM was calling the good CalTech professor "I-Don't-Like-It-Dr.-Langer." When asked whether his reasons for disliking certain scenes were scientific or dramatic, he would usually reply, "Both." When pressed, he would explain, "Scientists don't act that way."[25] By this he generally meant that no matter how tense the moment, a scientist would always remain calm. It is not hard to imagine what he would have thought of the movie that Huxley wanted to make, the one about the wife and the assistant.

A final shooting script written by Paul Osborn and Hans Rameau was not ready until Christmas 1942, some four years after Huxley and Fitzgerald had first been assigned the picture. Then, after so much writer trouble, the picture developed director trouble. Albert Lewin quit and all of the footage which he had shot was scrapped. Work stopped completely for two weeks until Mervyn Le Roy took over.

Madame Curie did not open until December 1943, by which time Fitzgerald was already three years dead. Begun in 1938, it had taken longer to make the movie (five years) than it had for the Curies themselves to carry out the experiments which led to the discovery of the radium (four and one half years). Of course the $1,400,000 which the long-delayed picture cost would have bought and sold many times over the leaky shack which the Curies used as their radium lab.

After all that time and money, the picture as finally made was much like the picture Fitzgerald had originally hoped for. Almost none of his words survived the years and years of rewriting, but the rewritten script captured the same spirit which Scott had captured. If Bernie Hyman had wanted a love story only, in the end Franklin won and was allowed to make a film which was true both to the Curies' romance and to their work, the one always depending on the other. And the critics generally appreciated what Franklin had made of his story.

Bosley Crowther, who replaced Frank Nugent as the *New York Times* film critic wrote:

Behind the discovery of radium, and behind the long years of patient toil which eventually contributed to humanity one of the greatest of all the elements, lay a story of personal devotion and loyalty to a high ideal which should be a lasting inspiration to all those who hold mankind in true regard. And it is this story—the story of the Curies, a French scientist and his famous little wife—which Metro has told impressively and with fine cinematic restraint. . . . The most absorbing action of the picture is that which has to do with the search for the elusive radium—and this is the more surprising because of the dramatic problem involved. . . . [The film] has made [the Curies'] absorption in science as comprehensible as the urge to read good books, and it has pictured their collaborative union as a warm and richly rewarding love.[26]

Time wrote, "*Madame Curie* emphatically establishes Director Le Roy in Hollywood's top drawer, and frail, modest Producer Franklin in the seven-league shoes of the late Irving Thalberg." The magazine went on to say:

[The movie] devotes itself to dramatizing matters seldom attempted on the screen: the beauty, dignity, and calm of a marriage earnestly, rather than romantically, undertaken, the binding and illuminating power of a rare intellectual companionship and a grinding work performed in common. *Madame Curie* is probably as unerotic and maturely human a romance as Hollywood has yet attempted.[27]

One could almost believe that *Time* was reviewing the script Fitzgerald himself had written nearly five years before.

With Sheilah Graham, Fitzgerald must have hoped to have a romance which would rival the romance he had written for the Curies—a romance where the lovers solved all their equations together, where each partner was half of a delicate balance. He ministered to Miss Graham's mind, teaching her literature, history, music, philosophy, in their College of One; Sheilah for her part took care of Scott's health and tried to keep him away from alcohol. They even worked together writing her radio broadcasts and filling his notebooks for the Hollywood novel he was going to write. But all too soon the balance's strong right arm began to weaken. The trouble began in earnest when Scott was fired from MGM.

Years before when Amory Blaine had received an envelope from the Princeton dean and had known that a blue slip meant failure and a white one a passing grade, he had torn the cover off and waved the slip in the air, shouting, "Blue as the sky, gentlemen."[28] But in California where the sky was really blue, Fitzgerald no longer had that kind of strength. Eddie Knopf, the man who had hired him in the first place, had already told him what was coming. When the notice finally arrived, signed only by the Metro treasurer—and not even an explanation—he tucked it away out of sight. He made no speeches. No one remembers his last words at the studio—perhaps he left without saying anything to anyone. He cleared out his desk and then toppled the long line of empty Coca-Cola bottles. They had done their job for a year and a half, but they would not be able to protect the alcoholic much longer.

Free-Lancing

1

At home, Tara, Scarlett O'Hara stood at the top of a tall stair-case like a fine porcelain teapot high up out of reach on the top shelf of the china closet. Beneath her at the foot of the stairs stood handsome Rhett Butler. But of course it wasn't really Tara. It was Belly Acres. And it wasn't really Scarlett. It was Sheilah—the former chorus girl who wanted to be an actress but who had settled for gossip columnist—playing Vivien Leigh playing Scarlett O'Hara. Nor was it really Rhett. It was Scott—the acting hopeful who had flunked out of the movies in 1927 when his screen test flopped—playing Clark Gable playing Rhett Butler. They were acting out the staircase scene to help Scott with his writing. He had worked on the scene for a week, asking himself, "What would she say to him? What would he say to her?"—until finally he and his helper decided simply to play the scene and find out what got said. Sheilah scampered to the top of their winding staircase and struck a strained pose; Scott took his place at the bottom. Nor was it enough for him to be the leading man and the writer in this production—he made himself the director as well. "Now, slowly," he told Sheilah, "—keep your eyes on me—"

Slowly, her head and skirts lifted, the mock Scarlett began her descent. From below Scott looked up and smiled that half smile he had learned back in the twenties, back when the public considered *him* one of the great lovers and Clark Gable was nothing but a heavy playing in road shows.

"Miss O'Hara," he said.

Scarlett waved an imaginary fan. "Captain Butler, I believe."

Rhett Butler broke up laughing.

Sheilah's reserved Scarlett suddenly gave way to a little girl skittering down the stairs and into her captain's arms. "Am I really such an awful actress?" she asked. "I tried to help."

Scott didn't hesitate. "Sheilah," he said, "it might be better if I work it out on paper."[1]

The man whom Fitzgerald was trying to "work it out" for was David O. Selznick, L. B. Mayer's son-in-law. When Selznick had been moved into Thalberg's old job as head of production at Metro back in 1933, the movie world wisecracked, "The son-in-law also rises."[2] But Selznick left MGM and his father-in-law's wing in 1935 to found his own independent company, Selznick International. The next year Kay Brown, his story editor, asked him to read a novel by an unknown Southern writer. When Selznick paid out fifty thousand of his fledgling company's small cash reserves for the screen rights, he had to listen to a lot of Hollywood pros lecture him about how Civil War stories never made any money.

When MGM fired Fitzgerald, he went directly to Selznick and landed a job on *Gone with the Wind*. The producer already had a script, but he couldn't leave it alone. Rewriting would continue right up to the moment a shot was filmed and printed. Scott was given a fat sheaf of papers bound in yellow, and asked to apply his art as if it were a kind of cosmetic—highlighting here, painting over ugly lines there. Not only was he not writing an original—he was required to make his rewriting as unoriginal as possible. As Fitzgerald later told Maxwell Perkins, "In that

Gone with the Wind job I was absolutely forbidden to use any words except those of Margaret Mitchell; that is, when new phrases had to be invented, one had to thumb through as if it were Scripture and check out phrases of hers which would cover the situation!"³

The man chosen to direct the picture was Scott's old friend George Cukor. But Selznick had reservations about George, especially about his reputation as a woman's director. "Look, don't let Scarlett romp all over Rhett Butler," Selznick told Fitzgerald one day. "George will try and throw everything to her. You and I have got to watch out for Clark."⁴

Selznick pushed his writers hard on the *Wind*, even staying up late with them some nights and working as a combination boss and collaborator. When Fitzgerald finally got a day off, he wrote his daughter:

> Day of rest! After a wild all-night working on *Gone with the Wind* and more to come tomorrow. I read it—it is a good novel—not very original, in fact leaning heavily on *The Old Wives' Tale, Vanity Fair,* and all that has been written on the Civil War. There are no new characters, new techniques, new observations—none of the elements that make literature—especially no new examination into human emotions. But on the other hand it is interesting, surprisingly honest, consistent and workmanlike throughout, and I felt no contempt for it but only a certain pity for those who consider it the supreme achievement of the human mind. So much for that—I may be on it two weeks—or two months.⁵

Fitzgerald gave Selznick his first bundle of *Gone with the Wind* revisions January 11, and more batches followed almost daily. His job encompassed more than reworking the script: he had to be a kind of salesman, making a special pitch for each of his "improvements." Following Selznick's orders, Scott was careful to mark all passages which he touched and to justify all his changes in marginal notes. He suggested some alterations for practical reasons which had nothing to do with his over-all motion-picture aesthetic. In one scene, for example, Scarlett

O'Hara (Vivien Leigh) wraps a yellow sash about the waist of Ashley Wilkes (Leslie Howard). The original script had Ashley say, "It looks like gold." Scott crossed out the line, reminding Selznick, "This is technicolor."[6]

Fitzgerald made more telling changes in a scene where Ashley tells Scarlett of the tragic plight of the Southern armies, who have "no arms—no food. . . ." In the margin, Fitzgerald asked sarcastically, "It's news that the South fought without arms?" He replaced this catalogue list of needed supplies with a moving line about yet another invader from the North, snow. "When our shoes wear out," Fitzgerald had Ashley say, "—well some of the men are barefooted now and the snow is deep in Virginia."

Ashley tells Scarlett that he can talk to her honestly of the impending doom awaiting the South as he never could to Melanie or Aunt Pitty. Fitzgerald crossed out the rest of Ashley's speech where he says that the other Southern women do not have Scarlett's fiber; that her strength comes from her Irish blood; and that she has the courage to look at life as it really is. In the margin beside the deleted lines, Fitzgerald wrote, "I still think it's dull and false for one character to describe another."

Many of Fitzgerald's changes amounted simply to crossing out script dialogue and restoring dialogue from the novel itself. Beside many of the screenplay's big speeches Fitzgerald wrote "trite and stagy." Time and time again he found Margaret Mitchell's "good dialogue . . . infinitely more moving" than the more sophisticated made-in-Hollywood lines. The ex-novelist was coming to the aid of his fellow craftsman.

Of all Fitzgerald's changes, perhaps the most poignant consisted simply of cuts with nothing added. By removing much of the original dialogue, he was attempting to make the drama quieter, more understated. In one scene Scarlett watches as Ashley and his new wife Melanie (Olivia de Havilland) start up to bed. The beautiful, spoiled Scarlett still loves Ashley, of course, and cannot comprehend how he could have chosen his plain cousin over *her*. The script which was given to Fitzgerald had Melanie and Ashley pause at the head of the stairs and look down at Scarlett; the wife says, "Good night, dear," and the husband, "Goodnight, Scarlett." Scott cut the pause and the dialogue, explaining, "I think they have said 'good night' downstairs. It seems to me stronger in silence." He knew that there were times when the most moving thing a screenwriter could say was nothing.[7]

These changes and many others Selznick agreed to: Scott left his footprints on *The Wind*.

Fitzgerald went on to rework the great movie's colorful ball scene where the belles and heroes of Atlanta are shocked when Rhett Butler buys a dance from Scarlett O'Hara; the midwife scene where with Atlanta in flames Scarlett delivers Melanie's child, Ashley's son; and the final flight from Atlanta with Scarlett and Rhett Butler on the front seat of a buckboard fighting their way through mobs of looters as the burning buildings collapse in great avalanches of fire. Perhaps it occurred to Fitzgerald as he rewrote someone else's script that he was pulling a Joe Mankiewicz, but that was what the movie business could do to you. Besides, for the most part his changes did make the script leaner, less flowery-sentimental.

Having survived work on the movie's major scenes, Fitzgerald finally lost his job over a minor episode involving a minor character. Aunt Pitty was simply more than he could handle. The trouble began when director George Cukor took out time to teach an important lesson about film-making. Scott described it afterward:

. . . George comes suddenly into Selznick's office. He looks worried. He says to Selznick, "Do I understand we start shooting tomorrow?" "Yes," says David. "But we're not ready," says Cukor, adding that he wants new scenes for Scarlett's arrival at Aunt Pitty's in Atlanta. "Then we'll just have to work all night," Selznick replies. One of the current authors on the picture [Scott] groans and telephones his fiancée [Sheilah] not to expect him for dinner. The conference begins.

"What worries me," says George, "is the character of Aunt Pitty."

"What's the matter with her?" says Selznick.

"She's supposed to be quaint," says Cukor, who is the brain behind the camera. "That's what it says in the book."

"That's what it says in the script too," says Selznick. He opens the script and reads: "Aunt Pitty bustles quaintly across the room."

"That's just what I mean," interrupts Cukor. "How can I photograph that? How do you 'bustle quaintly across the room?' It may be funny when you read about it, but it won't look like anything at all."

They argue about this question for three long hours, and the two writers try desperately to *make* Aunt Pitty funny and not just *say* she's funny. Which are two different things.

By midnight, Cukor and Selznick fire one of the writers. The other writer is sent home and immediately a telegram is dispatched saying that he [Scott] too will not be needed any more.[8]

While Fitzgerald labored over lesser films, *Gone with the Wind* was completed. The world première was held in Atlanta, once again bringing all manner of Yankees to the Southern city burned by Sherman. The chamber of commerce ballyhooed the grand event, and the Grand Theatre built a new false front which made it look like the portico of Twelve Oaks. Clark Gable was there along with his new wife Carole Lombard. When Vivien Leigh got off the plane, she pressed David Selznick's arm. "Listen," she said, surprised, "they're playing the music from the picture." He laughed and told the young English actress, "That's *Dixie*, dear."[9]

Gone with the Wind was a fair wind to the many who shared in its success. A star was born, Miss Leigh. Selznick became Hollywood's new wonder boy. In its first four months the picture grossed four million dollars; its first year it took in thirteen and a half million; by 1955 it had brought in fifty million; and in 1967 it was released again, this time on the seventy-millimeter screen and in stereo. But while other sails filled, Fitzgerald's only fluttered. Another historic production had swept past, leaving him worse off than before.

Nonetheless, a year after Fitzgerald was dropped from the Selznick payroll, he told his agent:

> Selznick International—I find this studio the pleasantest studio that I have worked in . . . but what Dave thinks of me I haven't any idea. I know that I was on the list of first choice writers on *Rebecca,* but that may have been Hitchcock's doing. I think that Dave is probably under the impression that I am a novelist first and can't get the idea as to what pictures are about. This impression is still from back in 1921 when he wanted me to submit an original idea for Elaine Hammerstein.[10]

2

"[After *Gone with the Wind*] I wanted to quit for a while," Fitzgerald later wrote, "—health bad and I was depressed about the Metro business. But Swanson argued me into a job with Wanger on *Winter Carnival* with a rise to $1500. This was a mistake."[11]

Producer Walter Wanger had hired Fitzgerald to collaborate with a young writer just three years out of Dartmouth named Budd Schulberg. Schulberg had already written a script based on Dartmouth's Winter Carnival, but neither the producer nor the young writer himself thought that it was any good. When Wanger started looking for someone to help doctor his college comedy, he naturally thought of the author of *This Side of Paradise.*

"My meeting with Scott Fitzgerald . . . still holds for me a dreamlike, legendary quality," Schulberg later wrote in *Esquire.* "Even while it was happening I felt as if the gods had swooped down and carried me off to serve as a minor player in one of their more extravagant myths." On the day it occurred, Wanger had called the unsuspecting Schulberg into his office and asked casually how he would like to team with F. Scott Fitzgerald. The younger writer shuddered, then wondered if his boss had

noticed. "My God," he asked, "isn't Scott Fitzgerald dead?"
Wanger answered, "On the contrary, he's in the next office
reading your script."[12]

When he was introduced to Fitzgerald, Schulberg saw a
figure who seemed to have been drawn with white chalk. He
recalls:

> There were no colors in him. The proud, somewhat too
> handsome profile of his earlier dust jackets was crumpled. To
> this day I am unable to say exactly what it was that left me
> with this lasting impression. The fine forehead, the leading
> man's nose, the matinee-idol set of the gentle, quick-to-smile
> eyes, the good Scotch-Irish cheekbones, the delicate, almost
> feminine mouth, the tasteful Eastern (in fact, Brooks Bros.)
> attire—he had lost none of these. But there seemed to be
> something physically or psychologically broken in him that had
> pitched him forward from scintillating youth to shaken old
> age.

Schulberg had happened to reread *The Great Gatsby* only a
few days before, and *Tender Is the Night* had been a favorite
of long standing. He remembers, "Scott was flattered and stimu-
lated and, it seemed to me, pathetically pleased to find any
product of the Depression thirties who knew, admired, and
could talk his books."

Fitzgerald, who was afraid that he had lost touch with the
young, had once written in his notebook, "Of course these boys
are more serious—this is the generation that saw their mothers
drunk."[13] The author who had heralded the speakeasy generation
of the twenties was so happy to find a young fan, and Schulberg
so pleased to have met a great writer, that they spent days just
getting to know one another. *Winter Carnival*, which Scott was
being paid three hundred a day to write, waited in a desk
drawer. Besides Fitzgerald's fiction, they also talked about politics, the cultural ebb and flow of generations, Hollywood and
movie making.

Schulberg was impressed by Fitzgerald's seriousness:

Scott was not a film snob. In fact he plunged into a study of film making that even included a card file of the plot lines of all the pictures he had seen. Although he thought of himself, naturally, as a novelist first and last, he was not, like so many novelists and playwrights I had known, in film work only for the fat Hollywood checks he neeeded to get back to his own line. He liked pictures and felt his talent was particularly well-suited to the medium.

Scott was not too good for film work in general, but when it came to *Winter Carnival* he was in no hurry to get started. On the one hand he was used to something better—*Three Comrades, Infidelity, Madame Curie,* or even *Gone with the Wind.* But on the other hand, since he had had trouble with the big movies he had worked on, now his confidence was crippled and he was not sure if he could handle even a small one.

Schulberg didn't worry. Why should he, with an Immortal helping him to write his script? He supposed that his collaborator was quietly working out the story and would presently interrupt their sprawling conversation to say, "Here's what we're going to do."

Meanwhile, in the quiet of the Valley nights, Sheilah Graham would hear Scott pacing back and forth, as if by moving the body he might trick the mind into motion too, or at least wear out his insomnia. "I was going to sleep every night with a gradually increasing dose of chloral," he wrote, "—three teaspoonfuls—and two pills of Nembutal every night and 48 drops of Digitalin to keep the heart working to the next day. Eventually one begins to feel like a character out of *The Wizard of Oz.* Work becomes meaningless and effort a matter of the medicine closet." One morning he announced, "My TB's flared up."[14] He began to run a low fever and to sweat his bed wet at night. Sheilah would change his sheets two or three times before morning.

The miles he walked within the confines of a single room, and the hours spent with a writing tablet to catch his thoughts as they fell, finally produced something tangible, a ten-page treatment for *Winter Carnival*. It began:

> First, as to the approach: Frankly, I haven't been able to look at this as a group picture in the sense that *Stagecoach* was, or *Grand Hotel*, with its sharp cuts between one melodrama scene and another. A winter carnival simply doesn't have that tense air of destiny that a journey has. It's a spread-out and expansive theme in itself. It has no real trajectory like a boat or stagecoach or a train. In the Dartmouth carnival the election of a queen is the committee's attempt to give it such a climax. So in my opinion this should be more akin to *She Loves Me Not*—it ought to have something of a plot.[15]

The author had studied his movie classics in the same way he had once studied classic novels.

The story Schulberg had written was about a glamour girl named Jill who takes her baby girl and flees her tyrannical husband, only to be stranded in mid-flight at Dartmouth during Winter Carnival when she gets off the train to stretch, and then stands helplessly by as the locomotive pulls off without her. To make matters worse, if Jill's husband catches up with her before she makes it across the border into Canada, he will take her child away from her. Even at a snow carnival with the temperature below zero, Hollywood could still make the old pot boil.

To Schulberg's brew, Fitzgerald wanted to add a villainess, a girl named Florine who in many ways resembled his own daughter Scottie. "She is a freshman at Vassar," he wrote, "and completely dazzled by New York—so much so that she has neglected her work and is on probation in college, a probation which she has broken to come to Dartmouth Winter Carnival, pretending she has been summoned home by the illness of her father. She is wild and feverish—in 1920, she would have been a flapper. At present she thinks she is ahead of the times, but she is really behind them."[16]

Scott also invented a "side-kick" for Florine, a girl known simply as the "little 'blind date' girl." "She never *does* meet her blind date, but goes *without a man* through the carnival,"

Fitzgerald wrote, "—a staid-faced, unsmiling little girl who might be good for a lot of laughs."[17]

In an effort to give the story some plot, the aging screenwriter suggested that they pit Jill and Florine against one another in the competition for the title of Carnival Queen. "Later in the day the girls are together in a fraternity house," he wrote. "There Jill learns that Florine is going to run for Queen and is sure to win. Jill realizes that if Florine wins, it will be in all the newspapers and she will be summarily kicked out of Vassar for breaking probation. Florine knows it too, but like a little fool is going to run. Jill in a friendly way warns her about this . . . and Florine is snippy, then furious—everything must yield to youth. Out of the way, last year's girl!"[18]

At the Carnival, Jill becomes re-acquainted with Instructor Stuart, who had been smitten by her four years before when she, then a college girl, visited the Carnival for the first time. But when he meets her this time he tells her that "years ago he knew she would never be the girl in his life because she objected to waxing her own skiis."[19] Scott was clearly tired of helpless heroines.

As a snowstorm arises—and Fitzgerald was about to learn just how miserable a Dartmouth snowstorm could be—Jill is crowned Queen. But before she can savor her victory beside a warm log fire, she learns that her child, its nurse, and a driver have been lost in the blizzard. When the car is finally located, it turns out to be on the other side of a swollen stream, and of course the bridge has been washed out. Instructor Stuart straps on a St. Bernard pack and prepares to ski jump the stream to rescue the stranded party. "There is suspense, Jill waxes Stuart's skis, torches blaze in the twilight. Then Climax—he jumps and makes it—torch in air."[20]

That was all the script they had, ten sketchy pages, when Wanger suggested that Fitzgerald and Schulberg accompany the camera crew which would shoot background footage at that year's Dartmouth Winter Carnival. Scott protested that he remembered the Carnival well enough from his own college days, but Wanger was going home to his alma mater and he wanted a prize to show off to his old teachers. Unfortunately, Wanger's trophy had dissipated much of its luster by the time the picture people reached Dartmouth. The dissipation began when B. P. Schulberg arrived at the Los Angeles airport to see his son off on his first big assignment and handed over a present, two bottles of vintage Mumm's. As soon as Budd and Scott, sitting next to one another in the plane, were in the air, the younger writer suggested a toast. The alcoholic writer said no at first, but was eventually persuaded.

They talked and toasted their way through the night. Fitzgerald seemed to have the same feeling about the twenties which some people have about their old school: he was chauvinistic about the entire decade. He reminisced about the writers of the twenties: "Bunny" Wilson, Ernest Hemingway, Carl Van Vechten, Gertrude Stein. About the athletes of the twenties: Bobby Jones, Red Grange, Babe Ruth, Jack Dempsey. About the movie stars of the twenties: Mary Pickford, Lillian Gish, Barbara La Marr, Gloria Swanson, Carmel Myers.

The closest they came to working on *Winter Carnival* was to discuss the picture's pipe-smoking Ivy League producer. Scott described him as "Ivy on one side, California palm on the other." The second bottle of champagne followed the first.

They decided to put off working on the script until they got to their hotel in New York; it would be easier to think once they had a room to do it in. But when they had checked into the Hotel Warwick, the four walls didn't help that much. They piled one dismally unworkable idea on top of another, but no progress was evident. Finally Budd decided to go out and look for some old friends. He asked if Fitzgerald minded. Not at all. Scott would take a long bath to relax and then make some notes on what to do about *Winter Carnival*.

When the young writer returned to the Warwick, Scott was missing. Instead of his collaborator, he found a note on his bed. "Pal you shouldn't have left me pal," it said in letters which seemed to stagger across the page, "because I got lonely pal and went down to the bar pal and started drinking pal, and now you may never find me pal. . . ."

As it turned out, Scott was easy to find. Budd rushed down to the street and then began systematically checking every bar he came to. A few doors from the Warwick, there he was, or at least there was a part of him, the part the alcohol had not dissolved. The younger man brought the older one back to the hotel and put him through the treatment: black coffees, cold showers. Fitzgerald sobered up enough to apologize and then Schulberg apologized, too. They promised each other to work, *work,* and the rest of the night they tried to. After all, they had a deadline. That morning they were supposed to report to Wanger's suite and tell him their Carnival story.

The two screenwriters really had not been able to appreciate how tired and even shabby they were until they saw how clean and rested the producer was. Wanger looked at them—an old story—and then decided to make the best of the uneasy situation. He asked about the plane trip—Had they seen anyone they knew? Schulberg answered innocently, "Let's see, oh, yes, Sheilah Graham was on the plane." She and Scott had seemed surprised. What a coincidence.

Wanger did what the Hollywood calls a "takem." Then he said disapprovingly, "Scott, you son of a bitch."

The story conference went as badly as the preliminaries had. After the disaster was over, Budd found himself apologizing once again.

"Holy God, Scott," he said, "I'm terribly sorry. I never would have mentioned her if I had . . ."

"All my fault," Scott said. "I should have told you. Maybe it's just as well it's out in the open with Walter anyway. I don't know why I feel I have to hide things from him like a schoolboy."

Scott Fitzgerald, the symbol of the younger generation in the 1920s, boarded a train in New York later that day along with carloads of girls who were seventeen, eighteen, nineteen—occasionally there would be a veteran of twenty or twenty-one. They were all going to the Winter Carnival to see several thousand boys who had been marooned on a lonely New Hampshire campus for too long. When the girls came home, they would make their adventures sound like the blurbs on the back of lurid novels. Like them, Fitzgerald too hoped to come home with a story, but one that could be filmed.

Schulberg called it a "wild, surrealist train ride north to Hanover." Fitzgerald started telling the students on the train— many of whom did not believe him—who he was and how much money he made. The students in turn mocked the middle-aged man who was obviously too old to be going to house parties.

The train stopped at a small town; the cars had become a trap to the two screenwriters, so they decided to get off, stretch, and have a cup of coffee. They could see the lights of an all-night diner and headed in that direction. Inside the warm shabbiness of the place a radio played tunes dedicated to people who lived nearby, people who would never be more famous than when the disc jockey read their names over the air. The two Hollywood refugees stayed on a little too long listening to the waitress flirt with some truck drivers.

They arrived back at the railroad tracks in time to see the train pulling away without them. The same thing had happened to Jill in Fitzgerald's *Winter Carnival* treatment, but it was too late for the screenwriter to remember that he might have known. They floundered about searching for a plan and then located a taxi, an old Model A which had somehow outlived the F. Scott Fitzgerald era and was still running in 1939. The cabbie agreed to drive them to the next town in the hope that they could get there before the train did. It was so cold that the two men found a blanket and pulled it up over their heads to make a tent, then sipped at the applejack the driver had given them as antifreeze. Sometime around four in the morning they finally caught up with the trainload of students and moving-picture people. Their careers were saved.

On the train once again, Scott fought back drink and cold and T.B. to come up with an opening shot for *Winter Carnival*. He was so excited about his inspiration that he hustled Schulberg down the corridor to Wanger's Pullman, where at just after five a.m. he hammered at the door until the producer let them in. What the hell did they want? Scott told him. He had a great opening and he had to tell Wanger all about it, cou'n wait, no shir. They would fade in on an Indian school with a roomful of young bucks all being solemnly addressed by a Great White Teacher. CUT TO: outside a pack of young squaws rush toward the school on snowshoes. CUT TO: Indian maidens bursting into schoolroom and waltzing around with the braves, bringing the lessons to a fast halt. FADE OUT. FADE IN ON the girls disembarking from train for Dartmouth's Winter Carnival.[21] Get it? Fantashtic, baby, jus' fantashtic. Wanger did not seem to like the opening as much as Scott did. He stared at the author with the unblinking eye of a potato and then went back to bed.

The two writers got no more sleep that night than the night before. They arrived at Dartmouth exhausted, in need of nothing so much as a bed. But there had been a slip-up: the producer had a suite and all of the directors, assistant directors, and cameramen had rooms, but no one had thought to make a reservation for the two men who were supposed to write the picture. Scott insisted on taking the whole thing as a metaphor for Hollywood's opinion of writers. At last the hotel manager found a place for them—a small room with no furniture except a metal two-decker bed up in the attic. This room was even less help than the one back at the Warwick—in fact, it was a positive hindrance. Schulberg remembers the room as a place where "for two days we fumed, labored, drank, suffered icy research, nerve-wracking deadlines and humiliating public receptions."

"One of the things that impressed me most in the course of that arctic weekend hell," says Schulberg, "was the quality of Scott's creative intelligence and the courage of his humor. He was constantly noticing little things that amazed me—details of academic life as exact as the lexicon of O'Hara. . . . At the very moment when the faculty and student onlookers were laughing at him as a drunk and a clown, his accuracy toward them was muffled but deadly."

At a party which one of the movie people gave, a group of professors took it upon themselves to criticize the picture Fitzgerald had come east to make. Scott sank into a chair and listened. From time to time, he would wave his hand and complain, "Lotta nonsense." When he had had enough, he rose and said, "You know, I'd love to be a professor in a university like this with all the security and the smug niceties, instead of having to put up with the things we have to put up with out there in the world. I bid you good night, gentlemen."[22] When the author left, the professors said wasn't it too bad about poor Scott.

Schulberg's "other memories of that nightmare weekend" include:

> Scott's trudging through the deep snow to the ski jump in his baggy suit, his wrinkled overcoat and his battered fedora, a gray, grim joke to the young, hearty Carnival couples in their bright-color ski clothes, and of his zombie walk to the door, saying, "I'm going to Zelda, she needs me, I'm going to Zelda. . . ." This was the first time he had mentioned his wife, whose unfortunate illness had dropped a dark curtain between them. I remember dragging him back from the door and throwing him down on the cot, hard. I remember thinking he had passed out again and beginning to take off his shoes, and his reviving enough to say, "Oh, you must be enjoying yourself, feeling so strong, so young, so damn sure of yourself. . . ." And I remember losing my patience and temper with him at last and running out to a friendly fraternity bar where I tried to drown our common sorrows, until mysteriously, inescapably, he tracked me down and we went out into the Carnival night laughing and improvising scandalous songs like any other two Carnival celebrants.

In their carnival mood the two screenwriters met Walter Wanger by accident in front of the Hanover Inn. Standing up on the steps, like a Puritan minister looking down on his congregation, the producer fired the two writers and told them to get out of town. They caught the Montrealer back to New York and then found that in their condition no New York hotel, not even the shabby ones, would take them in. Once again they had no room. They rode up and down Manhattan in a cab searching fruitlessly until finally Scott whispered "Doctor's Hospital." Scott Fitzgerald's Winter Carnival ended between snowy white hospital sheets.

When he returned to Hollywood, Schulberg was rehired to finish the picture—but not Fitzgerald. "Wanger will never forgive me for this," Scott told Schulberg at one point. "He sees himself as the intellectual producer and he was going to impress Dartmouth by showing them he used real writers, not vulgar hacks, and here I, his real writer, have disgraced him before the whole college."[23]

Malcolm Cowley has called Fitzgerald's Dartmouth Winter Carnival "his biggest, saddest, most desperate spree."[24] Scott himself said, "In retrospect, going east under those circumstances seems one of the silliest mistakes I ever made."[25]

3

"After a month's rest," Fitzgerald later recalled, "I took a job with [producer] Jeff Lazarus on *Air Raid*. We progressed for a month and then the picture was put aside for *Honeymoon in Bali* and I went to Cuba."[26] Working on *Air Raid*, Fitzgerald, like the blacked-out city in his story, was endangered by a bomb. The bomb, of course, was *Air Raid* itself. It was not really Scott's fault that the script was terrible. He had inherited the story from Donald Ogden Stewart and much of the credit must go to him. Actually, the picture had never been intended as anything more than an exploitation film. The German Blitzkrieg was under way in Europe and it had occurred to the American movie manufacturers, like the American arms manufacturers, that this war might be a gold mine.

Fitzgerald's version of the story began in a fashionable boutique where a very smart lady is trying on the latest things in very chic gas masks. The sales girl says that madame is "adorable." Madame replies through the mask, "Bd—ub—a—db?"[27] The script went downhill from there on.

After *Winter Carnival* Sheilah never knew when Scott was on gin. When she detected anything on his breath, she would demand, "Are you drinking? I'm sure you're drinking."

He: "That's none of your business."

She: "I hate you when you drink. You're not the person I like then. Why do you drink? When I fell in love with you you weren't drinking. Why are you doing it now?"

He: "I'm not drinking."[28]

But he was. Going through his bureau drawers, Sheilah found eleven empty gin bottles.

One morning Fitzgerald woke up and found that he could not move his arms. Actually his paralysis had as much to do with his being entangled in his pajamas as with gin, but the doctor decided to frighten his patient: continued drinking, he told the author, might paralyze him forever. Scott said, "I'd just blow my brains out."[29] The doctor asked the obvious question: Who would hold the gun?

Nonetheless, Scott kept on drinking, and one day Sheilah discovered a gun in his dresser drawer. She lifted it out, but before she could dispose of it, its owner came up. "Give me that gun!" he ordered. When she didn't, he tackled her, slamming her to the floor.

Miss Graham recalls the scene:

> We struggled wildly. Scott was like a madman. He grabbed at the gun, cursing as he pried my fingers loose. I gasped in pain. My fingers had been caught in the trigger guard and he had pulled them away so violently the flesh tore. Blind rage flooded me. With a tremendous effort I jerked the gun away and hurled it at the opposite wall. "Take it!" I screamed. "Shoot yourself, you son of a bitch! See if I care! . . . You're not worth saving, you're not worth anything!" I scrambled to my feet. I screamed at him, "I didn't pull myself out of the gutter to waste my life on a drunk like you!" I rushed downstairs and into my car and drove home.[30]

At this point, Scott headed for Cuba. He stopped off in Asheville, North Carolina, and took Zelda out of the sanitarium to accompany him, a mad companion for a mad trip. In Havana, Zelda went into a religious stupor, praying endlessly and reading the Bible. To escape her holiness, Scott went one night to a pit where they staged cockfights. But when the fight began, he was horrified. As he later told Sheilah, "One cock was slashing the other to bits and those men were egging them on."[31] Scott was no Papa Hemingway—he couldn't stand it. He jumped the guardrail and tried to separate the birds. That was when the spectators came down upon him, dozens of strong young cocks cutting up an old rooster. When the badly beaten Fitzgerald finally crawled back to his hotel, he found Zelda sitting in the dark room, still praying.

By the time he returned to California, Sheilah had forgiven him. Before long she was acting as his nurse.

"I found in the East that I was sicker than I had thought," Fitzgerald later recorded, "and came back here in May to lie around in bed till my health picked up. I had the refusal during these months of *In Name Only, Rebecca,* and half a dozen others, but by July, when I wanted to work again, the offers seemed to stop."[32] *In Name Only,* starring Carole Lombard, Cary Grant, and Kay Francis, and *Rebecca,* directed by Alfred Hitchcock and starring Laurence Olivier, Joan Fontaine, and George Sanders, were both fine films, as it turned out. In fact, *Rebecca* won the Academy Award and became a classic. Two more big ones had gotten away.

Scott grew more and more dependent on Sheilah, yet could not forget Zelda and what had happened to her. It was sometime during this period that he wrote out a proposal for a motion picture called *The Feather Fan.* "The real lost generation of girls were those who were young right after the war because they were the ones with infinite belief," Fitzgerald said in his treatment. "The sanitariums are full of them and many are dead."[33] But Scott could not interest the studios: his story of a broken flapper went uncourted.

Fitzgerald remained unemployed through an unhappy summer. At the end of July he wrote Zelda, "This last month has been too

much of a hell. . . . It was like 1935–1936 when . . . all my
products were dirges and elegies. Sickness and no money are
a wretched combination." A few days later, still sick, he wrote
his wife, "I am as annoyed at the unreliability of the human
body as you are at the vagaries of the nervous system."[34]

To pay the doctor, Fitzgerald began once again trying to write
magazine stories, but these did not sell immediately. Scott had
no savings from his movie work to draw on because he had
used his high salaries to repay much of the approximately forty
thousand dollars which Harold Ober and Scribner's had advanced
him, a few hundred at a time, over the past decade. And now the
author, who never tired of warning his daughter against economic,
emotional, and physical bankruptcy, found both his health and
his money running out at the same time. He needed to borrow
once again and so wired Ober for an advance against the price
of his stories when, or rather if, they sold. Ober refused. Fitzgerald fired him as his agent.

"I don't have to explain," the author wrote the man who had
represented him for almost twenty years, "that even though a
man has once saved another from drowning, when he refuses to
stretch out his arm a second time the victim has to act quickly
and desperately to save himself."[35] Like most people trying to
save themselves in deep water, Fitzgerald did little more than
thrash about wildly but unsuccessfully. He attempted to deal
with magazine editors directly, but few were interested.

Firing Ober meant firing Swanson too, since they were
partners. The writer and his Hollywood agent had already
quarreled, and at this point Scott broke off their business con-
nection altogether. To represent him in the movie capital Fitzgerald hired Leland Hayward. His next pay check did not come
until September, when he found a job rewriting a picture called
Raffles. Not only was *Raffles* no *Rebecca,* but this same movie,
based on William Hornung's 1899 novel *The Amateur Cracksman,*
had already been made three times before.

The artist would have to stay home for a while; this time
Fitzgerald was going to do the job as a businessman, for the

money only—one thousand a week. He looked the part of the businessman, pale hands and pale head poking out of the staid broker's suit. He even affected a businessman's prop, a bulging brief case. He would pick up his secretary, Miss Frances Kroll, on the way to work. Sometimes when they reached the small door in the side of what looked like a huge tobacco barn, the red warning light would already be burning. Shooting had already started. They were in a hurry to finish this one because their hero was anxious to go home and defend his country.

Inside, the man with the heavy brief case would see a night club with patrons already drinking at the tables and couples dancing on the dance floor. Here within the perpetual night of the windowless sound stage, night life had already begun at nine o'clock in the morning. It was hardly the kind of office a business-man dreams of, but Scott made the best of it. He would sit somewhere, open his brief case and draw forth his yellow pads, his stubby pencils, and a Coke. Every morning he packed a six-pack of Cokes along with his scripts and other writing ma-terial.

"For the benefit of the other people on the set, Fitzgerald used to laugh about it," Miss Kroll remembers. "He used to say that we should sell the idea of a pack of Cokes in every brief case to the Coca-Cola Company to use as an advertisement." But actually the Cokes were no laughing matter: they kept him alert—or so he believed. Fitzgerald could no more write without them than he could write without a pencil. And yet after what he called "a great orgy of Coca-Colas," he would often complain of "little aches around the elbows and shoulders."[36]

The man cast as the amateur cracksman, the man who was anxious to trade his white tie and silver pistol for a British uniform and a rifle, was David Niven. Opposite him beneath the bobbing microphone was Olivia de Havilland. "David Niven was very charming to Fitzgerald," Miss Kroll remembers. "They used to huddle on the set and talk when there was a break. Fitzgerald was envious of Niven, but not because he was a star. He was envious because of Niven's adventure. Niven was going off to war. Ever since he missed World War I, Fitzgerald had been something of a thwarted soldier."

Some days Samuel Goldwyn, Fitzgerald's new boss, would be on the set. In a sense, Sam and Scott both owed their starts in show business to the same man, Dustin Farnum. In 1904 Farnum, then a player in the Buffalo Tech Stock Company, had supplied the young Scott Fitzgerald with free tickets to his shows —shows which inspired the eight-year-old Scott to stage his own dramas up in the attic. Nine years later, Farnum met a man named Goldfish who was casting for his first picture, *The Squaw Man,* and won the title role. The movie made Farnum a movie star and set Goldfish up as an established producer. Changing his name to Goldwyn, the upstart impresario headed the Goldwyn Pictures Corporation until 1922 when he quarreled with his partners and quit with the immortal declaration, "You may include me out."[37] Later, when the Goldwyn company merged with Metro and Mayer, Sam was also included out of one of the most powerful movie machines in history. In fact, Goldwyn spent his life competing against Metro-Goldwyn-Mayer. Now Fitzgerald had come over to his side.

They made a strange team, the rough Polish immigrant, Sam, and the Princeton-educated man of letters, Scott. Fitzgerald had always been known for his felicity with words, Goldwyn for the exact opposite. Once while preparing a script for an Eddie Cantor film, he was heard to declare, "Tomorrow we shoot, whether it rains, whether it snows, whether it stinks."[38]

Joseph Breen had cost Fitzgerald his job writing *Infidelity* for Metro, but ironically the author had the censor to thank for landing the *Raffles* job. Goldwyn had submitted his script to the Hays Office and was preparing to start shooting when a letter from Breen informed the producer that *Raffles* was "unacceptable." Why? The censor made clear that it was "a violation of the Production Code" to show "a criminal, who is permitted to outsmart the police, and to go off 'scot free.' " Breen left Goldwyn some hope for his picture, however, by suggesting: "This basic difficulty could be easily remedied, if you could insert a line, possibly in the closing scenes of the picture, . . . which would indicate to the audience that Raffles knows that he cannot escape justice, that the police are waiting for him . . ." The censor then went on to say that "there should be no scenes at any time, showing 'ladies of the street' "; that the "action of Raffles planting the gun in the pit of Crawshay's stomach, will be deleted by political censor boards everywhere"; and that the producer should "eliminate the expression . . . 'Good Lord' " from his script. The censor's objections and the screenplay were turned over to Fitzgerald.[39]

There were other problems, too. "I came in on a violent quarrel between Goldwyn and Sam Wood," recalled Fitzgerald, who was caught in the crossfire between the producer and the director. Scott later told his new agent, Hayward, "Sam Wood and I had always gotten along before, but during this week that I worked on *Raffles* everything got a little strained . . ."[40]

The picture was to tell the story of a well-known cricket star (David Niven) who is deeply in debt, but who hides behind a tuxedo bought on credit in a desperate struggle to keep up appearances. In choosing Fitzgerald to help tell this story, Goldwyn was almost guilty of typecasting. The very week that Scott took on the *Raffles* job, he wrote Zelda, "I hocked the car again for $150.00."[41] When the author reworked the movie's opening scene, he put that in: he had Raffles hock his roadster, then grow paranoid about it. A certain Lady Melrose innocently calls to see if Raffles would like a car sent round to fetch him for one of her dinner parties. Raffles protests to his valet:

RAFFLES: Wait! I scarcely know the old dear. (*Pause.*) She couldn't know my roadster's in pawn, could she?

VALET: Scarcely. I can hardly believe it myself, sir . . .[42]

Arriving for the dinner party, Raffles is drawn magnetically to two beauties, a girl named Gwen (Olivia de Havilland) and an emerald necklace entwined about the stout neck of his hostess, Lady Melrose. Gwen has loved Raffles from afar for a long time, and now that she is finally up close, she makes her admiration plain. She asks Raffles to look at her. He does and asks her to part her lips.

RAFFLES: That's better. You know you're—you're a—

GWEN (*eagerly*): *What?*

RAFFLES (*passionately*): You've a magnificent dentist.[43]

Gwen is crushed.

(A good writer never wastes anything, not even a visit to the dentist. Fitzgerald told his secretary that back in St. Paul when he was a boy, "All I needed to fix my teeth was a broomstraw," but recently he had been having some complicated dental work done. Those trips to the drilling chair, Miss Kroll remembers, had given him the idea for the compliment paid to Gwen's dentist.)

Later that night we see Raffles and Gwen on "A Smart London Street such as Bond Street." This scene as originally written was one of those which Breen had complained about because the background props were to have included assorted "ladies of the street." Scott changed these ladies to "hurrying working girl[s]"[44] and evidently warmed Breen's suspicious heart.

But that was as far as Fitzgerald got. Goldwyn decided that he had done enough and took him off the payroll. In his notebook Scott wrote that he "liked Sam Goldwyn—you always knew where you stood with Goldwyn—nowhere."[45] Sam himself could not have put it better.

Raffles had turned out to be another disappointment. No one could have turned it into a great picture—it simply had not aimed at greatness. Moreover, as Scott worked on the film it must have occurred to him that this was where he came in. His first play, written at the age of fifteen and starring the boys and girls of St. Paul, had been called *The Captured Shadow* and had told the story of a gentleman burglar much like Raffles. Now at forty-three he tried to write like a fifteen-year-old once again, but he no longer had the enthusiasm. He was an old man trying to ride a child's vehicle and kept falling off.

But now at least the low had been reached. The avalanche of bad luck and bad health and bad reputation which had come down on Scott after *Winter Carnival* was over. The screenwriter was about to write his best screenplay.

☆ 12 ☆

Cosmopolitan:
Splicing It Together

1

Fitzgerald's telephone rang. Lester Cowan, the independent producer, was at the other end. He invited Fitzgerald to lunch. They went to one of those dark Hollywood restaurants which, like the dark Hollywood sunglasses, help protect the prominent from the stares of the curious. Not that Fitzgerald was afraid of being recognized—not anymore. What worried him was not the anonymous crowd but the man across the table. Cowan was not a big man, but he looked like and sometimes acted like a fighter, a bantam pugilist, and Scott simply did not trust him. He knew that a clever producer could loot the finer furnishings of a screenwriter's mind the way less talented Hollywood crooks cleaned out Beverly Hills homes. Scott was trying to remember to keep all the doors and windows locked. He had already said more than he planned to.

Fitzgerald ate quickly, but not Cowan. The producer lingered over dessert, over coffee, over his many questions, most of which had to do with Scott's ideas for turning his story "Babylon Revisited" into a full-length motion-picture. Where would he begin? What material would he add to stretch his short, evocative tale over an hour and a half? The producer was always fascinated with Fitzgerald's answers, wanted always to hear more, his appetite insatiable. Scott, sipping cup after cup of black, highly sweetened coffee, grew more and more nervous.

The next day the telephone rang. It was Cowan again. He and Liam O'Flaherty wanted Fitzgerald to go to the racetrack with them, but the author was afraid that he might lose more than the money he bet on the horses. "I told him," Scott later recalled, "I was otherwise engaged." After Cowan hung up, the author wrote his new agent, William Dozier, for help. One more long conversation, Scott complained, and Cowan would have "a good piece of me in his pocket for nothing."[1]

From then on Cowan had all his talks, not with the writer, but with his agent. A deal was finally made in late January; Fitzgerald sold his screen rights to his story for a thousand dollars, and agreed to do the adaptation for three hundred a week. By Hollywood standards, he was keeping a five-and-dime store. As he wrote Scottie, "You earned some money for me this week because I sold 'Babylon Revisited,' in which you are a character, to the pictures (the sum received wasn't worthy of the magnificent story—neither of you nor of me—however, I am accepting it)." A few months later, still sore about the money but not unhappy, he wrote her, "I am working on this 'Babylon Revisited' picture at a rotten salary but it is rather fun and may amount to something."[2]

Now it was Fitzgerald's turn to call Cowan. He wanted to read the producer the scene where the father in his story, wasted by alcohol and the prisoner of a hospital bed, is unexpectedly reunited with his daughter.

"How are you, dear? I've thought a lot about you. Haven't been very well," Scott read into the receiver, playing Cary Grant's role. Still in character, he pretended to shout at a nurse, "Bring me a comb. I asked for a barber."

Changing roles, playing Shirley Temple now, he read, "Perhaps you'd better rest, Daddy."

"Rest, rest. What's all this about rest? Is it something you take like a pill? I don't want to rest. I want to do something and go somewhere. Do you think that just *lying down* makes you sleep? Doctors and nurses seem to believe that all you have to do is say 'rest,' and immediately sweet sleep comes. My Heaven! They've given me every pill in their bags, and the miracle just doesn't happen. I'm going to Italy this afternoon. . . . I want you to help me get dressed. I want to get out of here."³

When he hung up the phone, Fitzgerald turned to his secretary Frances Kroll with a strange look on his face. He thought for a moment before telling her what Cowan had done. "He cried."

After that "the two seemed to get along well," Miss Kroll remembers. "Cowan would come up to the apartment to talk. Sometimes he would come up for lunch. I would fix them sandwiches and they would work."

Now that their lunches were more relaxed, Fitzgerald enjoyed answering Cowan's questions. "Cowan had intelligence," says Miss Kroll. "He wasn't like the others. And Fitzgerald respected that. Cowan was very respectful, too; he had a sense of regard for Fitzgerald's talent."

Since Fitzgerald did not sleep very much, he would think through his scenes at night. Mornings, he would put on his old bathrobe and walk back and forth as he dictated. He wrote very fast, setting himself deadlines and trying to meet them.

"Fitzgerald loved his screenplay, really," his secretary recalls. "He had complete control over it and Cowan always let him work at home. It was very different from going to the studios."

Fitzgerald had needed this job desperately. He had gone without work all through the winter. It was during a pinched January that he had written Leland Hayward, his agent at the time, that chilling letter which began, "Once Budd Schulberg told me that, while the story of an official black list is a legend, there is a kind of cabal that goes on between producers around a backgammon table, and I have an idea that some such sinister finger is upon me."⁴

Fitzgerald's only regular income during these months came from the Pat Hobby stories which he sold to *Esquire* at two hundred fifty dollars apiece. Scott said they were "done to pay the grocer."[5] Budd Schulberg remembers him coming down the stairs of the Encino house one night and announcing to a group of friends, "I've just finished an awfully good story."[6] He wanted to know if they would like to hear it. They would. He hurried upstairs and fetched it down. Some of the Pat Hobby stories were at least fine anecdotes, but not this one. Schulberg remembers that it was embarrassingly unfunny. The scene was reminiscent of that 1931 party at Irving Thalberg's house where Scott had flopped with his song about a dog, but this time, at least, he had had the good sense to flop in his own home.

Yet while Fitzgerald was chronicling Pat Hobby's misadventures with his left hand, with his right he was composing some of his finest prose. "Look!" he wrote his daughter in late October 1939, "I have begun to write something that is maybe great. . . ."[7]

In general Scott was very secretive about his new novel, but he told Budd Schulberg about it. "It's coming well," he said. "Just a few pages a day, except for a spurt when I wake up with a little of my old pep. But at least it's *coming*." He said that he hoped to finish a first draft before too much longer.

"Marvelous, I'll bring champagne," Budd kidded.

"Oh, God, not this time!" he laughed. "This time I know— I've got no choice—I'm on the wagon forever, baby."[8]

The prose in the new novel, *The Last Tycoon*, was so alive that it almost seemed to get up and walk, and yet Scott wrote most of it lying flat on his back. He was nursing his tuberculosis. He had a writing board and, sitting up in his bathrobe, he covered yellow pages with a scrawl that looked like a string of lopsided balloons. As he finished each sheet, he pushed it out of bed onto the floor.

When his doctor would call to give the author vitamin injections and other medication, he would climb the stairs, walk carefully across the floor trying to keep from stepping on the masterpiece, and sit down beside the bed while Scott continued to write, oblivious of his visitor. Sometimes minutes would pass before the writer would look up.

"Oh, hello," he would say. "Been waiting long?"

"No," the doctor would answer. "Only a minute or two."[9]

In November Scott took time off from being a novelist to become Sheilah's speech writer. Her syndicate, the North American Newspaper Alliance, had booked her for a two-week publicity tour of all the major cities where her column appeared. She wrote out a speech entitled "Now It Can Be Told" which was just the kind of talk it sounded like. Scott read the thing and informed Sheilah, "This really isn't very good. I can't let you do a lecture like this."[10] Solution: Scott wrote a lecture for her.

Fitzgerald made the director the hero of his Hollywood talk just as he would later make a director-producer, Stahr, the hero of his Hollywood novel. Scott, who had come to Hollywood hoping eventually to work his way up to a position where he himself could direct, knew that the directors and not Sheilah's much-publicized stars really stood at the center of the Hollywood stage. The lecture began:

> A few months ago I visited the enormous back lot of the Goldwyn studio. The picture was *The Real Glory*—the scene a Philippine village on the banks of a swift river. After a minute of absolute silence there was a quiet command from the man sitting under the camera. This was echoed through a loud microphone by his assistant—"All right, we're rolling"—and then a wild uproar filled the air. Filipinos jumped to the walls of the village, rifles crackling; screaming Moros rushed from the jungle; men were catapulted through the air from bent trees; David Niven died at the feet of Andrea Leeds; and down the raging stream came Gary Cooper on a raft. "Cut," said the director Hathaway quietly. "Print it."
> In the sudden lull I said, "It must be wonderful to be back of all this. It must give you a great sense of power."[11]

That sense of power and creation flowing together—that chance to command an army of stars, technicians, and extras and yet be an artist at the same time—still tantalized Fitzgerald as it had for so long. He was a thwarted soldier, a thwarted actor, who saw in the motion-picture director a special symbol:

> On the stage the director is merely the man who says, "Now, Miss Cornell, you cross left at this point. You'll have an amber spot following you."
>
> The duties of the motion-picture director are on an infinitely grander scale. From the first day of shooting until the word "printed" is uttered after the last take, he is the picture. *He* is its life, its *heart* and *soul*.

Where Sheilah's now-it-can-be-told gossip had once been, Fitzgerald wrote in some of the lessons he had learned as a Hollywood screenwriter. One of the most important had to do with that old gulf between *show* and *tell*, between writing pictures for the screen and pages for the bookshelf. "A writer's instinct is to think in words," he said.

> The director has got to work with the writer and turn the writer's words into visual images for the camera. We can do without speeches, but we've got to see, for on the screen, *seeing* is believing, no matter what the characters say.

Fitzgerald pointed out that in most great pictures "we are absorbed in seeing rather than hearing," but he went on to add:

> This accent on the visual need not mean we have to blow up a city or have schooners sailing the seven seas. The focus may be on something as small as the famous "kitten and boots" gag in Harold Lloyd's *Grandma's Boy.* You may remember that Harold Lloyd had greased his boots with a special ointment which proved unexpectedly attractive to cats, and at the crisis of his love affair, sitting on the sofa with his girl, a family of kittens kept licking at his boots.

Fitzgerald had watched the masters, done his homework. If his chance to direct ever came, he would be ready.

Toward the end of the talk, however, the fun of the kittens attacking Lloyd's boots as if they were size-nine mice was forgotten, and some of Scott's disappointment showed through. The movie industry is "too big for any of us," he wrote, "too big for most of the people who direct its destinies. Once in a while a great figure has appeared on the horizon and led it through a mighty exodus. Griffith was one, Thalberg was another. There is no such person now in Hollywood . . ."

Sheilah went on her publicity tour, leaving Scott behind. She couldn't write and yet she was being read all over the country. Scott was out of print. He was so anxious to get back before the public that when he finished the first chapter of *The Last Tycoon*, he had his secretary drive it to the airport and mail it to *Collier's* from there. The magazine had offered thirty thousand for the serial rights—*if* they liked it. Just as Sheilah was returning from her talk tour, word came. *Collier's* wanted to see more. It wasn't really a rejection but Scott took it like one. Furious at the magazine, he wired his old friend Maxwell Perkins: I HAVEN'T SEEN A PIECE OF FICTION IN THERE FOR SEVERAL YEARS THAT WOULD SERVE THE PURPOSES OF A SEARS ROEBUCK CATALOGUE.[12] Rather than submit more of his story to the ungrateful *Collier's*, he shipped his chapter off to an old ally, *The Saturday Evening Post*. They wanted to see more, too. Scott started to drink.

Drunk, he threatened Sheilah's life. It happened one night when Scott invited a couple of dead beats to the house and Sheilah threw them out. "Being rude to my friends—never so insulted in my life—" He picked up a bowl of soup she had made for him and hurled it against the wall. When his nurse attempted to come to Miss Graham's rescue, he whirled and kicked the nurse in the legs. Sheilah tried to leave the room, but Scott stopped her. "You're not going," he said. "I'm going to kill you." But nothing was working out for the author those days—he couldn't find his gun. He asked Sheilah, "Where's my gun?" but she wouldn't tell. He called his secretary, but she wouldn't tell either. Then Sheilah called the police.

A few days later, Scott slipped into Sheilah's Hollywood apartment and took the silver-fox fur he had given her—the one which made a short appearance in his draft of *The Women*. The next day Miss Graham's insurance agent called the author and informed him, "You have five days to return it. Then we—not Miss Graham—will start criminal action."[13] Scott said that it might take more than five days. He had mailed the coat to his daughter as a Christmas present.

The new job adapting "Babylon Revisited" for the movies brought the couple back together. They even began to act out some of the scenes in the new script the way they had done with *Madame Curie* and *Gone with the Wind.* This time the dramas staged in the Belly Acres Playhouse (their living room) went better than had Scarlett O'Hara and Rhett Butler on the staircase. Perhaps that was because their new roles were almost more than roles. Sheilah played the little girl in the story, Scott the father whom she looked up to. In a sense they had been rehearsing these parts as long as they had known one another.

He would slouch and shamble and say: "How would you like to see anybody walk like this?"

SHE: "Oh, Daddy."

HE: "You should try to walk like a queen."

SHE: "How do queens walk?"

HE: "Well, I've only met one queen, and she was an awful stumblebum."[14]

During his boom days, Scott had had trouble finding even one quiet room in which to work. People, usually trailing bottles, were always bursting in on him. But Encino was different. The room was quiet, the house was quiet, even the spreading Valley seemed a giant bowl of silence. There was only one noisy neighbor, an RKO Western lot which you couldn't see from the house but which you could sometimes hear. From faraway a voice: "Ev'rybody quiet! Camera—shoot!" And then the sound of hoofbeats and gunfire would roll up the valley. Now Fitzgerald enjoyed a little noise.

One night when it was quiet—all the RKO badman were being good that night—the silence was intruded upon by something other than noisy make-believe. The telephone rang loudly. It was Budd Schulberg, still at the hospital. His wife had just borne him a baby girl. They were calling her Victoria. Scott said that in her honor he would change the name of the little girl in his screenplay from Honoria to Victoria.

When the mother and baby returned home, Scott sent over a package. It did not matter to him that most babies cannot read: the present was a copy of *Tender Is the Night* with the inscription, "For Victoria Schulberg—in memory of a three-day mountain-climbing trip with her illustrious father—who pulled me out of crevices into which I sank and away from avalanches— with affection to you both."[15]

By May, Fitzgerald was enthusiastic about what he had accomplished so far. "My movie progresses," he wrote Scottie, "and I think it's going to be damn good:"[16]

But then in mid-June, with the writing and the finances both going well the weekly checks from the studio suddenly stopped with the screenplay only about half finished. Fitzgerald was forced to write his daughter:

> Here is your round-trip fare to Montgomery. I'm sorry it can't be more, but while my picture *is* going to be done, the producer is going to *first* do one that has been made for the brave Laurence Olivier, who will defend his country in Hollywood (though summoned back by the British government). This affects the patriotic and unselfish Scott Fitzgerald to the extent that I receive no more money from that source until the company gets around to it: so will return to my old stand-by *Esquire*.

Although the money stopped, Fitzgerald didn't. As he wrote Maxwell Perkins, "I finished the job for Shirley Temple, working the last weeks without pay on a gamble."[17]

2

Ignored as a novelist, Fitzgerald had determined to try to go beyond the novel. In a letter to Perkins the author said that he was enjoying his new movie "because it [is] my own picture *Babylon Revisited* and may lead to a new line up here." He sent off a letter to Zelda in her hospital which declared that his script, which he called *Cosmopolitan,* was his "great hope for attaining some real status out here as a movie man and not a novelist."[18]

To move beyond the novel, however, Fitzgerald took a page from one of his own books, *The Last Tycoon.* In that unfinished novel Stahr tries to teach the writer Boxley the difference between novels and pictures. To illustrate his point, the producer tells that story about the secretary who empties her purse on a table, spilling forth "two dimes and a nickel—and a cardboard match box."[19] In the first pages of his screenplay, which opens in Paris, Fitzgerald turned the device upside down: his eleven-year-old heroine, Victoria, packs a bag rather than emptying one. Socks, underwear, a toothbrush, and a comb all go into her book bag instead of schoolbooks; then when she leaves the house, she goes not to her classes but to the railroad station, the Gare de l'Est, where she boards a train bound for Switzerland. In *The Last Tycoon,* the girl in Stahr's story "takes her black gloves to the stove, opens it, and puts them inside . . . just as she lights the match, you glance around very suddenly and see that there's another man in the office, watching every move the girl makes—" In *Cosmopolitan* there are no gloves in the stove, of course, but we are still surprised when Victoria looks out her compartment window and sees a strange man watching every move *she* makes. As the train pulls out of the station, the man steps on board. Fitzgerald had learned something about making audiences ask— as Boxley asks Stahr—"What happens?"

At this point a flashback—one which Victoria herself helps to narrate—transports us back to New York harbor during the summer of 1929. Victoria and her father and mother, Mr. and Mrs. Charles Wales, are about to sail for Europe. Wales, who is retiring from the stock market, is the kind of broker whose colleagues tell him, "You play the market by ear . . . but you sure can play!" (Edmund Wilson once wrote of Scott, "It is true that Scott Fitzgerald plays the language entirely by ear. But his instrument, for all that, is no mean one."[20]) Wales' former business partner, Dwight Schuyler, comes down to the dock to see the family off and to try to persuade Wales to stay. A baby carriage breaks down near the group and the nurse hands the infant to Victoria to hold. The adults do not notice.

Fitzgerald had learned to write books which were told from a particular point of view as early as 1925, when he wrote *The Great Gatsby* as seen through the eyes of Nick Carraway. By the time he wrote *Cosmopolitan* he had learned to tell moving-picture stories the same way. But rather than one point of view, as in *Gatsby*, in *Cosmopolitan* there are two. Fitzgerald had planned to have his camera view the world in about half the shots from the child's point of view; the other contrasting shots were to be taken as if through the eyes of an adult.

All of the adult dialogue in the dockside scene is literally over Victoria's head, as Fitzgerald makes clear with his use of the camera:

CAMERA COMES DOWN TO VICTORIA'S LEVEL.

The men's faces are out of shot.

SCHUYLER: In other words, you're quitting.

WALES: Let's say it's on account of Helen. She needs me. . . . She'd probably be all right if she didn't hear the ticker in her dreams all night.[21]

A Western Union messenger arrives with the latest stock quotations. Wales, who is supposed to be getting out of the stock market, snatches the telegram out of Schuyler's hand and says:

WALES: Gaines is forming a pool. Don't let 'em fool you.

While her elders discuss stocks and mental illness, Victoria is preoccupied with taking care of her temporary charge. The child's vision has become a kind of test of the adult vision. All that is over her head becomes suspect. Her eyes are on what matters, the child and the buggy, and she does what she can to help the infant, rather than ignoring it as her elders ignore her. Here the technique and the moral are welded together. Fitzgerald used to enjoy quoting Conrad's dictum that it is the author's job "to make you see"[22]: here Fitzgerald, working as a screenwriter, satisfies both the literal and the implied meanings of "see." We see the picture, and seeing it, see its meaning.

On shipboard a day later, the captain and the retired tycoon meet and talk stocks—the captain has heard that rails are going up—while the camera, along with Victoria, peers at a pig's head with an apple in its mouth. As in the other scenes, the stage direction "over the shot" appears frequently, indicating that while we see one thing, we hear something else; when we *hear* the captain asking advice about the market, we *see* the little girl looking at the pig. Fitzgerald was stretching the movie medium so that the sound and the picture play off against one another, so that they give us the child's and the adult's world simultaneously. And in that one sight/sound experience he shows/tells us that the child is hungry for food while the piglike captain is hungry for money.

Later that night, while Wales is in the ship's brokers' room trying to help a friend save his investment, his neglected, de-mented wife throws herself into the ocean. The tycoon's boom, like America's, is over. In fact, when Wales says, "making money . . . making money . . . then a breakdown,"[23] his words seem to describe both himself and his country. His wife had seen him as a living stock ticker in her dreams, ticker tape pouring out of his mouth—the Market—incarnate, and the year 1929 was about to undo both the man and what he symbolized. Wales now faced what Fitzgerald himself had long feared, "emotional bankruptcy," just as his nation faced economic bankruptcy. Moreover, man and market would crash for the same reason: they had been living on margin, or as Fitzgerald put it in *The Crack-Up,* "drawing on resources that [they] did not possess . . . mortgaged . . . to the hilt."[24] Wales had ignored once too often the madness to which he was wed—and surely the twenties had taken the same bride—and that madness would now destroy everything. Wales, who in many ways stands for the author himself, was doomed, like "one of those delicate machines that register earthquakes ten thousand miles away,"[25] to record all the heart-shaking booms and busts of his era.

The idea of a 1929 crash which was personal as well as national had already been worked out, although not in such detail, as early as 1931 when Fitzgerald wrote "Babylon Revisited." But then he had not dreamed how bad the crash would be or how long the Depression would last. In fact, Scott's short story had really been about Zelda's crash, not his own. It was she who had gone into a mental institution in 1930, just as many of America's corporations were going into receivership. Scott felt a great loss, but in some ways it was the kind of loss a man feels when a stock hits bottom: his treasure had been smashed to bits but he himself was still intact. Four years after "Babylon Revisited" was published, however, the incredible happened: Scott's own head cracked. So in 1940, as he worked at turning "Babylon Revisited" into a movie, the author had a slightly different story to tell—the story of his own crack-up.

Actually, the carry-over from "Babylon Revisited" into *Cosmopolitan* was surprisingly slight. The mock courtship scene between father and daughter appears in the screenplay much as it does in the story. Wales says, "I want to get to know you . . . Who are you please?" And Victoria answers, "[Victoria] Wales, rue Palantine, Paris." "Married or single?" "No, not married. Single." And in both picture and story Victoria begs her father, "Daddy, I want to come and live with you . . . I love you better than anybody. And you love me better than anybody, don't you, now that mummy's dead?" "Of course I do," the father says. "But you won't always like me best, honey. You'll grow up and meet somebody your own age and go marry him and forget you ever had a daddy." "Yes, that's true." Then there is Marion's denunciation of Charles. "My duty is entirely to Helen," she says in both stories. "I try to think what she would have wanted me to do. Frankly, from the night you did that terrible thing you haven't really existed for me. I can't help that. She was my sister."[26] Almost all the rest of the dialogue in the screenplay Fitzgerald had to create fresh out of his imagination.

The basic situation, the problem, in both stories is the same: a father is separated from his daughter. But in the short story the father knows from the beginning what he wants: his daughter back. The screenplay, on the other hand, is actually the story of how the father comes to discover his need for that daughter.

Continually drunk, fast becoming an alcoholic, rude to everyone including Victoria, cracked up, Wales is put in the care of doctors and shipped off—like Pat in *Three Comrades,* like Nicole in *Tender Is the Night,* like Scott and Zelda both—to a Swiss sanitarium. He is cared for by a woman much like the nurse in "An Alcoholic Case." The author told his producer what he wanted her to be like—and what not like—at her first entrance: "She must not awaken a romantic pull in the audience, but rather she will justify or damn herself by her actions."[27] Rosalind, Gloria, Daisy, Nicole—they had all created a "romantic pull" when they stepped into a story. But Fitzgerald's new women, heroines like the nurse in the "Alcoholic Case" and especially Mme. Curie, were made beautiful by the work they did. In *Cosmopolitan,* Wales' nurse, Mary Waldron, works hard to put Wales back together again. Victoria liked Mary from the beginning, but it takes Wales longer to come around. When he does, he has taken the first step in pasting his broken family back together.

Cosmopolitan draws its moral richness and complexity from the two points of view, child and adult, and yet the action in the closing scenes has to do with erasing the gap between the father and daughter so finely portrayed through most of the story. In short, the father must learn to see through his daughter's camera. When he does, there will be only one level, only one viewpoint, and the story will have reached a happy resolution.

In telling such a story, Fitzgerald knew that he was taking certain risks. As he wrote Lester Cowan, "The effects have been attained by contrasting the innocence of a child's world with a series of adult situations," but if the child's world turned out to be too saccharine, then in learning to enter that world the father would be sinking into a second childhood. So Fitzgerald warned:

Any attempt to heighten the sentiment of the early scenes by putting mawkish speeches into the mouth of the characters —in short by doing what is locally known as "milking it"— will damage the *force* of the piece. Had the present author intended, he could have broken down the sentimental section of the audience at many points, but the price would have been *the release of the audience too quickly from tension*—and one would wonder at the end where the idea had vanished—or indeed what idea had been purchased. So whoever deals with this script is implored to remember that it is a *dramatic piece* —not a homey family story.[28]

The most important lesson that Wales learns from his daughter is that preserving what is left is more important than mourning what has already been lost. Incidentally, Fitzgerald seems to have been trying to teach himself the same lesson. Arthur Mizener writes that Fitzgerald began by writing stories about "the sadness of the lost past," but that in later stories, like "Babylon Revisited," "the past is used only for exposition; they are about the grim present."[29] But here the critic is only half right: in the story when Charles Wales comes into the Ritz Bar which is "not an American bar any longer,"[30] the air is rich with lost glory. In *Cosmopolitan*, however, the shadow of the past is lifted completely so that past events really do become only background. Perhaps this is because of the very nature of the motion picture, a medium which renders action in only one tense: the present.

Near the beginning of the picture, Victoria's Aunt Marion tells her, "I believe you think more about your father than about your—poor mother." Victoria, the eleven-year-old pragmatist, replies, "Mother's dead—Daddy's still alive."[31] What Wales must learn, of course, is to think more about Victoria than about his wife. In the end, he does.

Fitzgerald had begun *The Last Tycoon* before Lester Cowan hired him to turn "Babylon Revisited" into a movie, so like two mirrors facing one another it is hard to say which work reflects the other. Both are about heroes whose first heroines have died. Moreover, in *Cosmopolitan* (but not in "Babylon") Victoria continually reminds Wales of his dead wife, just as in *The Last Tycoon* Kathleen reminds Stahr of his own. Most interesting of all is the brotherhood which seems to exist between the two heroes: they are both, in their own ways, the end of a great line of tycoons. Wales is the literal tycoon: the big business operator, dealing in stocks and bonds. Stahr is a new type: the cinema tycoon. Neither man is small or selfish; they stand in bold contrast to men who "have merely gypped another person's empire away from them like the four great railroad kings of the coast."[32] Had the novel been finished, Stahr was to have interceded on the side of the workers at the studio. The night Wales' wife killed herself, her husband was not playing the market for himself but to save a friend. Stahr and Wales are benevolent tycoons, and the last of them.

Both Stahr's and Wales' rise are linked to the American Dream, to Manifest Destiny. Stahr goes west like the pioneers to be a kind of conquistador in California. Wales, of course, stays in the East, but nonetheless continues to think in American frontier terms. When the crash comes and he is forced to go back into the market to spend one last day "selling short" or be ruined completely, he explains his business deals to his daughter this way:

> WALES (*to Victoria*): About the market, dear—suppose I was a man whom just *loved* to hunt Indians—and then I decided not to . . . But one day the Indians came and attacked my house. I'd have to shoot them, wouldn't I?[33]

Gatsby, Wales, Stahr—they all follow the pioneers.

Even the endings of *Cosmopolitan* and *The Last Tycoon* were to have been mirror images of one another. In both stories the benevolent tycoons are threatened by a new breed of money men, destructive tycoons related not to the pioneers of early American history but to the gangsters of Prohibition. *The Last Tycoon* was to have ended with Stahr forced to hire men to murder his rival, Brady, because Brady has hired men to murder him. Wales' story ends with the young man who followed

Victoria onto the train trying to kill her father so that her father's former partners can collect his insurance to cover their losses in the crash. The gunman breaks into Wales' room and is about to fire when the telephone rings. The executioner looks for an instant in the direction of the sound, and Wales knocks the gun from his hand. It is Victoria calling.

Fitzgerald had spliced together all or most of what he had learned in Hollywood. In *Cosmopolitan,* the picture experiment begun with Rumpled Hair and Gray Hair in *Infidelity* is completed. Rumpled and Gray added a Nick Carraway touch at the beginning of the earlier screenplay; in *Cosmopolitan* that beginning is made to stretch over the entire length of the film. Victoria becomes a kind of Dr. T. J. Eckleburg, and through her eyes we brood over the wasteland of a boom/bust world. But this story does not live by pictures alone, as *Infidelity* sometimes seemed to. Rather, the sound track is now used to actually stretch that picture, to make us aware of worlds beyond the range of the camera. While we are looking at the adult world, we hear the child's. While we look at the child's, we hear the clacking ticker and the strained voices of the adult's. *Cosmopolitan* also reintroduces Fitzgerald's new breed of heroine, and with that heroine we see again the new marriage which she represents, a marriage where both husband and wife are able to work without damaging the other.

3

Scott was there to drive a hard bargain, to make a deal. That was the problem with writing for the movies. You had to be such a businessman, a wheeler-dealer, a Hollywood tycoon betting not on U.S. Steel or American Tel and Tel, but on properties like Stewart, Grant, and Hepburn. The problem was worse when your producer wasn't willing to put up much money to buy stars. Scott was an amateur, new to Hollywood high finance, while the actress he faced was a veteran who had been in the business most of her life. A latter-day prospector, she had found California gold in her curls. Across the bargaining table from Scott sat a real tycoon, Shirley Temple.

Fitzgerald wrote his daughter that he had met Miss Temple,

> with whom I spent the day yesterday. (Her mother was there so it was all right.) She really is a sweet little girl and reminds me of you at 11½ when you hadn't succumbed to the wiles of Fred Astaire, lovey dovey and the radio crooners. But I told her mother it wouldn't be long now. I don't know whether she's going to do my picture or not.

He finished the letter with, "Isn't the world a lousy place?— I've just finished a copy of *Life* and I'm dashing around to a Boris Karloff movie to cheer up. It is an inspirational thing called *The Corpse in the Breakfast Food.*"[34]

The same day the author wrote his wife to tell her about the eleven-year-old celebrity he was getting to know:

> I spent a silly day yesterday with Shirley Temple and her family. They want to do the picture and they don't want to do the picture, but that's really the producer's worry and not mine. She's a lovely little girl, beautifully brought up, and she hasn't quite reached the difficult age yet—figuring the difficult age at twelve. She reminds me so much of Scottie in the last days at La Paix, just before she entered Bryn Mawr. You weren't there the day of the Maryland Hunt Cup Race in the spring of '34 when Scottie got the skirt and coat from my mother which suddenly jumped her into adolescence.[35]

In a more business-like tone, Scott wrote Cowan:

> I was very impressed with the Temple kid—no trace of coyness or cuteness, yet a real dignity and gentleness . . . if the personality that she has in private life could be carried *almost without heightening* over into the picture, I believe she would be perfect. She has reached a point pictorially and by reason of natural charm where any attempt to strain and stress her prophetic conduct would seem a vulgarization. She is a perfect thing now in her way, and I would like to see that exquisite glow and tranquility carried intact through a sus-

tained dramatic action. Whoever you get for the part would have to forget such old dodges as talking with tears in her voice, something that a well brought-up child wouldn't.[36]

Miss Temple *was* like the little girl Fitzgerald had created in his script—in more ways than the author would ever know. Like Victoria, who stared at a roast pig while her father and the captain talked stocks, Shirley ignored the grownups' talk of money, but stared at the glass in Fitzgerald's hand, which had to be refilled time and time again. Miss Temple, now Shirley Temple Black, says that she remembers that the author "visited my home once and spent two or three hours speaking with great enthusiasm about 'Babylon Revisited,'" adding: "I remember Fitzgerald as a kindly, thin and pale man, who was recovering from an illness. The thing that impressed me the most as an eleven or twelve-year-old was that he drank six or eight Coca-Colas during his visit. As a young girl, I thought this to be a stunning accomplishment—in fact, I *still* do."

Negotiations dragged on and no contract was signed. The Captain of the Good Ship Lollypop had something of a pirate for a mother. "I'm afraid Shirley Temple will be grown before Mrs. Temple decides to meet the producer's terms," the husband wrote his faraway wife. "It wouldn't be interesting if she's thirteen."[37]

And while Scott was worrying about a star, he had to worry about a director, too. Cowan approached Garson Kanin at RKO to see if he would be interested in doing the picture, and Scott wrote immediately to encourage Kanin to take the job. "The idea," he said, "of an old-line director dipping this one in the traditional fish-glue would make me sad indeed." With the same worry on his mind, he wrote Cowan, "I want what happens in this picture to be felt in the stomach first, felt out of great conviction about the tragedy of father and child—and *not* felt in the throat to make a fat woman's holiday between chocolate creams."[38]

The picture never went up to the cameras, but Scott was spared knowing that he had failed once again. He died still believing that his picture had a chance.

Years later Victoria came home to the father who had named

her Budd Schulberg. He was given Scott's screenplay and
asked to rewrite it. "I read it," he remembers, "and thought it
first rate, just as it stood."[39]

Schulberg refused to touch the script, but others were not so
timid about rewriting Scott Fitzgerald. Later MGM, the studio
where Fitzgerald started, purchased the script for which Cowan
had paid five thousand. They paid the producer one hundred
thousand. At about the same time they bought an Elliot Paul
book about expatriate life in France. So when the story appeared
on the nation's motion-picture screens in 1954, someone else got
the money—Lester Cowan. And someone else got the credit—
screenwriters Julius J. and Paul G. Epstein. Metro even used
someone else's title, Elliot Paul's: *The Last Time I Saw Paris*.

Van Johnson played Charles, Elizabeth Taylor his wife Helen.
Donna Reed was the Aunt Marion with whom Victoria went to
live, and Sandra Descken was Vicky herself.

Bosley Crowther passed judgment in the *New York Times*
as follows:

> F. Scott Fitzgerald's poignant story of a father's lonely love
> for his little girl, told in "Babylon Revisited," has "inspired"
> Metro-Goldwyn-Mayer's big color film *The Last Time I Saw
> Paris*. . . .
> "Inspired" is a polite way to put it. For what has actually
> occurred is that Mr. Fitzgerald's cryptic story of a man's
> return to the scene of his wantonness—to Paris, that is—in the
> tense hope of recovering his child by his late wife, has excited
> the picture makers to an orgy of turning up the past and
> constructing a whole lurid flashback on the loving and lushing
> of the man and his wife before she died.
> . . . Richard Brooks, who directed this picture after polish-
> ing up an Epstein-brothers' script . . . changed the time of it—
> from the predepression days to the years just after the last war,
> when Paris was again full of American sports. Next, he has
> changed the hero's business. Now he is an ink-smeared jour-
> nalist who graduates from *Stars and Stripes* to a news agency
> and then to a hopeless try at authorship. And finally he has
> made the wife a daughter of an American expatriate, and has

arranged for the couple to get wealthy by a lucky strike of Texas oil. . . .

Money is the evil that defeats them. As soon as they strike it rich, they begin to behave like idiots and get themselves hopelessly involved. . . . Finally, after an odious marital mix-up—he with another woman and she with another man—the husband locks the wife out in a snowstorm and she dies of pneumonia. . . . The rest is loosely Mr. Fitzgerald's tale—how the husband, now sober and repentant, returns to Paris to get his child, how his sister-in-law resists him and how, in the end—unlike Mr. Fitzgerald's lady—she gives in.[40]

Time magazine praised the acting of Elizabeth Taylor and company, then added, "But all these excellent efforts are lost in the general effort to bring the twenties up to date—an attempt about as sensible in 1954 as mixing bathtub gin.[41]

At the end of *The Great Gatsby,* Nick Carraway returned to his dead friend's mansion and walked the lawns where Rolls-Royce head lamps once gilded the grass and the party guests. Nick passed the swimming pool where they had found Jay floating in the water mixed with blood. He went on to the front of Gatsby's Folly, that great palace where no queen had ever lived, and on up the steps. At the top, he stooped to erase the dirty word that a boy had scrawled in chalk against the doorstep.

Fifteen years later, Fitzgerald himself was not so lucky. After he was gone, the producers and their writers gathered about his best screen play like little boys with their boxes of chalk, but there was no one left to come along behind them and rub out the words they scrawled on Scott's monument.

☆ 13 ☆

"Action Is Character"

1

After a shower and a shave, Fitzgerald went to the closet to disturb the last rest of an old suit. As he slipped into the jacket, he found it an old friend, but not the kind of friend you much wanted other people to meet. When he was dressed, Scott went looking for Sheilah. She wasn't far away. She couldn't have been, not in the small apartment they had rented in Hollywood when the Encino summer turned too hot. Together they piled into the car and headed for Dorothy Parker's. The playboy of the twenties was on his way to his last party. At Mrs. Parker's, Scott found many old friends, but there were many whom he didn't find. Frank Tuttle of the old Film Guild was there, along with Deems Taylor—Scott hadn't seen them since those long party nights on Long Island in the twenties. But he missed the Hacketts, who had long since gone home to New York. Anita Loos was missing, too. She had wanted to leave two years before, but Metro had refused to release her from her contract. "So I wrote movies with one hand and a play for Helen Hayes with the other," she remembers. When her time was served, she headed for Broadway. Fitzgerald wrote Zelda that Fay Wray, the girl in *King Kong*, had been at the party, but that he had missed her husband, John Monk Saunders.[1] One night Saunders, whose chest had once mesmerized Zelda, had gone to his closet and taken down a robe much like the one which the young Fitzgeralds had ripped open back in 1927. He used the robe's cord to make a noose.

Fitzgerald was happy to see Dorothy Parker, that old friend from New York whom he had met again at Metro, where she once leaned out of a window in the writers' building and screamed, "Let me out of here. I'm as sane as you are!"[2] Mrs. Parker was one of the old crowd, but her entourage now included some new faces. Scott stuck to the older people, though he was very much aware of the others. "There was a younger generation there," he wrote Zelda. "I felt very passé and decided to get a new suit."[3]

The next morning Fitzgerald was back at the 20th Century–Fox studio, back in the little Spanish cottage with the red-tile roof, back in his chair looking at the telephone, waiting for it to ring. He couldn't go forward with his script until Darryl Zanuck approved his latest scenes. Meanwhile Zanuck's outer office was crowded with directors, producers, agents, and others who were nothing—only reputations waiting patiently to be made. When the executive got time, he would scan what Fitzgerald had written.

The writers' cottage where Scott sat was crowded, too—crowded with new people in new suits writing more pages for Zanuck to pass on. Sometimes while he was waiting Scott would go out into the garden that surrounded the cottage and pace its narrow walkways, but these paths, like the wires of a great communications network, always led back to the same telephone.

Darryl Zanuck, the head of 20th Century–Fox, had met Fitzgerald several times at parties in Europe back in the 1920s, and perhaps that was one reason why he had hired him. When Scott heard that Zanuck wanted him, he wrote Zelda, "I think I have a pretty good job coming up next week—a possibility of ten weeks' work and a fairly nice price [$7000 total] at 20th Century–

Fox. I have my fingers crossed, but with the good Shirley Temple script behind me I think my stock out here is better than at any time during the last year."⁴

What he did not write home about was the kind of picture he had been hired to rewrite. After completing his great original, *Cosmopolitan,* he was now back to adapting another writer's work for the screen. Moreover, it was only going to be a B picture. The author who had once set out to prove that he was "better than any of the other young Americans *without exception*"⁵ was being asked to write the hind end of a double feature. The story was about an artist who had once been applauded by everyone but who had been undone by drink. Now an old man, he tried to support his daughter by doing odd jobs. Fitzgerald must have wondered if he needed this much irony in his life.

After a script conference with Zanuck and several others, Fitzgerald got down to work. He was under orders to stick as close as possible to Emlyn Williams' London play *The Light of Heart,* but Christmas was not far off and the holidays gave him an idea for an original opening. He had learned the power of beginning a motion picture with a nearly silent scene, a Chaplinesque pantomime; he decided to open with a mute portrait of twelve Santas in the personnel room of a London department store. The first eleven Santas are sober—the last one in line adjusts his "beard so as to disguise his mouth as much as possible," and "reels a little on his feet." The personnel manager instructs his army of redcoats that the toys they carry are *not* for sale, then sends them out into the streets where "our Santa Claus . . . clutches an ash can and hangs there a second." The unsteady Father Christmas turns out to be Mackay Duncan, a former matinee idol who was washed off the stage in a tidal wave of booze. His biggest problem in his latest role, the one which the department store has hired him to play, is that he comes to believe that there really is a Santa Claus and that *he* is it. He offers a little boy one of his display toys, but the boy protests, "I haven't got a bob." Mackay answers dimly, "The displays are

not for sale."[6] When the department store discovers that Mackay
has given everything away, this Santa finds himself unemployed
on Christmas eve.

The failed Father Christmas stumbles home to tell his daughter Catherine. She is crippled and that makes it harder for
Mackay to confess. But before he can tell her, she informs him
that she has just been offered a job singing in a wedding. Fitzgerald understood the touching paradox immediately. Many of
his earlier characters had been sound of body but acted like
cripples, always leaning on others. But now in Emlyn Williams'
The Light of Heart Scott found a real cripple, a girl with a club
foot, who leaned on no one but instead was a crutch to her
father. In this sense, she was a kind of sister to Marie Curie in
Madame Curie and Mary Waldron in *Cosmopolitan,* women who
represented Fitzgerald's new heroines, women who supported
others. Fitzgerald had not planned it this way but still it was
appropriate that the last portrait in his gallery of heroines should
be Catherine.

Out of a job again, Mackay Duncan dries out and goes looking
for work once more. Here Fitzgerald decided to add an irony
not found in the play. He gave Mackay a position as guide at an
Ideal Homes Exhibition. Scott, of course, knew that his own
credentials for the job were no better than Mackay's. Ideal
Home?—why, a daughter away at school and a wife away at
the sanitarium wouldn't even be enough for a down payment.
Mackay is in charge of keeping the customers circulating.

> MACKAY: Move along please. MOVE ALONG PLEASE. Move
> a—long *please!* Move ALONG, please. *MOVE* along—please.
> . . . (*Bending forward confidentially*) There's a small fire in
> the basement, Madame . . .[7]

Mackay's creative approach to his job loses him this position too.

Just when it looks as if Mackay Duncan will go on drunkenly
staggering after jobs forever, help arrives in the form of a
dowager dea-ex-machina. Here name is Lady Machen, and she
idolized Duncan when he was a star. Now she resolves to make

him one once again. She invites Duncan and his daughter to her country estate. Fitzgerald described the change which the new chance has worked upon Mackay. The author was in a position to appreciate such transformations.

> CAMERA FAVORS Mackay who sits with a magazine on his knee. He looks ten years younger; his hair is cut, his suit is new, and he wears horn-rimmed spectacles. Now that he is neither drunk nor suffering from after effects, his true manner emerges for the first time—shy, good-humored and unpretentious. After eight years of desperation . . . this journey into the world of country houses, leisure, and luxury is a great adventure.[8]

Also present on the Machen estate—assembled there by the muse of melodrama—are a young musician named Robert McClure and a beautiful blonde named Eleanor who expects a proposal from him. Eleanor knows that Catherine is in love with Robert, too, and so refers to her jealously as "the girl with the heart of gold—and the foot."[9] The three sides of this triangle are brought together one afternoon on Lady Machen's veranda. There Fitzgerald put together a scene which not only accomplishes the engagement of a man and a women, but seems to wed the silent films of the twenties to the talking thirties. Many of the words are Emlyn Williams', but the technique is all Scott Fitzgerald—it was the kind of scene he had been working for almost four years to learn how to write:*

EXT. CORNER OF COUNTRY-HOUSE VERANDA—
   CATHERINE

Lazy chairs against a wall of ivy and climbing wisteria. Back of the chairs is the glassed-in part of the veranda, used as a semi-conservatory *into which we can see clearly.* In the glass wall is a glass door. Catherine is on a wicker chaise longue with a book.

---

* Quoted at such length not because it is Fitzgerald's best screenplay but because 20th Century–Fox proved to be the most generous studio with permissions.

ROBERT

approaching along the veranda, thoughtful . . .

ROBERT . . . (*suddenly strained*): Why do you think you're
constitutionally deformed?

CATHERINE: I'm not in the mood for your frank stunt, Robert.
. . .

ANOTHER ANGLE INCLUDING ROBERT, CATHERINE
AND THROUGH THE GLASS, ELEANOR

who has come into the conservatory and not yet seen Robert
and Catherine outside.

From this point on, we watch Eleanor behind the glass as if she
were a character in a silent movie, seen and not heard. Catherine
and Robert continue to play a talkie. He tells her what he has
just discovered by telephoning the doctor who delivered her.

ROBERT: . . . I've been trying to trace him for weeks. He's just
told me that you were one of the most perfect babies he ever
saw.

INT. CONSERVATORY—ELEANOR

looking impatient and pettish. She breaks off the stem of an
orchid and starts to pin it on her shoulder. Simultaneously she
sees Robert through the glass and brightens. *She cannot hear
them.*

For Eleanor, of course, the people on *our* side of the glass are
the ones in the silent film.

EXT. VERANDA—ROBERT AND CATHERINE

CATHERINE: But . . . he told my father I was born crippled.
Why should he have lied about it?

ROBERT: Because when you were a year old your father had a
bad fall with you in his arms. When they found something

was wrong, the doctor made out you'd been born like that, to save your father's feelings. You see, when he fell he— wasn't sober.

ANOTHER ANGLE—INCLUDING ELEANOR THROUGH GLASS

Robert turns and his eyes meet Eleanor's. He smiles abstractly, and nods as if to say "Just a minute." She smiles back—it won't be long now. . . .

ROBERT: Do you realize this means you can have a perfectly healthy child?

CATHERINE (*philosophically*): You mean I *could* have had. I don't see any husbands suddenly rushing at me from nowhere. . . .

ROBERT: Can't you see that I'm asking you to marry me? . . .

INT. CONSERVATORY—ELEANOR

looking out, frowning. In b.g. through the glass Robert regarding Catherine, whose face cannot be seen. . . . His face tells her everything, and she strains close to the glass trying unsuccessfully to hear and feeling outraged. . . .

TWO SHOT—CATHERINE AND ROBERT

. . . we can clearly see Eleanor through the glass in b.g. walking quickly from the conservatory.[10]

Fitzgerald's new heroine had beaten just the kind of girl whom the author had once so romanticized.

The weekend among the very rich ends for Catherine and Mackay, and they return to their small room in the great city. The actor and his daughter spend their days getting up the play which Lady Machen had chosen for Duncan's comeback—*Lear*. This Shakespearean tragedy was selected for the play within the play because Mackay is about to lose his own Cordelia. Not only is she to be married, but she and her husband plan to go to America to live. Fitzgerald, who felt that he had lost his own daughter, thumbed through his copy of *Lear* time and time again to find just the right Lear-Cordelia speeches for Mackay and Catherine to practice together.

MACKAY: . . . O, you are men of stone!
Had I your tongues and eyes, I'd use them so
That heaven's vault should crack. She's gone for ever!

On the day of the long-awaited opening, Duncan discovers— melodrama will out!—that his daughter is leaving him. He hears the news and cracks like an old plate. Suddenly he can no longer remember his lines. They find Mackay in the street, his body, like the window through which he jumped, shattered.

At first Fitzgerald had been very hopeful about *The Light of Heart*. Like the actor Duncan, he foresaw a comeback. Scott wasn't a star nor much competition for Tyrone Power, the studio's current *ne plus ultra*. But in playful moods the author sometimes felt like a star and would send his secretary telegrams affectionately signed TYRONE.

With a check coming in regularly now, he sent Zelda some extra money to "spend on something which you need," along with the following explanation: "This is the third week of my job and I'm holding up very well, but so many jobs have started well and come to nothing that I keep my fingers crossed until the thing is in production." At the end of the letter, however, he allowed himself a paragraph for hoping. "They've let a certain writer here direct his own pictures," he said, "and he has made such a go of it that there may be a different feeling about that soon. If I had that chance, I would attain my real goal in coming here in the first place."[12]

After six weeks on the picture the writing continued to go well. Fitzgerald was pleased when he reported to his agent that Zanuck was thinking of elevating *The Light of Heart* from a B production to an A. "I don't know what the next three months will bring further," he wrote Zelda, "but if I get a credit on either of these last two efforts things will never again seem so black as they did a year ago, when I felt that Hollywood had me down in its books as a ruined man—a label which I had done nothing to deserve."[13]

The euphoria could not last. Quarrels sprang up in the conference room at 20th Century–Fox. The Zanuck people thought Scott's story was too gloomy. They especially did not like a scene which pictured the girl with the clubfoot acting like a normal girl, dancing with the man she loved. One night Scott waited up even later than usual at 20th. It was well after midnight, but the author and his secretary were still at their posts beside the telephone. There was nothing to do to fill up the waiting time. The writer could not even try to think out his next scene—not until he was sure that this one had been okayed. The studio was quiet now. There were no typewriters, no conversations, only the sounds of many people waiting. And then, occasionally, a wastebasket would rattle. Offices which were impossible to get into during the day now opened immediately to admit cleaning ladies.

Fitzgerald listened, looked out at the dark, sharpened his pencils. As he grew tireder, the hours of walking up and down dictating began to tell. His feet hurt. The author hoisted one foot after the other up onto his desk. Carefully prying off his tight-fitting shoes, he confided to Miss Kroll, "I'm beginning to feel the squeeze."

In a letter to Zelda written a few days later, he reported, "I don't know how this job is going. . . . Things depend on such hairlines here—one must not only do a thing well but do it as a compromise, sometimes between utterly opposed ideas of two differing executives. The diplomatic part in business is my weak spot."[14]

On October 19 Fitzgerald wrote his agent, "You are a tactful man but I felt a certain tacit reproof in your voice this afternoon. You thought either I should have (a) rejected the script as gloomy or (b) done a better job at brightening it. Well, at the end of two weeks I did feel it wasn't good for a great movie, but Zanuck had been so stirred by my ideas at the first conference . . . that I thought I must be wrong."[15]

The Emlyn Williams play was passed on to the man whom Fitzgerald two years before had tried to order out of Hollywood. Nunnally Johnson, who hadn't taken the advice and who never knew that Scott had written an adaptation of *The Light of Heart*, turned out a script which was filmed in 1942 under the title *Life Begins at 8:30*. Fitzgerald's screenplay had been written by a grim man in a grim season, and it showed. Johnson had brightened up the movie so that Bosley Crowther, writing in the *New York Times*, called it "a tears-and-laughter story of a liquidated actor" which is sad but "not grim." The critic called Monty Woolley, who starred in the film, "the man who came to dinner— with a load."[16] Johnson had even contrived a happy ending where Fitzgerald's ending had been another dirge.

The day Scott discovered that there was no hope at all for his picture, he wrote Zelda. For the first time in weeks, he said nothing about his script. Instead, he was full of his book. "I'm trying desperately to finish my novel by the middle of December," he wrote, "and it's a little like working on *Tender Is the Night* at the end—I think of nothing else. . . . My room is covered with charts like it used to be for *Tender Is the Night,* telling the different movements of the characters and their histories. However, this one is to be short, as I originally planned it two years ago, and more on the order of *Gatsby*."[17]

The next week he wrote, "I am deep in the novel, living in it, and it makes me happy. It is a constructed novel like *Gatsby,* with passages of poetic prose when it fits the action, but no ruminations or side shows like *Tender*. Everything must contribute to the dramatic movement." At the end of the letter he said, "Two thousand words today and all good."[18]

Then the letters stopped for a fortnight. When they resumed, there was a worried irritation in the voice. "No news," Fitzgerald said, "except that the novel progresses and I am angry that this little illness has slowed me up."[19]

2

Fitzgerald was in Schwab's to buy cigarettes. Every American small town in the 1930s seemed to be built around not City Hall but the local drugstore, and Hollywood, the arch small town, was no different: it sometimes seemed to be built around Schwab's. It was like an extension of some studio's commissary, the kind of place where you might see Joan Crawford buying bobby pins. Scott was taking it all in, not missing a thing—a novelist could not afford to—when suddenly all his mental notes were erased. He had almost lost it all. Somehow he held on. He even got together the strength to walk home.

It was a dull November afternoon. Sheilah was on the sofa listening to Bach's *Singet dem Herrn,* so she did not hear Scott return. He wasn't making much noise. When she looked up, he was trembling as he lowered himself into a chair. "Is anything the matter, Scott?" she asked and hurried to turn down the music. He took his time about lighting a cigarette, lifting the match carefully; then he answered.

"I almost fainted at Schwab's. Everything started to fade. I think I'd better see Dr. Wilson in the morning."

The next day Fitzgerald drove downtown to his doctor's office. When he returned he announced, "I had a cardiac spasm."[20]

Not long before, he had written Zelda, "Weeks of fever and coughing—but the constitution is an amazing thing and nothing quite kills it until the heart has run its entire race."[21]

From the time of the heart spasm, movies were out. He wrote his daughter the day that it happened, but saved all news about his health for what tried to be a matter-of-fact postscript. "P.S. . . . The phone rang after I finished this letter," he said, "and the doctor after seeing my cardiogram has confined me to the house. So at this moment I *couldn't* go to the studios if I wanted to."[22]

Under a strange kind of house arrest—the only guard his own heart—Fitzgerald continued to work on his novel. He could not go near the studios but in a sense they were still very close to him. He even wrote most of the dialogue for his book the way they had taught him at the studios, walking up and down, dictating to his secretary. When he couldn't walk, the secretary would sit beside his bed.

And out of all that pacing and dictating came a dialogue and action that was different from anything Fitzgerald had written in any of his earlier books. In *Tender Is the Night* especially there had been very little that was actually said or done, but that was because, as Fitzgerald himself explained, *Tender* "was shooting at something like *Vanity Fair*." It was a psychological novel. Now, however, he was trying to write a dramatic novel and, as he said, that kind of writing "has canons quite different."[23] In fact, *The Last Tycoon* is so much more dramatic than any of his other stories that it sometimes seems to be a printed talkie.

On the black and white pages there could be no real pictures for the eye, but for the imagination there was much to see: the lights like fireworks as the plane dropped down into Los Angeles, the earthquake and even a flood with the heroine served up to the hero on a huge papier-mâché head of a goddess floating in a rampaging drainage ditch. Fitzgerald had learned that the best movies emphasize the visual, and he must have decided that a great novel needed bold visions, too.

In *Tender Is the Night* we must generally take Dick Diver's charm on faith, or infer it from his effect on others, but Stahr's leadership and his production genius are another matter. They are demonstrated for us, acted out in the story. We follow Stahr through a day at the studio and see him coach Boxley, review the day's rushes, remove a director who has been dominated by his star, help a cowboy who suddenly finds himself impotent, and preside over a story conference where he calmly tells his writers that they have written the wrong kind of story. As Fitzgerald wrote in his notes for *The Last Tycoon:* "ACTION IS CHARACTER."[24] This was perhaps the most important lesson Fitzgerald learned in Hollywood. It was an existential rule not only to write by but to try to live by. In the novel Stahr is a leader only to the extent that he leads, and the man behind the novel, Scott Fitzgerald, had come to realize that he was a writer only to the extent that he wrote. He had outgrown that old idea that character is a pretty face or a good profile or fine dreams. Like Mme. Curie, Mary Waldron, and even the crippled Catherine, Stahr finds his character, and therefore his integrity, his dignity, in hard work. And Fitzgerald too, writing in bed with the last of his life's strength, hoped to work for, to earn, his own character.

But to learn that "ACTION IS CHARACTER" is one thing, and to learn it in time is another. Fitzgerald returned to the novel too late, just as Stahr found Kathleen too late. Stahr and Fitzgerald had found their new heroine, but the producer lost her because for once he did not act in time, and the novelist lost her because he died before he could finish her portrait, enshrining in a book the kind of heroine he had already created for the movies.

Stahr liked Kathleen because she was not at all like the other girls he kept meeting, nor was she much like the girls to be met in the fiction Fitzgerald wrote before coming to Hollywood. "This girl had a life," the author wrote in his notes, "—it was very seldom he met anyone whose life did not depend in some way on him or hope to depend on him."[25] Had it worked out, she might have been to Stahr what Mary Waldron was to Charles Wales, what Marie was to Pierre Curie.

In *Cosmopolitan* Nicolas walked through the emptiness of his unused mansion, finally stopping in his bedroom where even the bed is covered to keep off dust. His tragedy is a house vacated before its time, just as Stahr's tragedy is the "Waste Land of the house too late." Stahr and Kathleen drive out to the producer's unfinished home together. It looks like the half-done houses on the sets at the studio, and what the man and woman say to one another there reads a little like a scenario, one of the good ones.

"I'm building a house out here," Stahr said, "—much further on. I don't know why I'm building it."

"Perhaps it's for me," she said.

"Maybe it is."

"I think it's splendid for you to build a big house for me without even knowing what I looked like."

"It isn't too big. And it hasn't any roof. I didn't know what kind of roof you wanted."

"We don't want a roof. They told me it never rained here. It—"

She stopped so suddenly that he knew she was reminded of something.

"Just something that's past," she said.

"What was it?" he demanded, "—another house without a roof?"

"Yes. Another house without a roof."

"Were you happy there?"

"I lived with a man," she said, "a long, long time—too long. It was one of those awful mistakes people make. I lived with him a long time after I wanted to get out, but he couldn't let me go. He'd try, but he couldn't. So finally I ran away."

He was listening, weighing but not judging. . . .

"We were too close," she said. "We should probably have had children—to stand between us. But you can't have children when there's no roof to the house."[26]

The studio is really Stahr's home, and his house—complete with prop department grass and a projector in the living room— is really a studio. Pictures might be begotten here, but nothing else. *The Last Tycoon* is a monument to new techniques, but also to a new sentiment. Over the course of Fitzgerald's writing career, there had been a shift from the nostalgia for what is lost in the past to a nostalgia for what will be lost in the future: the children that Nicolas and Althea will never have, the house which Stahr will never finish. Nicolas' and Stahr's defeats, of course, seem to prophesy the final, unintended nostalgia of *The Last Tycoon* itself, the great fragment.

During the 1930s the novel and the movies seemed to flow into one another, two fictional streams joining and altering one another's course. Novels helped to flesh the movies out, giving them fully developed stories to tell, but at the same time the pictures taught the novels to pick up their pace, so that they moved faster than a Victorian walk. In *The Last Tycoon* F. Scott Fitzgerald, the novelist who was also a screenwriter, was one of the first to

bring good movie writing and good novel writing together between the same covers. His first works had made him sound a
little like a late-blooming Victorian, but now as an old man of
forty-four he was putting together a story which was newer than
Hemingway. Hollywood had used him and cheated him and
neglected him, but it had also taught him.

On December 14 Fitzgerald wrote Zelda:

> The novel is about three-quarters through and I think I can
> go on till January 12 without doing any stories or going back
> to the studio. I couldn't go back to the studio anyhow in my
> present condition, as I have to spend most of the time in bed,
> where I write on a wooden desk that I had made a year and a
> half ago. The cardiogram shows that my heart is repairing
> itself, but it will be a gradual process that will take some
> months. It is odd that the heart is one of the organs that does
> repair itself.[27]

Fitzgerald used to say, however, that he sometimes knew more
in his books than he did in real life. And in the book which he
was writing now, the optimism of the letters was absent. At one
point he says of Stahr:

> He was due to die very soon now. Within six months one
> could say definitely. What was the use of developing the cardio-
> grams? You couldn't persuade a man like Stahr to stop and lie
> down and look at the sky for six months. He would much
> rather die. He said differently, but what it added up to was
> the definite urge towards total exhaustion that [the doctor]
> had run into before. Fatigue was a drug as well as a poison,
> and Stahr apparently derived some rare almost physical pleas-
> ure from working lightheaded with weariness. It was a perver-
> sion of the life force he had seen before, but he had almost
> stopped trying to interfere with it. He had cured a man or so—
> a hollow triumph of killing and preserving the shell.[28]

Epilogue

Here in the figured dark I watch once more
There with the curtain rolls a year away
A year of years . . .
                                        —Fitzgerald

Scott sat in the audience. He had been in the audience when the
Triangle Club's *Evil Eye* played St. Paul in 1916, not up on stage
as a chorus girl the way he should have been. And now as the
curtain was going up on the forties, he was *still* there, out front,
filling up a red plush seat in some gymnasium of a theatre in
Los Angeles. The author had once written in a short story, "We
make an agreement with children that they can sit in the audience
. . . but . . . after they are grown" they must help "to make the
play."[1] Yet Scott had failed in his attempts to make plays and so
was still trapped on the child's side of the footlights. The old
dream of love, money, and the stage coming together in an alliance with the writer had passed Fitzgerald by as surely as World
War I had passed him by. So, in the audience, Scott watched and
listened, just as Amory had, while "the violins swelled and
quavered on the last notes, the girl sank to a crumpled butterfly
on stage, a great burst of clapping filled the house."[2]

The girl was Helen Hayes. She no longer remembers what play it was, calling it simply "one of my bigger successes, one of those pompous plays I used to do." After all the opening night curtain calls and all the applause, the actress crept away to her dressing room where she was mobbed by "a lot of film people, all the celebrities." It was a long time before the room emptied and the actress was at last left alone with her flowers and her telegrams and the solvent which peeled off the make-up.

"Then I heard this quiet little knock," Miss Hayes remembers. "I looked up and saw Scott in the doorway with this little blonde beside him. I, of course, flung my arms around him and made a big fuss and we had a happy visit, I thought. I told him how nice it was of him to wait until all of the others had gone so that we could be alone together."

The next night the audience was just as large and just as enthusiastic, if not quite so distinguished, as the one on opening night. And there were almost as many flowers delivered to Miss Hayes' dressing room, even a large basket from Fitzgerald. Attached to the bouquet was a note from Scott which began, "Dear Helen, I know you despise me. I shouldn't have come backstage in that company . . ."

"That was the last I ever heard from Scott," the actress remembers.

Not long after, the novelist who had failed in his attempts to break into pictures spent the last evening of his life with a Hollywood gossip columnist at the movies. The feature was titled *This Thing Called Love:* it had a mechanical plot which revolved about a marriage of convenience. The date was December 20. Leaving the theatre, Fitzgerald staggered, so that Sheilah took his arm. For once, the proud man did not push her away. "I feel awful," he whispered, "—everything started to go as it did in Schwab's. I suppose people will think I'm drunk."[3] They didn't call the doctor that night because he was coming the next day anyway.

The following afternoon Fitzgerald sat in a chair in the apartment which he shared with Sheilah, passing the time while he waited for the doctor. He was thumbing through an alumni magazine from Princeton, the university which he left without a degree, making notes in the margin on next year's football team, the squad he hadn't made. He placed a check beside Bob Sandbach's name, remembering the field goal he had missed against Harvard so that the game ended in a 0–0 tie. But against Yale Sandbach had redeemed himself, kicking in three points from the twenty-six-yard line and winning the game for Princeton, 10–7. Scott had listened to the games on the radio. He was glad to see that the kicker would be coming back next year.

Fitzgerald's mind was on football when his heart stopped. He jumped to his feet, then fell dead. The body was taken to a Los Angeles mortuary where Dorothy Parker came and stood in front of the casket and said the same elegy for Scott which Owl Eyes had said for Gatsby: "Poor son of a bitch."[4] Twenty-eight years—almost to the day—after he had begun his first drama, *The Captured Shadow*, on a train running from Newman School to St. Paul for the holidays, his body was loaded onto a railroad car bound for Baltimore. Once again Scott Fitzgerald was going home for Christmas.

Tucked in with the author's notes for his unfinished novel was a short story about dying in Hollywood. The heroine was a young English girl named Pamela who was like Sheilah on the outside but on the inside was pure Scott. In the margin of one of the pages he wrote, "This has emotion—too sentimental but real." Pamela had come to Hollywood and attached herself to one of the studios much as Fitzgerald had. She wanted to break into the movie business, but something had gone wrong and she had been fired:

> She received her salary for some months—Jim saw to that—but she did not set foot on that lot again. Nor any others. She was placed quietly on that list that is not written down but that functions at backgammon games after dinner; or on the

way to the races. Men of influence stared at her with interest at restaurants here and there but all their inquiries about her reached the same dead end.

She never gave up during the following months—even long after Becker had lost interest and she was in want, and no longer seen in the places where people go to be looked at. It was not from grief or discouragement but only through commonplace circumstances that in June she died.

When the producer named Jim heard the news, he decided to get out Pam's screen tests. That was one way of saying good-by.

In the test Pamela was dressed as he had seen her that first night at the dance. She looked very happy and he was glad she had at least that much happiness. The reel of takes from the picture began and ran jerkily with the sound of Bob Griffin's voice off scene and with prop boys showing the number blocks for the takes. Then Jim started as the next to last one came up, and he saw her turn from the camera and whisper:

"I'd rather die than do it that way."[5]

☆ ☆ ☆

Notes

Preface

1. F. Scott Fitzgerald, "Handle with Care," *The Crack-Up*, ed. Edmund Wilson (New York: New Directions, 1956), p. 78.

2. F. Scott Fitzgerald, early MS version of *Tender Is the Night*, in Princeton University Library, pages not numbered consecutively.

3. F. Scott Fitzgerald, "Crazy Sunday," *The Stories of F. Scott Fitzgerald*, ed. Malcolm Cowley (New York: Charles Scribner's Sons, 1951), p. 407.

4. F. Scott Fitzgerald, *The Last Tycoon*, ed. Edmund Wilson (New York: Charles Scribner's Sons, 1941), p. 163.

1. A Day at the Studio, 1938

1. Andrew Turnbull, *Scott Fitzgerald* (New York: Charles Scribner's Sons, 1962), p. 288.

2. *The Letters of F. Scott Fitzgerald*, ed. Andrew Turnbull (New York: Dell Publishing Co., 1966), p. 28.

3. Story about Coke bottles told by H. M. Swanson, Fitzgerald's agent.

4. *Tycoon*, p. 21.

5. *Tycoon*, p. 48.

6. *Tycoon,* p. 7.

7. F. Scott Fitzgerald, *The Pat Hobby Stories,* ed. Arnold Gingrich (New York: Charles Scribner's Sons, 1962), p. 26.

8. *Tycoon,* p. 101.

9. *Letters,* pp. 30, 63.

10. F. Scott Fitzgerald, *The Great Gatsby* (New York: Charles Scribner's Sons, 1953), pp. 96, 40.

11. F. Scott Fitzgerald, *Infidelity,* MS in Metro-Goldwyn-Mayer archives, Culver City, California, p. 87.

12. *Tycoon,* pp. 94, 98.

13. This previously unpublished note is in a folder marked *The Last Tycoon* in the Fitzgerald Papers at Princeton University Library.

14. George Oppenheimer, *The View from the Sixties* (New York: David McKay Co., 1966), p. 105.

15. Note in *Tycoon* folder.

16. *Tycoon,* p. 110.

17. Sheilah Graham and Gerold Frank, *Beloved Infidel* (New York: Bantam Books Inc., 1968), pp. 165–66.

18. *Beloved,* p. 125.

19. Unpublished letter to Leland Hayward, December 6, 1939, in Princeton University Library.

20. Unpublished letter to Leland Hayward, January 16, 1940, in Princeton University Library.

21. Lillian Hellman, *An Unfinished Woman* (Boston: Little, Brown, 1969), pp. 67–68.

22. Carlos Baker, *Ernest Hemingway: A Life Story* (New York: Charles Scribner's Sons, 1968), p. 316.

23. Hellman, p. 68.

24. "Sleeping and Waking," *Crack-Up,* p. 67.

25. "Sleeping and Waking," *Crack-Up,* p. 68.

26. Note in *Tycoon* folder.

27. Arthur Mizener, *The Far Side of Paradise* (Boston: Houghton Mifflin Co., 1965), p. 317.

28. F. Scott Fitzgerald, "Pasting it Together," *Crack-Up,* pp. 83–84.

29. Sheilah Graham, *College of One* (New York: Bantam Books, Inc., 1968), p. 183.

30. *Tycoon,* p. 136.

31. *Gatsby,* p. 182.

2. Flashback

1. Bosley Crowther, *The Lion's Share: The Story of an Entertainment Empire* (New York: E. P. Dutton & Co., 1957), pp. 13–14. Crowther gives a good account of the evening that motion pictures were born, quoting from newspaper stories of the day and emphasizing the agitation of the crowd when they saw the ocean rolling toward them.

2. Fitzgerald's ledger is in the Princeton University Library.

3. F. Scott Fitzgerald, "My Lost City," *Crack-Up*, p. 23.

4. "The Freshest Boy," *Stories*, p. 340.

5. F. Scott Fitzgerald, "Head and Shoulders," *Flappers and Philosophers*, ed. Arthur Mizener (New York: Charles Scribner's Sons, 1959), p. 73.

6. F. Scott Fitzgerald, "The Adjuster," *Six Tales of the Jazz Age and Other Stories* (New York: Charles Scribner's Sons, 1960), p. 158.

7. F. Scott Fitzgerald, "Who's Who—and Why," *Afternoon of an Author*, ed. Arthur Mizener (New York: Charles Scribner's Sons, 1957), p. 83.

8. F. Scott Fitzgerald's scrapbook in Princeton University Library.

9. F. Scott Fitzgerald, "The Captured Shadow," *Stories*, p. 360.

10. Unpublished letter from Fitzgerald to Edwin H. Knopf, October 26, 1938, in Princeton University Library. Fitzgerald seems to have been serious about the importance of reducing one's ideas in the picture business. In *The Last Tycoon* he wrote:

> "I keep wishing you could start over," Boxley said. "It's this mass production."
>
> "That's the condition," said Stahr. "There's always some lousy condition. We're making a life of Rubens—suppose I asked you to do portraits of rich dopes like Bill Brady and me and Gary Cooper and Marcus when you wanted to paint Jesus Christ! Wouldn't you feel you had a condition? Our condition is that we have to take people's own favorite folklore and dress it up and give it back to them. Anything beyond that is sugar. So won't you give us some sugar, Mr. Boxley?" [p. 105.]

11. Scrapbook.

12. "Who's Who," *Afternoon*, p. 84. On other occasions Fitzgerald said that he went to Princeton because he admired their football team.

13. Turnbull, p. 44.

14. "Who's Who," *Afternoon,* p. 84.

15. Turnbull, p. 54.

16. Arthur Knight, *The Liveliest Art: A Panoramic History of the Movies* (New York: The New American Library Inc., 1957), p. 35.

17. "My Lost City," *Crack-Up,* p. 28.

18. Scrapbook.

19. *Letters,* p. 86.

20. "Who's Who," *Afternoon,* p. 84.

21. F. Scott Fitzgerald, "Handle with Care," *Crack-Up,* p. 76.

22. "Who's Who," *Afternoon,* p. 85.

23. F. Scott Fitzgerald, *This Side of Paradise* (New York: Charles Scribner's Sons, 1960), pp. 30–31.

24. *Paradise,* p. 40.

25. *Paradise,* p. 184.

26. Turnbull, p. 67.

27. "Pasting It Together," *Crack-Up,* p. 82.

28. Heywood Broun, *New York Tribune,* undated, in Fitzgerald's scrapbook.

29. Unpublished letter to Maxwell Perkins, July 1922, in Princeton University Library.

30. Arthur Mizener, "Introductory Essay," *Flappers,* p. 13. Not long after, Fitzgerald sold "Myra Meets His Family" to 20th Century–Fox and the story was produced as *The Husband Hunter.* Like "The Offshore Pirate," this story uses the device of actors who are hired to play roles—in this case to act as members of the family Myra meets. The ruse is meant to test Myra's love.

31. "Head and Shoulders," *Flappers,* p. 72.

32. "Head and Shoulders," *Flappers,* p. 27. Ardita Ford, about whom the story was written, gave a theatre party when the movie played in St. Paul so that everyone could "see what I am like in the movies" (*Far Side,* p. 373).

33. "Head and Shoulders," *Flappers,* p. 46.

34. Turnbull, p. 127.

35. F. Scott Fitzgerald, *The Beautiful and Damned* (New York: Charles Scribner's Sons, 1950), p. 422.

36. *Beautiful and Damned,* pp. 214–15.

37. Turnbull, p. 113.

38. Unpublished letter to Maxwell Perkins, April 15, 1922, in Princeton University Library.

39. James Gray, *St. Paul Dispatch,* March 2, 1926, p. 15.

40. F. Scott Fitzgerald, "The Diamond as Big as the Ritz," *Stories,* pp. 7, 25.

41. Unpublished letter to Maxwell Perkins, January 1922, in Princeton University Library.

42. *Letters,* p. 180.

43. *Far Side,* p. 170.

44. *Far Side,* p. 161.

45. F. Scott Fitzgerald, "How to Live on $36,000 a Year," *Afternoon,* pp. 93–94.

46. *Far Side,* p. 377.

47. B. F. Wilson interview in scrapbook.

48. F. Scott Fitzgerald, "Notes on *This Side of Paradise,*" eleven-page MS in Princeton University Library.

49. "Handle with Care," *Crack-Up,* p. 77.

50. *Far Side,* p. 214.

51. Frederick James Smith, "Fitzgerald, Flappers and Fame: An interview with F. Scott Fitzgerald," clipping in Scribner's file, Princeton University Library. Fitzgerald made several notes for changes. For one thing, he decided that the "Christlike" look spoiled the effect. "I don't think Amory should ever be sanctimonious or Christlike," he wrote, "so I believe in a semi-miraculous Christlike effect to convey the fact *directly* to the audience . . . a rich piglike suitor of Eleanor's might be introduced—and he later might fire the shot through Amory's hand." He also had second thoughts about the wedding scenes: ". . . instead of Amory going for flowers let her just run out in a panic and let him pursue her and then weep in his arms, going home unmarried in a taxi cab. . . . Somehow the groom with flowers in his hand and the bride gone is always faintly ridiculous."

3. Beginning in Hollywood

1. F. Scott and Zelda Fitzgerald, "Auction—Model 1934," *Crack-Up,* p. 58.

2. *Far Side,* p. 224.

3. In a note in the *Tycoon* folder, Fitzgerald mentions a "talk with Eisenstein" about "cross cutting."

4. Turnbull, p. 136.

5. *Gatsby*, p. 2. Milton Hindus also makes the point about the actor in Jay Gatsby in *F. Scott Fitzgerald: An Introduction and Interpretation* (New York: Holt, Rinehart and Winston, 1968):

> There is some evidence for believing that in making Gatsby resemble an actor who regarded life itself as his stage, Fitzgerald thought that he was drawing a universal human characteristic—as Shakespeare did when he called life a stage and all men and women players. [p. 42.]

6. *Gatsby*, p. 106.

7. *Gatsby*, pp. 106, 108.

8. F. Scott Fitzgerald, "Rags Martin-Jones and the Pr-nce of W-les," *All the Sad Young Men* (New York: Charles Scribner's Sons, 1926), pp. 140–41, 156, 157, 159.

9. F. Scott Fitzgerald, "The Adjuster," *All the Sad Young Men*, p. 190.

10. *Far Side*, p. 210.

11. *Far Side*, p. 180.

12. *Letters*, p. 201.

13. Unpublished telegram from John Considine to Fitzgerald, December 30, 1926, in Princeton University Library.

14. Unpublished telegram from Fitzgerald to Maxwell Perkins, January 4, 1927, in Princeton University Library.

15. F. Scott Fitzgerald, "Magnetism," *Stories*, p. 220.

16. F. Scott and Zelda Fitzgerald, "Show Mr. and Mrs. F. to Number —," *Crack-Up*, p. 47.

17. "Magnetism," *Stories*, p. 227.

18. *Far Side*, p. 225.

19. James Montgomery Flagg, *Roses and Buckshot* (New York: G. P. Putnam's Sons, 1946), pp. 210–11.

20. *Letters*, pp. 29, 435.

21. "Magnetism," *Stories*, p. 224.

22. "Magnetism," *Stories*, p. 225.

23. Turnbull, p. 171.

24. F. Scott Fitzgerald, *Tender Is the Night* (New York: Charles Scribner's Sons, 1934), p. 24.

25. F. Scott Fitzgerald, *Lipstick*, MS in Princeton University Library, p. 2.

26. *Lipstick*, pp. 3, 5.

27. *Lipstick*, p. 24.

28. Unpublished telegram from John Considine to Fitzgerald, April 3, 1927, in Princeton University Library.

29. *Letters*, p. 29.

30. *Lipstick*, pp. 1, 10.

31. *Lipstick*, p. 35.

32. *Tycoon*, p. 139.

33. Note in *Tycoon* folder.

34. *Tycoon*, pp. 134–35.

35. "Magnetism," *Stories*, p. 224.

36. *Far Side*, p. 227.

4. The Wrong Kind of Picture

1. *Tycoon*, p. 52.

2. *Tycoon*, p. 53.

3. The story of Harlow pointing to Eddie Mannix's picture is told by Edwin Knopf. Actually, *Hell's Angels* made Harlow a star, but she had dropped from sight. *The Redheaded Woman* was her first picture at Metro and gave her a whole new career.

4. "Handle with Care," *Crack-Up*, p. 78.

5. Dorothy Speare, "Hollywood Madness," *The Saturday Evening Post*, October 7, 1933, p. 60.

6. F. Scott Fitzgerald, "Crazy Sunday," *Stories*, p. 405.

7. Speare, p. 60.

8. *Letters*, pp. 29–30.

9. F. Scott Fitzgerald, "Teamed with Genius," *The Pat Hobby Stories*, p. 36.

10. Malcolm Cowley, "Third Act and Epilogue," *F. Scott Fitzgerald*, ed. Alfred Kazin (New York: Collier Books, 1967), p. 150.

11. F. Scott Fitzgerald, *The Redheaded Woman*, MS in Princeton University Library.

12. *Redheaded Woman*, p. 56.

13. *Tycoon*, pp. 40–41.

14. "Crazy Sunday," *Stories*, pp. 403–404.

15. Dwight Taylor, *Joy Ride* (New York: G. P. Putnam's Sons, 1959), p. 241.

16. "Crazy Sunday," *Stories*, p. 404.

17. "Crazy Sunday," *Stories*, p. 406.

18. Taylor, p. 243.

19. Taylor, p. 244.

20. "Crazy Sunday," *Stories*, pp. 406–407. George Oppenheimer tells the story about Gilbert's gun at a party. It was a dinner party and Gilbert came in apparently drunk and wearing a holstered pistol strapped to his leg. Since Gilbert was known to be a little wild, everyone tried to ignore the gun even as the Great Lover took it out and laid it on the dinner table. After dinner, Gilbert left and Herman Mankiewicz arrived. Oppenheimer told Mankiewicz the whole scary story. "Don't get so excited," Mankiewicz said. "After all, how much can a gun eat?"

21. Taylor, pp. 246–47.

22. Turnbull, p. 203.

23. "Crazy Sunday," *Stories*, p. 408.

24. Speare, p. 60.

25. *Letters*, p. 30.

26. "Crazy Sunday," *Stories*, p. 418.

5. *Tender Is the Night* and the Movies

1. Early MS version of *Tender*, in Princeton University Library.

2. Turnbull, p. 151.

3. *Letters*, p. 384.

4. Grace Moore, *You're Only Human Once* (New York: Doubleday & Co., 1944), pp. 108–109.

5. *Tender*, pp. 64, 72, 105.

6. "Magnetism," *Stories*, p. 228.

7. *Tender*, p. 70.

8. *Tender*, pp. 291, 209.

9. F. Scott Fitzgerald and Charles Warren, "Summary Treatment of Fitzgerald's *Tender Is the Night*," MS in Princeton University Library, p. ii.

10. *Tender* treatment, p. 1.

11. John Keats, "Ode to a Nightingale," quoted on title page of *Tender*.

12. *Tender* treatment, pp. 3–4.

13. *Tender* treatment, p. 4.

14. *Tender*, p. 27.

15. *Tender* treatment, pp. 4–7.

16. *Tender* treatment, pp. 8–9.

17. *Tender* treatment, p. 12.

18. *Tender* treatment, p. 16.

19. F. Scott Fitzgerald, "How to Live on Practically Nothing a Year," *Afternoon*, p. 116.

20. *Tender* treatment, pp. 18–19.

21. Unpublished letter from Fitzgerald to Bess Meredyth, dated May 23, 1934, in the possession of Charles Warren.

22. Unpublished letter from Fitzgerald to F. Warburton Guilbert, dated May 22, 1934, in the possession of Charles Warren.

23. Unpublished letter from Fitzgerald to George Cukor, dated May 23, 1934, in the possession of Charles Warren.

24. Turnbull, p. 248.

25. Unpublished Fitzgerald outline in the possession of Charles Warren, envelope postmarked June 19, 1934.

26. *Letters*, pp. 294–95.

27. F. Scott Fitzgerald, "Financing Finnegan," *Stories*, p. 449.

28. *Tender*, p. 267.

29. *Letters*, p. 388.

30. *Tycoon*, pp. 31–32.

31. *Letters*, pp. 589–90.

6.   *A Yank at Oxford:* Pictures of Words

1. "Sleeping and Waking," *Crack-Up*, p. 68. The story of the movie based on Fitzgerald is told by Edwin Knopf.

2. F. Scott Fitzgerald, "The Note-books," *Crack-Up*, p. 165.

3. "Pasting It Together," *Crack-Up*, p. 80; "The Note-books," *Crack-Up*, p. 232.

4. Unpublished treatment titled "Open That Door," in the Princeton University Library.

5. "The Crack-Up," *Crack-Up*, p. 72.

6. "The Crack-Up," *Crack-Up*, pp. 72–73.

7. Quotations from Otis Ferguson's review of the picture *The Wedding Night*, in *The New Republic*, April 3, 1935, p. 214.

8. Note in *Tycoon* folder.

9. "On the Current Screen," *The Literary Digest*, March 30, 1935, p. 32. I do not mean to suggest that the picture is a romantic fairy tale. The hero, married to one woman, falls in love with another (Anna Sten). At one point the wife tells the other woman, "With you he's got nothing more than he had with me before it wore off, but what he and I have now, after these five years is . . . well after all,

five years." Yes, the author on the screen has problems, but he comes to terms with them, whereas Fitzgerald was a long way from coming to terms with his.

10. F. Scott Fitzgerald, "Afternoon of an Author," *Afternoon,* p. 182.

11. Note in *Tycoon* folder.

12. *Tycoon,* pp. 71–72.

13. George Oppenheimer, *The View from the Sixties,* pp. 77–78.

14. Turnbull, p. 288.

15. *Tycoon,* p. 26.

16. Graham and Frank, *Beloved Infidel,* p. 131.

17. *Tycoon,* p. 73.

18. *Beloved,* p. 132.

19. *Beloved,* p. 133.

20. *Beloved,* p. 139.

21. "Crazy Sunday," *Stories,* p. 411.

22. Alistair Cooke, "A Yank at Oxford," *The New Republic,* March 23, 1938, p. 195.

23. Cooke, p. 195.

24. *Tycoon,* p. 58.

25. F. Scott Fitzgerald, *A Yank at Oxford,* MS, unnumbered script pages dated July 13–24, in the archives of the MGM studio, Culver City, California.

26. *Letters,* pp. 574–75.

27. Crowther, *The Lion's Share,* p. 248.

28. Oppenheimer, *The View from the Sixties,* p. 152.

29. Review of *A Yank at Oxford,* in *Time,* February 28, 1938, pp. 63–64.

30. Cooke, p. 195.

31. Frank S. Nugent, "The Screen," *The New York Times,* February 25, 1938, p. 15.

7. *Three Comrades:* Words, Words, Words

1. *Tycoon,* p. 51.

2. *Beloved,* p. 176.

3. *Letters,* pp. 585–87.

4. Unpublished letter from Joseph Mankiewicz to John Biggs, May 1, 1944, in Princeton University Library. Biggs, as Fitzgerald's literary executor, had written to Mankiewicz on Edmund Wilson's behalf to

ask Mankiewicz' permission to publish the now-famous Fitzgerald letter.

5. *Letters,* p. 30.

6. *Letters,* p. 301.

7. *Letters,* pp. 576, 578.

8. *Letters,* p. 33.

9. *Beloved,* p. 175.

10. Unpublished telegram from Joseph Mankiewicz to Fitzgerald, September 9, 1937, in Princeton University Library.

11. *Beautiful and Damned,* pp. 262, 275.

12. *Letters,* pp. 580–82.

13. Turnbull, p. 289.

14. Note in *Tycoon* folder.

15. *Beloved,* p. 175.

16. "Crazy Sunday," *Stories,* pp. 411–12.

17. Conference notes, December 17, 1937, in MGM archives.

18. Note in *Tycoon* folder.

19. F. Scott Fitzgerald, *Three Comrades,* MS, dated September 1, 1937, in MGM archives, p. 20.

20. F. Scott Fitzgerald and E. E. Paramore, Joseph Mankiewicz, and others, *Three Comrades* final shooting script, dated February 1, 1938, p. 16.

21. *Comrades* MS, p. 65.

22. Erich Maria Remarque, *Three Comrades,* trans. A. W. Wheen (New York: Little, Brown, 1937), p. 152.

23. "Handle with Care," *Crack-Up,* p. 75; *Comrades* MS, p. 65.

24. *Comrades* final shooting script, p. 57.

25. Conference notes, December 20, 1937.

26. Conference notes, December 27, 1937.

27. *Letters,* p. 586.

28. *Comrades* MS, p. 80.

29. *Letters,* pp. 586–87.

30. *Letters,* p. 584.

31. *Comrades* MS, p. 36.

32. *Letters,* pp. 70–71.

33. *Comrades* MS, p. 167.

34. Note in "Pictures" folder in Princeton University Library.

35. *Letters,* pp. 588–89.

36. *Gatsby,* p. 182.

37. *Beloved,* p. 176.

38. Philip T. Hartung, "Joie de Vivre—in Germany, in France, and in Kentucky," *Commonweal,* June 10, 1938, p. 188.

39. Review of *Three Comrades,* in *Time,* June 6, 1938, p. 41.

40. Otis Ferguson, review of *Three Comrades,* in *The New Republic,* June 22, 1938, pp. 188–89. The most lengthy discussion of *Three Comrades* to date appears in Henry Dan Piper's *F. Scott Fitzgerald* (New York: Holt, Rinehart and Winston, 1956). But since Piper obviously never saw the movie, his comments are not as valuable as they might be. He writes:

> Fitzgerald wanted to emphasize the novel's mood of feverish gaiety mixed with cynical despair, that expresses so well the attitude of German youth during the sad decade following World War I. To convey this on the screen, he wanted to write scenes of serious social and political significance, leavened with others of broad comic satire. Instead, Mankiewicz and Paramore preferred to center the story dramatically around the friendship of the "three comrades," played by three well-known stars: Robert Taylor, Jimmie Stewart, and Robert Young. [p. 247]

First of all, the All-American Jimmie Stewart never considered the role of the German Otto Koster—it was played by Franchot Tone. Moreover, Mankiewicz did not take scenes of serious social significance leavened with satire and reduce them to scenes about friendship. If he had, he would not have had to fight the Hays Office censors as he did.

41. Frank S. Nugent, "The Screen," *The New York Times,* June 3, 1938, p. 17.

42. Letter from Mankiewicz to John Biggs, May 1, 1944.

43. *Hobby,* p. 143.

44. *Far Side,* p. 305.

8. *Infidelity:* A Picture Worth a Book of Words

1. Story told by Frances Goodrich and Albert Hackett.

2. Bob Thomas, *Thalberg: Life and Legend* (New York: Doubleday & Co., 1969), p. 210. See also Thomas, *King Cohn* (New York: Bantam Books, Inc., 1968), p. 63.

3. Hedy Lamarr, *Ecstasy and Me: My Life as a Woman* (New York: Fawcett Crest World Library, 1968), pp. 29–31.

4. *Tycoon,* p. 84.

5. *Beloved,* p. 166.

6. *Letters,* p. 575.

7. *Beloved,* pp. 163–64.

8. *Beloved,* p. 177.

9. Thomas, *Thalberg,* p. 105.

10. Notes in MGM archives dated February 8, 1938.

11. *Letters,* p. 446.

12. *Beloved,* p. 161.

13. *Letters,* pp. 303, 305.

14. Notes in MGM archives dated February 3, 1938.

15. Notes in MGM archives dated February 23, 1938.

16. Notes in MGM archives dated February 22, 1938. Fitzgerald makes a big point of the fact that he was writing an original—which he was. The title, however, was not original: it was taken from a story by Ursula Parrot which was printed in *Cosmopolitan,* February 1938, and which MGM had purchased. At first, Fitzgerald and Stromberg had considered adapting her story for the screen, but Fitzgerald did not think Miss Parrot's tale lent itself to adaptation, so they kept her title but threw out her plot. Fitzgerald wrote Stromberg on February 3, 1938:

> The Ursula Parrot story is well written in the first two-thirds, but in the last and most important third, it attains its effect by going into an orgasm of sentimental hysteria which is impossible to translate into drama. I have brought forth such effects myself in writing short stories, and I know the trick and know that it won't dramatize because it depends upon the sheer emotional power of the descriptive word. [MGM archives]

17. *Beloved,* p. 174.

18. *Tycoon,* pp. 32–33.

19. Notes in MGM archives dated February 11, 1938.

20. Knight, *The Liveliest Art,* p. 174.

21. F. Scott Fitzgerald, *Infidelity,* MS, dated March 7, 1938, in MGM archives, pp. 1–2. René Clair was so repelled by the first talkies that for a time he thought of abandoning film to write fiction. When he came to accept sound as inevitable, he satirized it. In *Sous les Toits de Paris,* for example, the director slammed a glass door in the face of the microphone and then filmed the action on the other side of the door. We see but cannot hear the people talking. Fitz-

gerald, of course, does the very same thing when he films through the opera glasses.

22. Zelda Fitzgerald, *Save Me the Waltz* (New York: Charles Scribner's Sons, 1932), pp. 109–10, 130–31.

23. Notebooks, I.

24. *Infidelity*, pp. 4, 8, 11.

25. *Infidelity*, p. 87.

26. *Tycoon*, p. 142.

27. Note, February 11, 1938.

28. *Gatsby*, p. 162.

29. *Tycoon*, p. 107. Fitzgerald thought that it was important for people to be able to see themselves in another's place as Althea sees herself in Iris's. On the other hand, he knew the dangers of actually trying to live someone else's life. Iris Jones, for example, has long been infatuated by the rich Nicolas just as Fitzgerald was long infatuated by The Rich, period. When she agrees to visit the Gilberts' apartment, she tells Nicolas: "I've always wanted to go behind the scenes—and see how it was" (p. 61). When Nicolas explains why he took Iris to his apartment, he echoes what she has said: "Two years ago there was a poor girl that wanted to see how the rich lived, so I threw my apartment open to her in a magnificent gesture" (p. 80). By not only seeing herself in the place of Nicolas' wife but actually putting herself in the wife's place, Iris damages all their lives. This pattern is a familiar one in Fitzgerald's fiction. In "Two Wrongs," for example, we meet Bill McChesney, the poor boy who makes good as a Broadway producer and tries to run first with the fashionable Long Island social set, then with the lords and ladies of England. Finally, the lords and ladies literally throw him out, his coat and cane following him out the door. Gatsby, of course, bought a white elephant of a mansion, hoping to be welcomed into Daisy's set. Failing, he is found shot to death in his own expensive swimming pool. Nor were these characters much different from the author himself. He too tried to throw open the door of the leisure class "in a magnificent gesture" and claim a place in the drawing room. But his desire to move among the very rich only led him so far into debt that he had to go to Hollywood to try to write himself out of bankruptcy.

30. George Bluestone writes: "Externalized and clothed in . . . factual reality . . . dreams and thought lose their qualitative properties.

They cease being dreams and thoughts" (*Novels into Film* [Baltimore: Johns Hopkins University Press, 1957], p. 210).

31. *Letters*, p. 43.
32. *Tycoon*, p. 28.
33. Note in MGM archives dated May 10, 1938.
34. *Beloved*, pp. 190–92.
35. *Letters*, p. 77.

9. *The Women:* Epitaph for the Spoiled Heroine

1. Note in *Tycoon* folder.
2. *Tycoon*, p. 92.
3. "The Crack-Up," *Crack-Up*, p. 181.
4. *Beloved*, pp. 162–63.
5. F. Scott Fitzgerald's few script pages for *Marie Antoinette* are located in the Princeton University Library.
6. Note in MGM archives, June 17, 1938.
7. Note in MGM archives, July 2, 1938.
8. Note in MGM archives, June 6–7, 1938.
9. F. Scott Fitzgerald, "Mightier than the Sword," *Hobby*, p. 145.
10. Unpublished passage in *Tycoon* MS. Siegfried Kracauer in his book *Theory of Film* (New York: Oxford University Press, 1965) agrees with Stahr about preludes to adapations of stage plays. He notes that many adaptations tack on what amount to documentary shots at the beginning and end of a play to give the illusion that the action covers great time and distance, whereas the main action is usually in reality quite a cramped affair. He writes:

> The device consists in framing the theatrical film by scenes which are apt to divert our attention from its staginess and indeed pass it off as an episode. . . . Hence the nuisance character of the framing scenes: they reduce the film to an illustration; they force it to illustrate the very message you would expect it to convey on its own account. These scenes transform the film from a cinematic communication into a whole with an ideological center. [pp. 260–61]

To an extent what Kracauer says does apply to *The Women,* for it was indeed Fitzgerald's intent that his prologue montage should focus our attention on the excesses of the privileged class and prepare us for the retribution which is to follow. But to have an "ideological center"—to point a finger—is not necessarily bad manners in the cinema.

11. Thomas, *King Cohn,* p. 65.

12. *Letters,* pp. 45–46.

13. Clare Booth, *The Women,* in *Sixteen Famous American Plays,* ed. Bennett A. Cerf and Van H. Cartmell (New York: Modern Library, 1941), p. 608.

14. F. Scott Fitzgerald, *The Women,* MS, dated July 9, 1938, in MGM archives (hereafter cited as *Women*), p. 25.

15. Booth, *The Women,* p. 609.

16. *Women,* p. 18.

17. *Women,* p. 7.

18. *Women,* p. 54.

19. Treatment of *The Women* in MGM archives, June 6–7, 1938.

20. *Letters,* pp. 46–47.

21. *The Women* treatment, June 6–7, 1938.

22. Anita Loos, *The Women,* in *Twenty Best Film Plays,* ed. John Gassner and Dudley Nichols (New York: Crow Publishing Co., 1943), p. 130.

23. Notebooks, K.

24. Unpublished letter from Fitzgerald to Phil Berg, February 23, 1940, in Princeton University Library.

25. Draft of *The Women* in MGM archives, dated August 15, 1938, p. 73.

26. Crowther, *The Lion's Share,* p. 272.

27. Thomas, *Thalberg,* p. 205.

28. Crowther, p. 272.

29. Review of *The Women,* in *Time,* September 11, 1939, p. 58.

30. Philip T. Hartung, "Clouds over Woman," *Commonweal,* September 22, 1939, p. 500.

31. Otis Ferguson, "It's Not the Humidity," *The New Republic,* September 6, 1939, p. 132.

32. Frank S. Nugent, "The Screen," *The New York Times,* September 22, 1939, p. 27.

33. Unpublished letter from Fitzgerald to Leland Hayward, December 6, 1939, in Princeton University Library.

34. *Letters,* p. 600.

35. "Pictures" folder in Princeton University Library.

36. *Letters,* p. 53.

10. *Madame Curie:* Brave New Heroine

1. Aldous Huxley, *The Genius and the Goddess* (New York: Bantam Books, 1956), p. 138. Huxley's research into Mme. Curie's past is related as remembered by Anita Loos.

2. Aldous Huxley, *Madame Curie* treatment MS in MGM archives, pp. 2, d, 43.

3. *Goddess*, p. 3.

4. Crowther, p. 187.

5. Letter to Leland Hayward, January 16, 1940.

6. "Pictures" folder.

7. Crowther, p. 277.

8. *Beloved*, p. 201.

9. *Beloved*, p. 141.

10. *Letters*, pp. 307–309.

11. *Beloved*, pp. 180–81.

12. F. Scott Fitzgerald, "An Alcoholic Case," *Stories*, p. 440.

13. Note in MGM archives, dated November 7, 1938.

14. F. Scott Fitzgerald, *Madame Curie*, MS, dated January 1, 1939, in MGM archives.

15. *Letters*, p. 367; *Curie*, pp. 73–74.

16. *Letters*, p. 53.

17. *Letters*, p. 57.

18. *Letters*, p. 59.

19. *Letters*, p. 61.

20. Letter to Hayward, December 6, 1939.

21. Letter to Hayward, December 6, 1939.

22. Unpublished telegram from Fitzgerald to Bernard Hyman, January 6, 1939, in Princeton University Library.

23. Fred Stanley, "Hollywood Goes All Out on Spending Spree," *The New York Times*, April 25, 1943, II, p. 3.

24. "The New Picture," *Time*, December 20, 1943, p. 61.

25. "Discovering Radium for the Screen," *The New York Times*, November 15, 1943, X, p. 4.

26. Bosley Crowther, "The Screen in Review," *The New York Times*, December 17, 1943, p. 23.

27. "The New Picture," *Time*, December 20, 1943, pp. 60–61.

28. *Paradise*, p. 97.

11. Free-Lancing

1. *Beloved*, p. 202.
2. Crowther, p. 205.
3. *Letters*, pp. 311–12.
4. Graham, *College of One*, p. 169.
5. *Letters*, p. 65. In another letter Fitzgerald wrote, *"Dorian Gray* . . . is in the lower ragged edge of 'literature,' just as *Gone with the Wind* is in the higher brackets of crowd entertainment" (p. 113).
6. F. Scott Fitzgerald, *Gone with the Wind,* MS, in Princeton University Library, script pages dated January 11–24, 1939, p. 78.
7. *Wind*, pp. 75–76, 80.
8. *College*, pp. 169–70.
9. Crowther, p. 269.
10. Letter to Hayward, December 6, 1939.
11. Unpublished letter from Fitzgerald to Messrs. Berg, Dozier, and Allen, February 23, 1940, in Princeton University Library.
12. Budd Schulberg, "Old Scott," *Esquire*, January 1961, pp. 97–99.
13. *Tycoon* folder.
14. *Letters*, p. 60; *Beloved*, p. 203.
15. F. Scott Fitzgerald, *Winter Carnival* treatment MS, in Princeton University Library, undated, p. 1.
16. *Winter Carnival*, p. 3.
17. *Winter Carnival*, p. 4.
18. *Winter Carnival*, pp. 6–7.
19. *Winter Carnival*, p. 8.
20. *Winter Carnival*, p. 10.
21. Unpublished letter from Fitzgerald to Budd Schulberg, February 28, 1939, in Princeton University Library.
22. Turnbull, pp. 295–96.
23. *Far Side*, p. 317.
24. Quoted in "Old Scott," p. 99.
25. Letter to Schulberg, February 28, 1939.
26. Letter to Berg, Dozier, and Allen, February 23, 1940.
27. F. Scott Fitzgerald, *Air Raid,* MS, Princeton University Library, March 30, 1939, pp. 1–2.
28. *Beloved*, p. 208.

29. *Beloved*, pp. 210–11.

30. *Beloved*, p. 212.

31. *Beloved*, p. 214.

32. Letter to Berg, Dozier, and Allen, February 23, 1940.

33. Unpublished treatment titled "The Feather Fan," in Princeton University Library.

34. *Letters*, pp. 125, 128.

35. *Letters*, p. 42.

36. *Letters*, p. 623.

37. Crowther, p. 69.

38. Oppenheimer, *A View from the Sixties*, p. 97.

39. Unpublished letter from Joseph I. Breen to Samuel Goldwyn, September 6, 1939, in Princeton University Library.

40. Letter to Berg, Dozier, and Allen, February 23, 1940; to Hayward, December 6, 1939.

41. *Letters*, p. 142.

42. F. Scott Fitzgerald, *Raffles*, MS, in Princeton University Library, script pages dated September 11, 1939.

43. *Raffles*, September 9, 1939, pp. 20–21.

44. *Raffles*, September 11, 1939, p. 21.

45. Note in *Tycoon* folder.

12. *Cosmopolitan:* Splicing It Together

1. Unpublished letter from Fitzgerald to William Dozier, March 1, 1940, in Princeton University Library.

2. *Letters*, pp. 79–80, 87–88.

3. F. Scott Fitzgerald, *Cosmopolitan*, MS, in Princeton University Library, draft dated May 29, 1940, pp. 64–65. There is a second draft dated August 13, 1940 (the Victoria draft). Hereafter drafts will be indicated by roman numerals I and II.

4. Letter to Hayward, January 16, 1940.

5. *Hobby*, p. xxii.

6. "Old Scott," p. 100.

7. *Letters*, p. 77.

8. "Old Scott," p. 101.

9. *Beloved*, p. 216.

10. *Beloved*, pp. 216–17.

11. *College*, pp. 165–69, 192.

12. Unpublished telegram from Fitzgerald to Perkins, November 29, 1939, in Princeton University Library.

13. *Beloved*, pp. 224–29.

14. *Cosmopolitan*, I, p. 23.

15. "Old Scott," p. 101.

16. *Letters*, p. 89.

17. Unpublished letter from Fitzgerald to Perkins, September 15, 1940, in Princeton University Library.

18. Letters, pp. 315, 144.

19. *Tycoon*, p. 32.

20. Edmund Wilson, "F. Scott Fitzgerald," *F. Scott Fitzgerald: Twentieth Century Views*, ed. Arthur Mizener (Englewood Cliffs, N.J.: Prentice-Hall, Inc., 1963), p. 81.

21. *Cosmopolitan*, II, pp. 23–26.

22. *Letters*, p. 271.

23. *Cosmopolitan*, I, p. 70.

24. "The Crack-Up," *Crack-Up*, p. 72.

25. *Gatsby*, p. 2.

26. F. Scott Fitzgerald, "Babylon Revisited," *Stories*, pp. 390, 392, 394.

27. *Cosmopolitan*, I, p. 58.

28. The first quotation is from a note appended to the first draft of *Cosmopolitan*, the second from a note appended to the second draft.

29. *Far Side*, pp. 283–84.

30. "Babylon Revisited," *Stories*, p. 385.

31. *Cosmopolitan*, I, p. 49.

32. *Tycoon*, p. 135.

33. *Cosmopolitan*, I, p. 102.

34. *Letters*, p. 101.

35. *Letters*, p. 140.

36. *Letters*, pp. 627–28.

37. *Letters*, pp. 144–45.

38. Letter from Fitzgerald to Garson Kanin, September 23, 1940, in Princeton University Library; *Letters*, p. 627.

39. "Old Scott," p. 100.

40. Bosley Crowther, "The Screen in Review," *The New York Times*, November 19, 1954, p. 20.

41. Review of *The Last Time I Saw Paris*, in *Time*, November 22, 1954, p. 102.

13. "Action Is Character"

1. *Letters,* p. 145.
2. Story told by Lillian Hellman.
3. *Letters,* p. 145.
4. *Letters,* p. 142.
5. Turnbull, p. 151.
6. F. Scott Fitzgerald, *The Light of Heart,* MS, in Princeton University Library, dated October 11, 1940, pp. 1–3.
7. *Heart,* p. 37.
8. *Heart,* p. 72.
9. *Heart,* p. 59.
10. *Heart,* pp. 86–92.
11. *Heart,* p. 107.
12. *Letters,* p. 143.
13. *Letters,* p. 146.
14. *Letters,* p. 144.
15. Letter from Fitzgerald to Phil Berg, October 10, 1940.
16. Bosley Crowther, "The Screen in Review," *The New York Times,* December 10, 1942; p. 35; December 13, 1942, VIII, p. 3.
17. *Letters,* p. 147.
18. *Letters,* p. 196.
19. *Letters,* p. 151.
20. *Beloved,* pp. 244–45.
21. *Letters,* p. 146.
22. *Letters,* p. 116.
23. *Letters,* p. 388.
24. *Tycoon,* p. 163.
25. *Tycoon,* p. 152.
26. *Tycoon,* pp. 80–81.
27. *Letters,* p. 152.
28. *Tycoon,* p. 108.

Epilogue

1. "The Adjuster," *Jazz Age,* p. 158.
2. *Paradise,* p. 30.
3. *Beloved,* p. 248.
4. *Far Side,* p. 336. Biographers have reported that Fitzgerald was

laid out at the mortuary which still stands next door to Metro-Goldwyn-Mayer. It would have been highly ironical if he had been, but the mortuary has no record of a Scott Fitzgerald in 1940.

    5. Story in *Tycoon* folder.

☆ ☆ ☆

Index

"Adjuster, The," 48, 275n.
Adventures of Tom Sawyer, The, 119
"Afternoon of an Author," 103
Ah, Wilderness, 7
Air Raid, 24, 229–30
Akins, Zoë, 127
"Alcoholic Case, An," 203, 251
Alexander's Ragtime Band, 119
Alice in Wonderland, 128
All About Eve, 124
Allen, Jay, 133
All Quiet on the Western Front, 125
All the Sad Young Men, 47
Amateur Cracksman, The, 232
Ameche, Don, 119
Arnold, Benedict, 158
Assassination of the Duc de Guise, The, 28
Astaire, Fred, 56, 127, 255
Austen, Jane, 197

"Babes in the Wood," 65
"Babylon Revisited," 24, 238–40, 245–58
Bach, Johann Sebastian, 269
Balanchine, George, 4
Balcon, Michael, 108, 112, 117

Barnum, P. T., 47
Barretts of Wimpole Street, The, 199
Barrymore, John, 50–51
Barrymore, Lionel, 117
Barthelmess, Richard, 86
Bartholomew, Freddie, 29
Beauclerk, Topham, 22
Beautiful and Damned, The, 37–38, 130, 181, 188
"Beautiful Chord Come True, The," 92
Beery, Wallace, 209
Beloved Infidel, 16
Benchley, Robert, 106–107
Benét, Stephen Vincent, 127
Ben Hur, 45, 55, 58, 72
Berg, Phil, 267–68n.
Berkeley, Busby, 59
Bernhardt, Sarah, 28
Bickford, Charles, 86
Big House, The, 67
Big Parade, The, 102
Big Pond, The, 101
Birth of a Nation, The, 31
Blondell, Joan, 14, 17
Blonde Venus, 67
Bogart, Humphrey, 107–108

Booth, Clare, 24, 180, 183, 185–87, 189, 192
Bornhapt, Charles, 32
Borzage, Frank, 147
Bow, Clara, 62
Boyer, Charles, 153
Boylan, Malcolm Stewart, 116, 118
Boys' Town, 119
Brackett, Charles, 14–15
Brackett, Elizabeth, 14–15
Breen, Joseph, 145, 150–52, 154, 165, 170–71, 186, 198, 234–36
Bride Wore Red, The, 123
Bringing Up Baby, 119
Broken Soil, 101
Brooks, Richard, 257
Broun, Heywood, 35
Brown, Kay, 214
Brush, Katharine, 65
Bryan, Gertrude, 28
Buck, Gene, 46
Butterfield 8, 106
Byron, Lord, 22

Camille, 23
Campbell, Alan, 11, 16, 106, 155, 158
Candide, 191
Cantor, Eddie, 234
Capra, Frank, 85
Captains Courageous, 144
Captured Shadow, The, 29–30, 277
Chained, 156–57
Chaplin, Charlie, 30, 32–33, 43, 46, 127
Chopin, Frederic, 206
Chorus Girl's Romance, The, 36
Clair, René, 39, 46
Claire, Ina, 28, 86, 111
Cobb, Buff, 200
Cohan, George M., 34, 46
Colbert, Claudette, 155
College Humor, 10
Collier's, 244
Colman, Ronald, 86
Columbia Pictures, 176
Connelly, Marc, 108
Conrad, Joseph, 100, 249
Considine, John W., 49, 55–56, 58, 158
Conway, Jack, 63, 74–75, 112
Cooke, Alistair, 109, 118

Cooper, Gary, 101–102, 158, 168, 242
Cosmopolitan, 24, 126, 208, 238–40, 245–58, 261–62, 271
Cowan, Lester, 238–40, 251–52, 255–57
Coward, The, 30
Cowley, Malcolm, 67, 229
Crack-Up, The, viin., 21n., 22, 28, 31, 35, 43, 45n., 64, 97–99, 102, 125, 134, 140, 249
Crawford, Joan, 17, 116, 123, 127, 129, 148, 156–58, 160–61, 170, 185–86, 192–94, 202, 269
"Crazy Sunday," vii, 71–73, 75, 108n., 136n.
"Crickets Are Calling, The," 65
Crowd, The, 102
Crowther, Bosley, 211, 257–58, 268
Cukor, George, ix, 10, 92, 192–93, 215, 217–18
Curie, Eve, 197, 199
Curie, Marie Sklodowska, 24, 196–198, 202–207, 209–211
Curie, Pierre, 197–98, 202–206, 209–11
Czarina, The, 100–101

"Dance, The," 49
Daniels, Bebe, 58
Davies, Marion, 71, 127
Davis, Owen, 10, 48, 93
de Havilland, Olivia, 216, 233, 235
del Rio, Dolores, 86
De Mille, Cecil B., 39, 55
Dempsey, Jack, 224
de Sano, Marcel, 65–68, 91
Descken, Sandra, 257
"Diamond as Big as the Ritz, The," 38, 179
Dickens, Charles, 33, 100, 201
Dietrich, Marlene, 71, 97 101, 155
Disney, Walt, 150
"Dixie," 218
Dreyer, Carl, 55
Duchess of Buffalo, 49
Duchin, Eddie, 160

Ecstasy, 154
Eddy, Nelson, 176
Edison, Thomas A., 27, 44
Eisenstein, Sergei M., 46

Eliot, George, 33
"Emotional Bankruptcy," 143
Epstein, Julius J., 257
Epstein, Paul G., 257
Esquire, 132, 241, 246
Evil Eye, The, 31–32, 275

Fairbanks, Douglas Jr., 86
Fame, 148
Famous Players, 40–44, 58
Farewell to Arms, A, 147
Farnum, Dustin, 27, 234
Farrell, James T., 201
Far Side of Paradise, The, 125
Faulkner, William, vii
Feather Fan, The, 231
Ferguson, Otis, 147, 193
Ferris, Walter, 116, 118
Fie! Fie! Fi-Fi!, 31
Fields, W. C., 85
Fifth Column, The, 201
"Financing Finnegan," 94
Finney, Ben, 80
First National Pictures, 49–51, 54–60
Fitzgerald, Annabel, 35
Fitzgerald, Mrs. Edward, 30, 255
Fitzgerald, Frances, *see* Mrs. Grove Smith
Fitzgerald, Zelda, 5, 14, 33, 35–38, 44–46, 52–53, 61, 63–65, 73, 77, 83, 90, 98, 100, 105, 110–11, 130, 139, 142–43, 165–68, 170, 184, 187–89, 202–203, 228, 230–32, 235, 246, 250, 255, 259–60, 266–269, 273
Flagg, James Montgomery, 52–53
Flappers and Philosophers, 36
Fleming, Victor, 192
Flesh and the Devil, 199
Fonda, Henry, 123, 125
Fontaine, Joan, 95, 185–86, 192, 231
Fontanne, Lynn, 199
Ford, John, 85
For Whom the Bell Tolls, 177–78
Four Horsemen of the Apocalypse, The, 33
Francis, Kay, 86, 231
Franklin, Sidney, 18, 190, 198–99, 208–11
Freaks, The, 74

"Freshest Boy, The," 28, 112
Front Page, The, 126, 193

Gable, Clark, 9, 12, 17, 119, 150–52, 157, 191–92, 213, 215, 218
Garbo, Greta, 23, 71, 97, 101, 128, 155, 185, 199
Garland, Judy, 29, 170, 191, 209
Garson, Greer, 197, 199
Genius and the Goddess, The, 197n., 198
Gibbons, Cedric, 91–92
Gilbert, John, 73
Gilbert and Sullivan (W. S. Gilbert and Sir Arthur Sullivan), 28
Gingrich, Arnold, ix, 132–35
Gish, Lillian, 37, 51, 224
Goddard, Paulette, 185, 192–94
Goethe, Johann Wolfgang von, 22
Goldbeck, Ruth, 80
Gold Rush, The, 46
Goldwyn, Samuel, 4, 101 234–36 242
Goldwyn Pictures Corporation, 234
Gone With the Wind, 6, 10, 24, 70, 117, 153, 192, 213–19, 221
Goodbye Mr. Chips, 199
Good Earth, The, 199
Goodman, Benny, 160
Goodrich, Frances, ix, 7–9, 11–12, 14, 17, 55–56, 150–53, 158, 175–176, 259
Graham, Sheilah, ix, 16–17, 21, 106–108, 122, 128–29, 132–35, 146, 154–55, 163, 168–69, 171–73, 176, 179, 184, 187–88, 199–203, 211–214, 221, 225, 230–31, 242–45, 259, 269, 276–77
Grand Hotel, 185, 222
Grandma's Boy, 243
Grange, Red, 224
Grant, Cary, 119, 231, 254
Grapes of Wrath, The, 173
Great Gatsby, The, 10, 13n., 23–25, 45–49, 92–94, 101–102, 115, 119, 145, 148, 164, 168–69, 201, 220, 248, 250n., 258, 268
Green Pastures, The, 108
Griffith, D. W., 31, 51, 91, 244
Guardsman, The, 199
Guilbert, Warburton, 92
Gunsmoke, 92

Hackett, Albert, ix, 7–8, 14, 17, 55–
    56, 150–53, 158, 175–76, 259
Haden, Sara, 170
Hamlet, 28, 95
Hammond, Percy, 48
Harding, Ann, 86
Harlan, Kenneth, 38
Harlow, Jean, 61–63, 70, 151–53,
    185
Hathaway, Henry, 242
Hartung, Philip T., 146–47, 193
Hayes, Helen, ix, 86, 126–28, 187,
    259, 276
Hays, Will H. (Hays Office), 69,
    125, 149–50, 153, 170–71, 193,
    234
Hayward, Leland, 18–19n., 194,
    208–209n., 219n., 232, 235, 240
"Head and Shoulders," 28, 36
Hearst, William Randolph, 127
Hecht, Ben, 126
Hellman, Lillian, ix, 19–20
Hemingway, Ernest, 19–21, 82, 92,
    100, 124, 133, 176–79, 199, 201,
    224, 231
Hepburn, Katharine, 86, 99–101,
    119, 254
Her Night of Romance, 49
His Honor the Sultan, 30
Hitchcock, Alfred, 164, 219, 231
Hitler, Adolf, 129
Holden, Fay, 170
Honeymoon in Bali, 229
Hopkins, Miriam, 86, 155
Hopkins, Robert, 9
Hornung, William, 232
Horton, Edward Everett, 199
Howard, Leslie, 216
"How to Waste Material," 49
Huxley, Aldous, 9, 12, 15, 196–98
Hyde, Alice, 172
Hyman, Bernard, 18, 78, 208–210

Ibañez, Blasco, 33
Imaginary Voyage, 46
Infidelity, 13n., 23, 90, 149, 152,
    158–73, 180, 185, 194, 202, 221,
    234, 254
In Name Only, 231
It Happened One Night, 85
It's a Gift, 85
Ivens, Joris, 19

"Japanese Sandman," 65
Jarrett, Mrs. Edwin, 95
Jazz Singer, The, 55
Johnson, Marion, 172–73
Johnson, Nunnally, ix, 172–73, 268
Johnson, Van, 257
Jones, Bobby, 224
Jones, Jennifer, 95
Josanne, Edouard, 165–66, 168

Kanin, Garson, 256
Kaper, Bronislau, 118
Karloff, Boris, 225
Katz, Sam, 102, 144
Kaufman, Beatrice, 105
King, Ginevra, 110
King Kong, 259
King Lear, 265–66
King of Kings, The, 55
Knopf, Alfred, 105
Knopf, Edwin, ix, 13, 16, 18, 29, 55,
    95–96, 100–104, 108, 118, 121,
    138, 159, 212
Kroll, Frances, ix, 233, 236, 240, 267

La Marr, Barbara, 224
Lamarr, Hedy, 153–54
"Land of the Never Never, The," 92
Langer, Rudolph M., 209–10
Lardner, Ring, 5, 40, 47
Lasky, Jesse L., 116
Last of Mrs. Cheney, The, 198
Last Time I Saw Paris, The, 257
Last Tycoon, The, 7, 10, 13n., 24,
    32, 39, 59–63, 65, 68–70, 94, 104,
    106–107, 110–11, 120–21, 154–
    155, 163–64, 167, 169, 171, 173,
    177–78, 185, 203, 241, 244, 247,
    252–53, 268–73
Laughton, Charles, 199
Lazarus, Jeff, 18–19, 229
Leeds, Andrea, 242
Leigh, Vivien, 117, 213, 216, 218
Le Roy, Mervyn, 210–11
Letty Lynton, 67
Lewin, Albert, 210
Lewis, Sinclair, 121, 124
Life, 255
Life Begins at 8:30, 268
Life of Emile Zola, The, 203
Life of Madame Curie, The, 199,
    203

Light of Heart, The, 261–68
Lillie, Beatrice, 127
Lipstick, 55–59, 78, 81
Little Boy Blue, 28
Little Caesar, 67
Little Millionaire, The, 34
Little Red Ridinghood, 55
Lloyd, Harold, 43, 243
Loew, Marcus, 27, 33
Lombard, Carole, 9, 218, 231
Loos, Anita, ix, 3–5, 9, 12, 74–75, 153, 191–92, 197, 259
Lorimer, George, 144, 159
Lost Patrol, 85
Lost Weekend, The, 14
Louis XVI, 181
Loy, Myrna, 86, 168, 185
Lubitsch, Ernst, 20, 192
Lukas, Paul, 86
Lunt, Alfred, 199

MacArthur, Charles, 4, 80, 126–28
MacDonald, Jeanette, 176, 185
MacLeish, Archibald, 19
Madame Curie, 6, 9, 24, 89, 195–199, 202–11, 221, 262
"Magnetism," 50–51, 54–55, 78
Making a Living, 33
Mankiewicz, Joseph, ix, 121–25, 129–30, 135–42, 144–48, 158–59, 199, 217
Manners, Diana, 51
Mannix, Edgar, 18, 63, 102, 138, 144
March, Fredric, 86, 116, 198
Marie Antoinette, 6, 152, 180–81
Marshall, Herbert, 86
Marx, Chico, 66
Marx, Groucho, 8, 66
Marx, Harpo, 8, 66
Mary Poppins, 169
Maugham, Somerset, 155
Maxwell, Elsa, 190
Mayer, Edwin Justus, 106–107, 126, 172
Mayer, Louis B., 10, 39, 63, 102, 109, 117, 119, 129, 138, 145–46, 153–54, 178–79, 209, 214
Mayer, Paul, 172
Meehan, Johnny, 9
Méliès, Georges, 55
Meredyth, Bess, 68, 91–92

Merton of the Movies, 93
Methot, Mayo, 107
Metro-Goldwyn-Mayer, 3–25, 27, 29, 33, 60–63, 65–75, 79, 82, 89, 102–212, 214, 219, 257
"Mightier than the Sword," 184–185*n.*
Mitchell, Margaret, 215–16
Mix, Tom, 59
Mizener, Arthur, 39, 49, 125, 251
Montgomery, Robert, 71–72, 75, 86, 95, 116
Moore, Gary, 82
Moore, Grace, 80
Moran, Lois, 53–54, 61
Morgan, J. P., 22
Mrs. Miniver, 199
Muni, Paul, 199
Murfin, Jane, 191
Myers, Carmel, 45–46, 51, 64, 73, 224

Nash, Ogden, ix, 8, 17, 21, 121–22
Nazimova, Alla, 106
Negri, Pola, 62
New Yorker, The, 201
Nineteen Eighty-Four, 197
Ninotchka, 192
Niven, David, 233, 235, 242
Novarro, Ramon, 72
Nugent, Frank S., 118–19, 147, 193–194, 211

Ober, Harold, 40, 103, 159, 232
Ober, Mrs. Harold, 116
"Offshore Pirate, The," 36–37
O'Flaherty, Liam, 239
O' Hara, John, 106
Old Wives' Tale, The, 215
Olivier, Laurence, 197, 231, 246
One Night of Love, 80
Oppenheimer, George, ix, 8–9, 14–15, 17–18, 101, 104–106, 116, 118, 121
Orwell, George, 197
Osborn, Paul, 210
O'Sullivan, Maureen, ix, 110–13, 116
Othello, 160
Our Daily Bread, 102
"Our Life Will Be a Wow," 82, 88

Paderewski, Ignace, 206

Paramore, E. E., 124, 130–32, 135–137, 146, 148
Paris Qui Dort, 39
Parker, Dorothy, 7, 11, 19–20, 106–107, 158, 259–60, 277
Passion of Joan of Arc, The, 55
Pasteur, Louis, 203
Paul, Elliot, 257
Perelman, S. J., 8
Perkins, Louise, 157
Perkins, Maxwell, 20, 35, 49–50, 93, 126–27, 132, 159, 201, 214, 244, 246
Pickford, Mary, 37, 51, 224
Poet Lore, 32
Potemkin, 46
Povah, Phyllis, 186
Powell, William, 15
Power, Tyrone, 266
Prevost, Marie, 38
Pride and Prejudice, 9, 197, 199
Public Enemy, The, 67
"Puccini Cowboy," 92

Quaker Girl, The, 28, 86, 111
Queen Elizabeth, 28

Raffles, 24, 232–36
Raft, George, 86
"Rags Martin-Jones and the Pr-nce of W-les," 47–48
Rainer, Luise, 185, 199
Rameau, Hans, 210
Real Glory, The, 242
Rebecca, 219, 231–32
Redheaded Woman, The, 62–63, 65–70, 82, 91, 112, 153
Reed, Donna, 257
Remarque, Erich Maria, 125, 138–139, 147
Rennie, James, 49
RKO, 245, 256
Road Back, The, 137
Robards, Jason Jr., 95
Robinson, Edward G., 67, 119
Rogers, Buff, 172
Rogers, Cameron, 172
Rogers, Ginger, 116
Rogers, Howard Emmet, 9
Romeo and Juliet, 23
Rooney, Mickey, 29, 119, 170
Rose and the Ring, The, 60

Russell, Lillian, 46
Russell, Rosalind, 116, 185–86, 192–194
Ruth, Babe, 224
Rutherford, Ann, 170

Safety First, 32
St. Francis of Assisi, 22, 40
St. John, Jill, 95
St. Paul, 186
Sandbach, Robert, 277
Sanders, George, 231
Saturday Evening Post, The, 144, 156, 159, 244
Saunders, John Monk, 52–53, 109, 260
Save Me the Waltz, 165–66n.
School for Scandal, 186
Schulberg, B. P., 58, 224
Schulberg, Budd, 219–29, 240–41, 245–46, 257
Schulberg, Victoria, 245–46
Secret Six, The, 67
Selznick, David O., 15, 18, 119, 192, 214–19
Selznick International, 214–19
Sennett, Mack, 28
Seventh Heaven, 147
Shakespeare, William, 95, 130, 160–161, 265
Shaw, George Bernard, 22, 40
Shearer, Norma, 15, 70–72, 74–75, 127, 173, 186, 192–94
She Loves Me Not, 222
Sherwood Robert, 69
Shining Hour, The, 122
Shoulder Arms, 33
Shy, Gus, 27
Simpson, Reginald, 52–53
Singet dem Herrn, 269
Sin of Madeleine Claudet, The, 128
Sister from Paris, 49
Slight Case of Murder, A, 119
Smart, Dave, 133
Smith, Mrs. Grove (Scottie), ix, 4–5, 12, 14, 37, 64–65, 73, 106, 116, 126–28, 143, 170, 173, 186, 188–189, 207–208, 215, 222, 239, 246, 255, 269
"Snows of Kilimanjaro, The," 177
So What, 82
Spanish Earth, 19

Speare, Dorothy, 64–65, 74
Squaw Man, The, 234
Stagecoach, 222
Stein, Gertrude, 224
Steinbeck, John, 201
Sten, Anna, 101
Stewart, Donald Ogden, 190, 229
Stewart, James, 254
Stone, Lewis, 170
Story of Louis Pasteur, The, 203
Strickling, Howard, 117
Stromberg, Hunt, 11, 17, 150–52, 158–59, 161, 163–64, 168–71, 174–76, 181, 183–85, 189, 191–92, 194–95
Suez, 203
Sullavan, Margaret, 23, 120–22, 129, 147
Sullivan, C. Gardner, 68
Sun Also Rises, The, 84
Susan Lenox, 67
Swanson, Gloria, 224
Swanson, H. N., viii, 10, 52, 96, 103, 219, 232
Swinburne, Algernon Charles, 16

Tales of the Jazz Age, 38
Talmadge, Constance, 37, 43, 49, 56, 60
Taylor, Deems, 259
Taylor, Dwight, 71–74
Taylor, Elizabeth, 257–58
Taylor, Robert, 109, 112, 116–19, 120–21, 129, 147
"Teamed with Genius," 66
Temple, Shirley, ix, 5, 155, 246, 255–56, 261
Temptress, The, 199
Ten Commandments, The, 39
Tender Is the Night, viin., 53, 55–56, 75–95, 102, 119, 128, 142–43, 165, 172, 181, 187, 201, 203, 220, 246, 251, 268, 270
Test Pilot, 119
Thackeray, William Makepeace, 60
Thalberg, Irving, 39, 60–63, 65–66, 68–75, 86, 104, 109–10, 159, 180–181, 185, 193, 198, 211, 241, 244
There Was a Crooked Man, 123
They Gave Him a Gun, 137
Thin Man, The, 7, 176

This Side of Paradise, ix, 33–36, 40–44, 49, 82, 86, 108, 110, 181, 190, 201, 212n., 219, 275
This Thing Called Love, 276
Three Comrades, 6, 23, 120–26, 129–32, 135–49, 156, 163–64, 181, 185, 190, 221, 251
Time, 201
Tone, Franchot, 129, 147
Tracy, Spencer, 9, 12, 119, 129, 191
Trip to the Moon, A, 55
Truex, Ernest, 40
Tuttle, Frank, 259
Twentieth-Century Fox, 260–68

Unfinished Woman, An, 19–20

Vanity Fair, 215
Van Vechten, Carl, 51, 54, 224
Vegetable, The, 39–40, 180
Vidor, King, 102
Vivacious Lady, 147

Wanger, Walter, 219–20, 223–29
Warner, Jack, 111
Warner Brothers, 51, 101
Warren, Charles (Bill), ix, 76–77, 82–84, 86–94, 172, 176–80
Waste Land, The, 167, 271
Wead, Frank, 109–10, 112, 118
Wedding Night, The, 97–102, 158
West, Mae, 152
"When the Hounds of Spring," 16
Whoopee, 59
Wife Versus Secretary, 150–53
Williams, Emlyn, 261, 268
Wilson, Edmund, 31–32, 39, 69, 124, 224, 247
Wilson, Woodrow, 31
Winter Carnival, 24, 219–29, 237
Wister, Owen, 131
Wizard of Oz, The, 221
Woman, The, 157
Women, The, 10, 24, 174–75, 180–194, 198, 244
Wood, Sam, 235
Woolley, Monty, 268
World's Fair, 157
Wray, Fay, 259

Yank at Oxford, A, 6, 22–23, 108–
    119, 129, 147, 175, 180
"Yankee Doodle," 112
You Can't Take It with You, 119
Young, Loretta, 129
Young, Robert, 129, 147

"Your Way and Mine," 49

Zanuck, Darryl, 260–61, 266–68
Ziegfeld, Florenz, 46–47
Zola, Emile, 203
Zukor, Adolph, 116